WHY DID OUR FAMILIES DO THAT

RESEARCH AND STORIES TO UNCOVER WHY WE ARE WHAT THEY WERE.
DID ANYONE MENTION BRIBES?

GEORGE KROLOFF

Copyright © 2025 by George Kroloff

All rights reserved.

ISBN: 979-8-89324-762-6

No part of this book may be reproduced, stored in a retrieval system, or transmitted in any form or by any means—electronic, mechanical, photocopying, recording, or otherwise—without prior written permission of the publisher, except for brief quotations used in reviews or articles.

The opinions expressed by the Author are not necessarily those held by the Publishers.

The information contained within this book is strictly for informational purposes. The material may include information, products, or services by third parties. As such, the Author and Publisher do not assume responsibility or liability for any third-party material or opinions. The publisher is not responsible for websites (or their content) that are not owned by the publisher. Readers are advised to do their own due diligence when it comes to making decisions.

Published by Franklin Publishers

Printed in the United States of America

For permissions, inquiries, or additional copies, contact:

Franklin Publishers

www.franklinpublishers.com

A fresh, fun, and accurate twist on genealogy and family history.

Note To Reader

This book is sort of different. You can read it from start-to-finish like most books. Some of it is about actual people who happened to be part of my wife Susan's and my families. Much is a variety of stories, reminiscences, news reports, excerpts from history books, and other sources that helped me understand the lives of my forefathers and foremothers ... and why they did what they did that still affects our lives. Your close and distant ancestors probably lived similar lives.

Much of it involves the Orthodox Jewish experience under the Tsars. But, there is a lot about the Orthodox Catholic experience in Europe and with American Unions. A few essays are about the American South from first landing of Englishmen in Virginia to 400 years later my wife Susan's birth in San Diego.

Hopefully, most of what is written is information you never thought about as being really important to your upbringing.

Pick a headline from the Table of Contents that tickles your fancy and dip your brain into a topic that might help explain why you are what they were.

For instance, I discovered the key to unlocking my father-in-law's hidden past by tripping over one hard-to-read border crossing document online.

INTRODUCTION

Storytelling is a way to discover why we are what they were.

**I retired
I was bored
I began gathering string.**

In journalism, gathering string is a term for saving the bits and pieces of information needed to weave together a complex story.

My general idea was to try to see the world through the eyes of my family's long-gone relatives. Also, to discover the greater changes in the world that affected them. Some of those changes they felt, but they didn't know why.

Of course, we are what they were because we were created with their DNA. Our lives also have been shaped by the local and worldwide events that influenced their lives and how they taught us to think.

The winds of change, the chaos in their lives, led them to make decisions that affect you and me today.

I thought building a family tree might be interesting. But Cousin Julie decided one of her best contributions to society was to abandon a budding career as an opera singer. While looking for a new job, she put together a gigantic Redwood-sized Kroloff family tree. I discovered that Julie wasn't the only smart cousin who prepared family trees. The woods were full of them. I became less interested in who begat whom and more interested in What they did and Why?

Because my wife Susan's and my families are so diverse, there likely is overlap with your families.

Much of this collection of stories looks at what was happening between 1880 and 1920. Several of the stories discuss what people were seeing and thinking in their own words or their kid's recollections. Much of the information I found is old-fashioned desk research or investigative reporting. And much of it, at least to me, was surprising.

All too often, ten massive changes that affected our recent ancestors are not mentioned in family stories. They are outlined below. These are important influences that shaped how our parents were raised and how our parents raised us.

My hope is you will find these stories and the appendices to be interesting "good reads." They are historically based. For example, increased medical knowledge led to fewer babies dying at birth or as infants. This led to bigger families. In turn, that led to overpopulation, lack of jobs, not enough food, and much more.

People who put together family trees usually are confronted with "brick walls." They try to find out birth dates and other information about someone they are sure existed but couldn't find the data.

I walked around the walls and found several ancestors and their environments. Some were Orthodox Jews, some Orthodox Catholics, some Protestant and some probably were none of the above, the uncommitted. Almost all of our families that I write about had roots in ancient and modern Europe and the Middle East. Most emigrated to the Americas, South Africa, and a variety of European nations. Today Susan's and my extended families come from every inhabited continent and reflect multicultural and ethnic backgrounds, physically and culturally.

I hope you will recognize many influences your ancestors didn't realize. They may explain why you do something, such as how you think about food, or how you internalize world events, or why some stray sperm paired up with an attractive ovum that eventually became your family and you. And not only why you are what you are, but also where you are. Or, at least help you figure out why you were born, plus why you were born where you were born.

How many times have you been talking about family histories, only to be interrupted by a cousin across the dinner table saying, "Well, what I heard was?" Whenever possible, I followed the dictum of an early journalism professor who proclaimed, "If your mother says she loves you, check it out."

For instance, you will find Uncle Jake's perilous escape from Ukraine is what he wrote in his autobiography for his kids. It reads like a B movie plot. But what I found most interesting was his reporting on bribes. How many times have we heard about bribes influencing how and when we were born?

The fact that a young Jewish couple named Mary and Joseph started it all is an intriguing way for my cousin Shelly to introduce stories about our grandparents. Much more about Mary's neighborhood is based, in large part, on research done by the women of Hull House in the late 1800s. The discussion about Mary's environment led to a look at the impact of the

Industrial Age on our families and the difference in thinking between small-town and big cities residents around 1900.

Susan's birth father was named Simmons. The first Simmons I could locate appears to have been a laborer who arrived in Jamestown, Virginia, in 1608. That was about a decade before the Pilgrims stepped onto Plymouth Rock. William "Simons" probably was an indentured slave. It took his descendants 400 years to travel across the "South" to San Diego, where Susan was born in 1939. I visit a few of the Simmons family stops along the way, including difficulties during the Civil War in rural Mississippi. Separately, similar difficulties were experienced by my Uncle Leon in rural South Africa during the Boer War.

Abigail, our eldest daughter, married into a family that traces its history back to Richard Warren, who arrived on The Mayflower. Thus, their kids, our grandkids, carry DNA from two of the first English people to settle in North America, or at least that part of the continent becoming the United States. I found an estimate somewhere online that I interpreted to mean Abby's kids have a minimum of 40 million cousins.

After the tragic death of Susan's father when she was seven years old, her mother married into the Gordick Orthodox Catholic family whose members suffered under the thumbs of the Barons of Galicia (a large region in the Austro-Hungarian Empire, not the Galicia in Spain). Meanwhile, my Orthodox Jewish grandparents, a few hundred miles to the north, were experiencing many of the same problems being squashed under the Tsar's thumbs.

Several Gordicks settled in Eastern Pennsylvania, where they were squashed under the thumbs of the Robber Barons of Wall Street.

While doing research on our South African Helfet family at the University of Cape Town, a librarian urged me to "follow the footnotes." I did and found juicy information that even my cousins born there didn't know.

Instead of footnotes, this book contains several long appendices and internet addresses that include contemporaneous stories and academic research of what our ancestors life really was like. They range from details about how people traveled from Europe to their final destination in "New Worlds" to quotes from old storytellers about the places our grandparents grew up.

For instance, I found stories about day-to-day life in Kapulia, Byelorussia, a Jewish sthetl with Muslim and Russian Orthodox citizens. The stories included news about devastating fires in the wooden homes and a link to a video from a man who grew up in that small village. He even mentions the erection of the first public privy.

Fires helped shape my ancestors' lives and, thus, my life. The Great Chicago Fire of 1873 was big in many more ways than one.

Maybe you knew about immigrant trains, or train travel in general, around the year 1900. I didn't until I found vivid descriptions and pass them along to you.

Finally, I was heavily influenced by two items of science:

1. The famous astronomer Carl Sagan said everything in our universe existed at The Big Bang about 14 billion Earth years ago. That stuff in The Big Bang eventually formed stars that later exploded. The remnants of those stars formed the stuff that got together to create all the atoms in our bodies and everything else in our Universe ... yes, everything. Sagan said we are made of star stuff.

2. The Chaos Theory and its extension, The Butterfly Effect, seems to be even more revealing. It says everything, no matter how big or small, is an individual component of a pattern. A rainstorm is a single unit in a larger system. The tiny small whiff of air disturbed by a butterfly flapping its wings in the Tsar's garden could have joined with millions of other whiffs of air and been part of a rain cloud over your great aunt's vegetable garden in Warsaw or have contributed to a hurricane or cyclone devastating Guam. Hurricanes look like the Milky Way, which is the spiral-shaped galaxy our solar system inhabits in the vastness of space. I read that most of the trillions of galaxies, each of which may contain trillions of stars, are spiral galaxies like ours. (Pictures: Hurricane Dorian, European Space Agency [left] Milky Way composite from NASA [right]. Both are available copyright free for educational purposes.)

My aging grandfather told me there was nothing new on Earth. I didn't ask Why.

My father tried to explain complicated matters by using simpler examples and telling me, "It is the same thing but different." And I never asked Why.

A friend who is a former criminal investigator said that while he was in "cop school" and I was in journalism school, our teachers said the explanation of every situation required a When, Who, What, Where, Why, and How? All too often, the Why is the most difficult to discover.

I hope you might learn from these stories about some of the pressures your ancestors suffered from and overcame … the history portions … and observe some techniques for telling stories that will inform your family about the lives of their forefathers and foremothers.

Basically, I took on the challenge of trying to discover our families' Why.

People who work in and around family trees often can't find ancestors they think existed. Generally the genealogists complain they have hit a brick wall. This picture was taken by Susan on a trip to Europe. I saw the other side of a brick wall.

The intriguing butterfly below was created by Sauci Churchill. She was Susan's dearest friend. Sauci's image reminds us of the tiny air disturbance by a butterfly in the Tsar's garden that might have joined with other tiny disturbances to produce a dramatic system called a hurricane.

Each of our families is like a fragile butterfly existing among and adding to a greater system all around us that we call society, civilization, or chaos. Sometimes, we can make sense of the chaos surrounding us and to which we contribute. Sometimes, we can't and are carried along with a physical trend (windstorm, climate change), and sometimes, we can make a small or major change (be active in a political movement or maybe just recycle).

In my life, Sauci's butterfly is always active in the background.

TABLE OF CONTENTS

Ten Items That Probably Didn't Make It Into Our Family Stories Or Legends.	1
Why They Emigrated, The Abbreviated Version	4
New Chapter	5
You Could Say It Began With Mary And Joseph	10
A Bit Of Family History, Including Chicago, The Capone Mob And Marshall Fields	12
Several Subjects Starting With S	16
This Draft And "The Draft"	19
My Family Hit The Shores Of North America … 255 Years After Susan's	22
Our DNA Took A Great Circle Route	23
Antisemitism Visualized	25
The Mostly Dark Road To The Pale	27
Meanwhile, 300 Miles South Of Kapulia, Two Orthodox Catholic Peasants In The Austro-Hungarian Empire Lands Called Galicia Take Front And Center Stage In Hazelton, Pennsylvania	29
The Big Picture	31
Pressures Crushed John Calvin's Family In Europe In About 1880	34
Hazleton	40
One Final Look At Old Vs. New Country	42
Why Anthracite Coal?	43
Mines	45
Unions, John Goes To War, Marries Edith, The Family Expands	47

A Smart Elek?	52
Uncle Jake's Dramatic Escape From Ukraine	54
The Unusual Part Of The Back Story	56
Excerpts From Jake's Autobiography	59
Liverpool, Mid-1890s Helfets And Dobrofskys	64
The Helfet Sisters Had Two Brothers, One Was Leon	68
Cape Town And Calvinia … A Little More Context	73
The Brutal Torture Of Abraham Esau	79
January 7, 1901, Leon's And Abraham's Fates Were Sealed	80
Appendix #1 : Ukraine And South Africa	82
Warmed Over Hash Going Back 2600 Years	84
Immigration To Poland-Lithuania Until 1600; Jewish Communities In The 17th Century	88
Separate And Unequal, With A Common Heritage And Language … Sort Of	91
Why So Few Jewish Farmers	93
Coming To America	94
Entering The USA At New York City	99
Fear And Fleeing, Keep Coming Up	101
Back To Europe	106
Kapulia, Around 1850, A Sense And Scent Of Life	109
What The Krulevitskys On-The-Lam Brought With Them	112
If It Wasn't For Them, There Would Be No Us In The Us	115
A Few More Characters From Kapulia	116
The Pall On The Pale Darkened	118
The Law(S)	120
The Labors, Neighbors And Trades	122
And Then It Ended	124

Appendix #2: This Is Long With Few Pictures	125
The Great Trans-Atlantic Migrations…	151
Train Travel In The 19th Century	159
Manifest Destiny	162
Chicago	164
What Mary Left	168
In 1878, Mary Was A Toddler, And Chicago Was A "Toddlin" Town	171
More about Mary's neighborhood and intro to the White City	175
Death, Marriage, Urban To Rural	181
Boston And Chicago Notes	184
Why They Came To America And Chicago	186
Chicago	187
The Seminal Event Occurred October 8, 1871	189
The Levys' Chicago Was The Same Thing As The Levy's Warsaw, Poland … But Totally Different	196
They Came From A Land That Considered Itself Polish, But …	200
Backtracking On The Levy Exodus	202
Trains, Taverns, Tenements, And Tidbits About Even More Stuff	204
Short History Of Chicago Jews Before 1900	211
Born In Rural Russia, Not All Had Roots In Their Communities	214
Short Review Of Items That Might Be Useful For Students Seeking Help With The Dreaded School Paper Due Tomorrow About Their Family History	216
Sioux City, Iowa…The Chicagowanna-Be	219
Who Came First?	221
How They Were Doing	223
Six Sidebars	225

What Was It About Both Chicago And Sioux City From 1880 To 1900?	227
Prairie Palaces And King Corn	231
Help From Native Americans	232
Sioux City Was What They Considered To Be World Famous	233
Sioux City In Full Force During 1889-90	235
Why Palace?	237
On The Other Hand, In Chicago	238
The Fair … Day And Night	241
Euphoria	245
Setting The Scene For The Family's Early Days In Sioux City	247
For All The Problems Of Daily Life	249
Globalization Is Not New. Our Family Was Part Of The Evolution	251
Pre-WWI	254
Riding The Rails West	257
Back To The White City	260
More Of What Mary Saw	263
Another Quick Recap	267
The Simmons, The South, And US History 1608 - 1945	271
Unmasking A Fake Voldemort Mapping A Road To Tippah	274
The Trek To Tippah Began With, And Was Pushed Along By, The Columbian Exchange	279
On The Road To Blue Mountain	282
US Expansion Geopolitical Barriers.	285
The Gap And Another Recap	289
A History For Dummies Moment	291
1860 Map President Lincoln Used Showing Slavery By County	292
Back To The Beginning	298
A Final Review	299
About The Author	304

TEN ITEMS THAT PROBABLY DIDN'T MAKE IT INTO OUR FAMILY STORIES OR LEGENDS.

Just as a furious thunderstorm is but a tiny cell in a bigger weather system, each family, including yours and ours, was a cell fighting furious high and low pressures and raging winds. At times it was like all the forces on Earth were enveloping and battering them.

In my view ten big-picture forces hit our families from all sides in the late 1800s. These forces shaped their lives and, in turn, they shaped how we were brought up and taught to think.

- **Weather change.** Severe droughts in Europe were bad karma for people who worked the land. Ages ago while a staff member of the US Senate Foreign Relations Committee I read an unclassified CIA report about the wars, deaths and migrations caused by weather and climate changes. You and I today were born, in part, because of these global events.

- **Mechanization**. When the man who ran the farm for the nobleman acquired a new-fangled mechanical reaper, he could fire about 15 workers, likely peasants or serfs such as Susan's Gordick ancestors. Weaving fabric on huge block-long looms attended by 12-year-olds was one near-to-home cause of the rise of unions. All experienced by the Gordicks. Illustration from Scotland where mechanization was slightly different.

Background at https://en.m.wikipedia.org/wiki/Scottish_Agricultural_Revolution Illustration at File:George Heriot Swanston03.jpg

- **Medical advancements and overpopulation.** They produced more people than jobs. Today we may look at the 19th Century (which means the 1800s) as a time of primitive medicine, using leeches, etc. There actually were dramatic advancements. Small Pox vaccinations, for example, were widespread in late 1700s. A century later in numerous societies people were living longer. Fewer mothers and babies died at childbirth, yet the baby production-line was not slowed.

- **The money economy replaced barter.** Banks were formed that dealt with all kinds of people, not just the landed gentry or kings and queens. Loans were available, credit and cash were being used. One reason for my great-uncle Leon's success in the god-forsaken wilds of South Africa's High Karoo (semi-desert) was his ability to help the local Boer-Dutch farmers figure out the new economy that had grown from simple barter to cash/money. Leon bought their crops and sold them to others.

- **Wars, the draft, egos, and taxes.** Royals and Emperors continued to get greedier and greedier, demanding more and more young men to become cannon fodder so they could expand the areas they commanded. To pay for those wars, people were being taxed and suddenly young men drafted.

- **Transportation.** A spider web of railroads expanded to cover most of Europe and much of the USA. The cost of producing many goods was cheaper in the big city factories. The cost of shipping was going down as the speed of transportation was going up. Jobs or crafts, like making clothes, were moving to the cities. Skilled and educated people also were moving to the cities. The Kroloff family's rural inn in today's Belarus closed in part because the rutted road that passed the inn was not getting as much traffic after the railroad opened nearby. Well, it probably wasn't his inn, it was the baron's, or some other upper-class person for whom my ancestor ran it. I am pretty sure Jews couldn't own property where he lived.

- **Education and unions.** In America there were new affordable land-grant colleges in most states, plus 2,509 Carnegie libraries, and public education. It wasn't perfect, but it helped. In Slovakia, the Austro-Hungarian Empire didn't provide education except for a very few. In Northeast Pennsylvania where John Calvin Gordick, my wife's stepfather grew up, there was public education and most kids, certainly not all, went to school. Yet, child labor was a big issue. Unions became a major political and labor force, bringing about the 40-hour work week and other benefits that dramatically changed industrialized nations. More about this in the story "The Smart Elek."

- **Information and Communication.** New technologies reduced the price of paper and lowered the cost of printing presses. There were more books, newspapers, posters, and pamphlets available. People who couldn't read were told about the outside world by those who could. Also, they learned about other people's aspirations, and glittering possibilities they never thought about. Introduction of the telegraph was huge, even when it was a mere eight words a minute via undersea cable from New York to Europe.

- **Crushing cultures.** As always new rulers wanted to change those they crushed to be more like the crushers. This was widespread, such as the "Magyarization" from 1880 to 1920 as the Austro-Hungarian Empire tried to digest much of a sprawling region called Galicia. It was characterized as a brutal destruction of political, cultural, social and economic life. The Magyars of Hungary were almost as vicious as their neighbors, the tyrannical Tsars of Russia.

- **Mass marketing.** By the 1800s companies and states or provinces were sending agents throughout Europe encouraging people to emigrate to the US and Canada. They had intriguing deals, including free land and jobs.

Overall, there developed an A-List of countries that were a magnet for immigration ... America, Argentinia, Africa (especially South Africa) ... among others like Canada. That's where it appeared the jobs were, and the local population might be more open to immigrants to fill jobs and fuel economic growth. There was little interest in the S list ... Somalia, Surinam, Siam ... where the jobs weren't.

WHY THEY EMIGRATED, THE ABBREVIATED VERSION

We have to start somewhere, so today, I am starting in the middle. As said above, our family stories or legends often are reduced to one sentence or one word, if they still exist at all. A man once asked me if Kapulia was a real place or a mythological kingdom made up by his parents, where, like Oz, people or rulers behaved in an "unbelievable manner." Unlike Oz, Kapulia was real. It was like hundreds of small rural towns across Central Europe. Some with a majority of Jews, some with a minority. Almost all had names that are different than those that appear on Google Maps.

Our Jewish Orthodox relatives who came from these Sthtels, as far as we can remember, told us they came to America to escape oppressive Russian antisemitism, the draft of young men into the army, fear of programs (which was organized violence against Jews), and/or because a relative said America was the place to be. And that's about all we remember.

Our Orthodox Christian relatives said the same thing, replacing Russia with the Austro-Hungarian Empire and attempting to convert them to a different religion. Those short statements are true as they stand, but the reality was more complex. Further essays in this collection, "Why Did Our Families Do That" put their actions in a larger context. For instance, the village from which Elek Gordizuk was born was a shtetl, like Kapulia. But he lived in the ghetto outside the Jewish Ghetto. And the equivalent of the famed Kapulia Fair was a few miles away, in the next town. He and his family were illiterate peons or peasants. The barons who owned the land wanted them in their place. For very different reasons, the Robber Barons of Wall Street wanted them in the Pennsylvania coal mines.

Pictured is Kapulia south of Minsk in what today is a country called Belarus. The Kroloff's and numerous relatives lived in and around Kapulia (now Kopyl) before coming to the USA. Kapulia was a shtetl or small village with some Jews.

It was not much different from hundreds of others in Central Europe under Russian or other nations' control. Around the year 1900, Kapulia (Kapulie, Kopil, Kopyl) was home to about 2,700 Jews and a reported 1,800 of other religions.

The Pale of Russia, where Jews were confined, was big. It was almost the size of the American states of Texas, California and New York combined. There are maps of The Pale in these essays. It included most of what later became known as Eastern or Central Europe. The 1897 Russian census of The Pale found 5 million Jews and 45 million others. About 2 million Jews emigrated to the USA. At that time, Jews, Catholics and just about everyone else in Europe were popping babies as fast as the popcorn machine behind the food counter at a movie theater. Much faster than people were emigrating.

Russia's millions of Jews were forced to live in The Pale, pay numerous taxes and suffer indignities because they would not convert to the Russian Orthodox Religion. Catholics in Poland and Orthodox Catholics in the Austro-Hungarian Empire had similar problems. More about that later.

Quite a bit is known about Kapulia because of a stroke of luck. A couple of prominent authors lived there.

Abraham Jacob Papirna wrote, "Christians and Muslims were on the side streets on and behind the mountain. The Jews took the best part of the shtetl on the highest part of the mountain where the marketplace was located. This included the street where the synagogue courtyard was situated. All the special Jewish religious and community institutions were there. Occupying such a respected place with its large Jewish population who carried on such lively commerce, Kapulia gave the impression of a clean Jewish community." (Clean is a relative term. Not sure what he meant, but assume it was supposed to be positive.)

Only ten percent of the 20 million emigrants to the USA between 1800 and 1920 were Jewish. Most of the other 90 percent were from all over Europe. People of color, especially Asians, who earlier had built the infrastructure of the American West, the railroads, for instance, were no longer invited in.

Like our relatives, most of the other emigres saw no great future for themselves in The Old Country. A majority of the non-Jews knew that they could return home if they made enough money in the USA. Some did. But, going back to The Pale, where most Jews who emigrated to the US between 1880 and 1920 was darn near impossible or not attractive… either way, they came to stay.

   This is another version of the information above about the main unspoken reasons for emigration with more contest.

NEW CHAPTER

1. The kings and queens of Russia were called Tsars, Russian for Caesar. High on all their agendas was the conversion of every non-believer within their realm to the Russian Orthodox religion. Though many others were persecuted, Jews historically felt they were more restricted and highly taxed, but usually not to the point where they couldn't pay. The picture is Tsar Ivan the Terrible, which he was. The story for our Catholic Gordick family is similar, only the Tsar was replaced by the rulers of the Austro-Hungarian Empire. That series of essays starts on p. 26. In picture, Ivan the Terrible from https://en.wikibooks.org/wiki/Brief_History_of_Europe/Print_version

2. Before 1900, there were highly publicized deadly pogroms (organized, devastating, anti-Jewish riots, usually sanctioned by local government officials). Fear of pillage, killing, and rape was an increasingly darker cloud that spread across The Pale's Jewish population. After 1900, the number and severity of pogroms accelerated. An over-simplistic explanation of the government's lackadaisical attitude toward the organized attacks was that the Tsars not only wanted to be the Popes of a unified Russia, but they wanted to ape the Western European kings and be considered very European, like the French. Antisemitism was about as French as one could get. Most forget that the Inquisition began in France. The Dreyfus Affair, accusing an innocent French Jewish military officer of treason, split the country. In the end, while he was innocent, antisemitism flourished, and in a convoluted way, his trial was the initial kick-start for the idea of Zionism and the start of the State of Israel.

3. The Russian military was busy putting down revolutions inside Russia and stirring up battles to expand the country's borders. (As of this writing, things haven't changed.) That led to higher draft quotas overall, but especially for Jews and Roman Catholic Poles once they came under Russian rulers. The pressure was so intense that there were unrefuted reports of some shtetls that met conscription numbers by kidnapping youngsters from other shtetl and offering the captured teens and pre-teens to the army.

4. The Tsar's wars and those fought by other rulers, like in the Austro-Hungarian Empire, created huge government debt. That led to new taxes and further restrictions on Jewish residents, especially in The Pale, which, in several ways, was run as a colony, at least for Jews, Mennonites, Gypsies and others.

Context: *The colony concept certainly has been a force in history. For instance, a few more essays in this series focus on American history through the lives of my wife Susan's ancestors, the Simmons and Mitchell families of Tippah County, Mississippi. A part of their story includes the French and Indian Wars of the mid-1700s and, later, the American Civil War. Also, Susan's New England relatives who migrated down from Canada fought in those wars and the War for Independence.*

England demanded its American colonists do much of the fighting against the French and their Indian allies west of the Appalachian Mountains. Then, London levied taxes upon the colonies to pay for the war. The new taxes were big factors in inciting the fight for Independence. King George III lost 13 colonies. The Tsars also waged wars and forced their "colonials" to pay for them in manpower and taxes. Tsar Nicholas II's actions were among the matches that lit the 1917 Bolshevik Revolution. He not only lost his country, he lost his life.

The after-shocks from the brutal 1904-05 Russo-Japanese War reverberate today. (This was edited during the Russian/Ukraine war.)

5. The Jews, Italians, Poles, Scandinavians, Slavs, Serbs, Irish, Greeks, and other poor European and second generation Americans, who came to the Missouri River Valley, where Sioux City sat, were influenced by the:

    - **Industrial Revolution,** which introduced machines to do the work of people and electricity that brought light to the night and lengthened the work day. The Industrial Revolution first occurred in the larger cities, then it stole jobs from the shtetls in Russia and small towns across all of Europe. This was a serious problem for Kroloff and Gordick's ancestors.

    - **Transportation Revolution**, which lowered travel time and prices for ships and railroads and helped lead to the concentration of production in cities. That eradicated many rural jobs. Among them were tailoring, making alcoholic beverages, and running inns for travelers.

    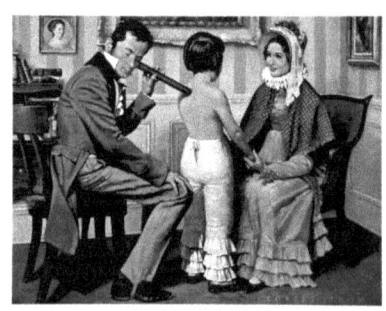

    - **Medical Revolution**, which increased lifetimes, decreased deaths at birth and led to over-population across Europe. Even as plagues still plagued Europe. Illustration downloaded free from
    https://www.researchgate.net/publication/262040079_The_Art_of_Listening/fulltext/5af72ec44585157136d2165e/The-Art-of-Listening.pdf

    - **Communications Revolution**, which reduced prices for printing presses and, more importantly, for paper. Suddenly, non-religious books in Yiddish, the common language of most European Jewish immigrants to the USA, appeared along with newspapers and posters. Telegraphed news replaced word of mouth. Salesmen spread across

Europe seeking workers for real jobs (tailors were needed in New York, and land was cheap for farmers). Advertising promoted the newer, bigger, and faster railroads and ships that had to fill seats and beds at almost affordable prices.

- **Economic Revolution**, which meant coins and paper money became a larger piece of people's lives than barter. Banks began to lend money to others than the nobility. That was huge.

- **Education Revolution**, which helped more people become literate. Suddenly, there was a Yiddish press. A Norwegian press. People read and saw that their lives could be rosier in other places and learned about those who shared their woes.

Below, is the cover of a Soviet Yiddish edition of Tevye der milkhiker, the story of Fiddler on the Roof. The situation in Galicia amongst the Slovak and other serfs was different. There was an effort by the government and church to keep the lower classes illiterate. As you will see, that was just fine with the Americans who owned mines in Pennsylvania and hired the newly arrived Galicians, who Anglicized their names to Gordick in the late 1800s. Writing in Yiddish, opened new worlds to Jews, just as publishing in other languages helped numerous ethnic groups learn about themselves. This is an early version about Tevya, The Fiddler on the Roof. https://traditiononline.org/the-best-tevya-the-dairyman/ Writing in Yiddish, https://www.wikiwand.com/en/articles/Yiddish_orthography

YOU COULD SAY IT BEGAN WITH MARY AND JOSEPH

Mary was my grandmother, my mother's mother. She was born in Chicago, Illinois, a few years after the devastating 1871 Chicago Fire left most of the center city covered in smoldering ashes. For more images and background Google "Great Chicago Fire Library of Congress."

Joseph was Mary's husband, my grandfather. He was a small man from a town called Slutsk in what is now Belarus. According to a family legend, the young "Joseph" climbed onto a barn roof and peed on pogrom attackers. A pogrom is a deadly anti-Jewish riot. Joseph's pee might be a myth. I haven't found any reference to a pogrom in Slutsk when he lived there, but my mother repeated it several times, so it must be true. (For a history of pogroms: http://www.encyclopedia.com/history/modern-europe/russian-soviet-and-cis-history/pogroms)

Joseph arrived in Sioux City as a youth. His trip was part of a deal brokered by two brothers who wanted their sister to divorce Joseph's father, still in Slutsk. It's complicated and explained later. As a young adult, Joseph prospered in Sioux City.

In 1900, my mom said he set out with friends on a train from Sioux City to Chicago to find a bride. There, he found and was fond of Mary Levy. She liked him, and soon they married. Big City Mary moved to the Small Town of Sioux City, Iowa, where Mary and Joseph raised a large family.

I vividly remember walking along Pierce St. in Sioux City, Iowa, with Joseph during a steaming summer in the 1940s. We went from Uncle Dave Ginsberg's typical small corner neighborhood grocery store down a steep hill to the apartment my aging grandparents shared. As we rambled along, Joseph was totally demolishing, a large orange… rind and all.

He was a quiet presence. For a long time, Joseph was the only male in his household of five daughters, one wife, one mother-in-law and at least one sister-in-law. His mother lived on the same block. That's a lot of females. I don't remember him ever saying much. My mother,

Florence Blossom Kauffman Kroloff, claimed her father was an avid and brilliant reader. The picture is of Joseph in later life, as I remember him.

Mary Levy Kauffman's parents were Sarah Mann and Louis Levy (originally Levinsky, I think). They were from Warsaw, Poland. They seem to have arrived about 1875 and settled in what is nicknamed "The Windy City." Some of the family was in Chicago earlier. According to my mother, Louis' father, my great-great grandfather Reuben, arrived in Chicago before the 1871 fire. Soon, he brought over members of his family, including at least two sons.

A BIT OF FAMILY HISTORY, INCLUDING CHICAGO, THE CAPONE MOB AND MARSHALL FIELDS

The growing Levy family eventually lived above their grocery store on Dekoven St. It was a very short walk to where an earlier Dekoven St. resident and her cow lived, the fabled Mrs. O'Leary. That cow allegedly kicked over a lantern, which set her barn aflame. It ignited half the neighborhood, which then spread further north and east. Soon, downtown Chicago was aflame and under a blanket of fallen embers.

Chicago History Museum for more information. This illustration depicting Mrs. O'Leary and her cow kicking over a lamp to start the Chicago Fire of 1871, Chicago. Lithograph by the Kellogg & Buckeley Co. CHM, ICHi-034703

The O'Leary's cow story is a big hit. Unfortunately, it is probably a myth, too. The barn and cow part are OK, but the fire likely started when someone carelessly lit smoking tobacco that fell on hay.

Fast forward. In 1935, I was born in Chicago. We lived across the street from the site of the Chicago World's Fair of 1893. Much, much more about that later. My parents had moved from Sioux City in the midst of the 1930s Great Depression because there were not any jobs in Iowa for my dad, Archie, a commercial artist.

(Coincidentally, Archie had been born about 30 years earlier in Chicago when his parents also moved from Sioux City seeking work. That didn't work out, so they returned to Sioux City. As I said, it's complicated, but soon it will seem simpler.)

By the early 1960s, I was manager of media relations for the massive Chicago Metro Chamber of Commerce. I felt as if the long-departed Mrs. O'Leary and I were joined at the hip. She and the kicking cow seemed real. My employers loved the cow's story.

In Chicago, my maternal grandmother was raised in a family of observant Orthodox Jews. That meant the 24 hours after sundown each Friday was supposed to be devoted to study and religious matters.

They followed a long tradition of hiring a Shobbos (Sabbath) Goy. That would be a non-Jew who would do chores forbidden to be performed on the Sabbath, such as lighting a fire in the stove. I have no clue why lighting a fire or turning on an electric light is a no-no.

As luck would have it, earlier in the mid-1950s, I had worked with a man who claimed to be the Levy's Shobbos Goy. By then, he was in his besotted "later years." I'm the guy in the middle of the picture. The supposed Shobbos Goy has a very soiled shirt.

All of our crew were members of the Capone Mob-run warehousemen's union. We were dust-covered order-fillers in a decrepit Pittsburgh Paint and Glass building behind Tribune Tower. It was home to a swarm of smelly, chubby cats brought in to control an ever-growing number of randy rats. In case you are a trivia fan, a big rat pack is called mischief, which kind of works with Frank Sinatra's Rat Pack. A herd of cats is called a clowder.

Our mischievous rats and clowdering cats peed a lot. There were uncovered gaps between the ceiling slats in the warehouse. The advice from day one was not to look up with your mouth open. Pay was ok.

Drenched in sweat, I often stared out of a 5th-floor window to glimpse at Michigan Avenue just a block away. There, I saw dapper men in sharply pressed suits and clean white starched shirts, chatting up their well decked-out high heeled secretaries. Fresh from their three-martini lunches, they headed back to jobs in advertising agencies, probably with air conditioning or big fans.

Seeing the ad-men was a great motivator to return to college as soon as possible. I had dropped out of work because our family was on the dole. Mom and Dad's sisters were regularly sending us money for food and rent. Paying for higher education was up to me. My father was an incredibly bright and good man. It wasn't until I became an adult I realized he was my best friend. Unfortunately, when I was a teen, he became somewhat incapacitated and unemployable because of heart problems.

I learned little from my workmate Vince (or was it Vic?), who I will assume was the Levy's Shabbos Goy, except that by Prohibition, he was a driver for the Capone Mob, which controlled much of the illegal activity in Chicago. And a lot of the legal activity, too.

The infamous Al Capone had a brother named "Bottles." Vince/Vic said he was Bottles Capone's chauffeur. He probably was.

One of Vince's exploits made The Chicago Tribune. I fact-checked him at the city's huge central library to read his story preserved on microfilm. While driving a mob-connected politician, Vince/Vic stopped at an intersection. Gun-totting gangsters forced open a door, and slugs ripped through the body of the surprised backseat passenger.

Poof, the guys with the gats were gone. Never to be found. Photo is a different car, but the same sorry story. https://49639813.weebly.com/prohibitions-significance-in-history.html

Well, according to the old newspaper story, he was right about the murder. Maybe he also was right about being my great-grandfather's Shobbos Goy. There were at least four, maybe five, Archie Kroloffs. One day in the 1970s, my dearest right-wing friend Jerry Lipson and I finished our regular lunch. He worked for the Republican leader of the House of Representatives, and I worked across Capitol Hill for the Democratic Chair of the Senate Foreign Relations Committee. After lunch at the House-side of the Hill, Jerry asked, "Do you wanna meet Mr. Rhodes (from Phoenix)?" Of course, I said, "of course." Wanna is a Chicago expression right up there with sitting at a hamburger joint and being asked if you want "a side of fries?" All one word, sideafries.

So we walk into his office. Mr. Rhodes was behind his desk, absorbed by something on a piece of paper. I don't know about the House, but Senate staffers like me were directed to write memos to Members on a page or less.

Jerry says, "Mr. Rhodes, I would like you to meet my friend, George Kroloff." Rhodes slammed his paper down, looked at me and shouted, "Kroloff!" my best friend is Archie Kroloff." Scared the living devil out of me.

In the 1900s, there were four, maybe five, Archie Kroloffs. My dad was the Chicago Archie Kroloff, an almost always sick, struggling advertising artist. Mr. Rhodes's friend was the affluent Phoenix Archie Kroloff, a man and his wife who seemed to have very trendy society tastes. Both Archies had accounts at Marshall Field's high end Chicago department store. Sometimes, Dad received his cousin's bills. Whew.

SEVERAL SUBJECTS STARTING WITH S

This may be the most confusing essay in this collection because I willy-nilly introduce a bevy of brothers and sisters with similar names but differing stories. Later essays are much simpler to follow.

The Levys, as noted before, came from Poland. The Kroloffs and Kauffmans from Belarus and Ukraine. Others you will meet from my family came from what now is Ukraine and Latvia/Lithuania, with stop-overs in England and South Africa.

Stories of my wife Susan's family are the same thing but very different. They appear to be among the very earliest English settlers in Virginia, even before the Mayflower arrived at Plymouth Rock. Coincidentally, our oldest daughter married a man whose family traces back to a businessman named Warren, who not only arrived on the Mayflower but signed the Mayflower Compact.

Susan's birth father's family traces back to the first supply ship to the Jamestown Settlement in Virginia, which arrived a decade before the Mayflower.

Another branch of Susan's family arrived much later, also from the British Isles. They initially settled north of Maine in Canada and eventually migrated down to New England. And finally, there were the former serfs or peasants from central Europe who emigrated to Pennsylvania's coal mining county. (Serfs were uneducated, unskilled and owned by the landowner. Peasants worked for the land owners or their managers, often paid taxes and could move to a different manor. Both were at the bottom of the social system and expected the landowners' protection.)

In a few pages, you will meet my dad's uncle, Jacob (Jake) Dobrofsky. He came from Mena, Ukraine. Jake disproves the myth that every small-town Jewish family under the thumb of the Russian Tsar was as poor as Tevye in Fiddler on the Roof. Jake's family was very wealthy, according to his memoir. Because of servants, he jokingly said his feet never touched the ground until he was about ten.

Suddenly, because of scandal, sex, deceit and meanness, the Dobrofskys were flat-out broke. The man handling his dad's money took all the cash and a girlfriend off to America. Jake's recollection of escape from deep disasters and debilitating losses to a somewhat lighter life in Liverpool is filled with bribery, stealth and danger. It is gist for a heart-thumping B-movie.

After following her to Sioux City, Uncle Jake married Esther Helfet. She was one of the Helfet sisters of Liverpool, England. Another sister, Sarah (Helfet) Kroloff, was my dad's mother. Jake and the Helfet kids were born in Ukraine but in towns far away from each other. He met the Helfets in Liverpool and fell in love with Esther.

Egads, this is complicated and boring. Maybe you want to skip to another essay.

Earlier, as a mere child, the seasick Sarah Helfet, Esther, Leon and their parents and siblings arrived in England aboard what probably was a storm-tossed cattle and cargo ship with bare-bones accommodations for a few passengers.

After growing up in Liverpool as a very prim young Victorian lady, Sarah and her two sisters sailed on the Cunard passenger line's ship Ivernia in 1903. The illustration is from an Ivernia promotional brochure. It shows that accommodations for steerage passengers (lowest class) on some vessels became rather tolerable after the shipping lines figured out how to make money on the poor, huddled masses yearning to breathe free.

Sarah and her sisters went through Ellis Island near New York City and headed for Sioux City, Iowa because relatives and/or friends of the family were already there, including brother Isaac, who changed his name to Harry, why Sioux City is a mystery to me. Travel promotion picture of Karoo desert, South Africa, I guess for people who dig deserts.

Sarah's other brother, Leon, like everyone else in the family mythology, seemed to have an independent streak. While still a teenager, Leon shipped himself from Liverpool to South Africa, where he prospered in a god-forsaken small town (a "dorp" in native Afrikaner language). The diminutive village is named Calvinia. It rests in the usually barren South African high desert called the Great Karoo (right), Far, far from a city.

Curiously, Leon and most of his siblings settled, at least for a while, in frontier towns half a world away.

Leon's traumatic adventures in the Anglo-Boer War were crucial to his noteworthy success. After the war, he married Lithuanian-born Sarah Levin, who also was brought up in Liverpool. She, like my grandmother, the other Sarah Helfet (Sarah Helfet Kroloff), was a prim stone-willed Victorian maiden. (Too many names? Skip over them for now. There will not be a test.)

My mother said that people in rural Sioux City joked about the three English "Helfet Girls" (actually young women) weekly washing the steps and sidewalk in front of where they lived, just as in England.

At the very same time, rural Calvinia's Boer residents would gossip about Leon Helfet's wife, Sarah, as she walked the dusty streets in the up-to-date Victorian wardrobe she brought with her from Liverpool.

Those Helfets had a flair for fashion that continued two generations later. Among them is Keith Helfet, Leon's grandson. Keith designed the fabled Helfet Jaguar and is featured in a book about the finest designers of the 20th Century. Photo is of Keith and one of his designs. His brother Clive was an art director in New York. (Reed Kroloff is possibly the most quoted architect in the USA over the past few decades.)

One family myth claims that Leon Helfet of Calvinia had a very profitable business selling horses to both sides in the brutal South African war between the Boers (descendants of Dutch emigrants) and the British. The typical life of a horse in that combat was six weeks. It is unclear how he produced the horses to be sold, but business was brisk.

For years, the situation in the small town of Calvinia was out-of-this-world tense. Everyone in town knew every other person's business. Just about everyone was in a faction. Boer vs. British supporters. White vs. Brown. If Leon actually was double-dipping and selling horses to both, and either side found out, he probably would have been shot on the spot. It's an interesting family myth. Doesn't seem credible. He also was a civilian quartermaster for the Brits.

He was a British citizen. South Africa was a British colony. Young Winston Churchill was a newspaper correspondent during The Boer War. He was imprisoned there for a while (not in Calvinia).

On occasion, Calvinia had been overtaken by the Boer military, who committed appalling atrocities. The British were equally brutal. But Leon Helfet skipped town. Wars do have consequences for the victims, and he was no dummy. Later, Leon married Sarah Levin, who became Sarah Helfet.

Also, about that time, my granddad, Samuel Kroloff (Krulevitsky), met and married Leon's sister, Sarah Helfet, after she and her three siblings settled in Sioux City.

The name of almost everybody in my family and my wife Susan's family duplicates the exact name of someone else in our family. When researching the Simmons of Virginia, Tennessee, and Mississippi, over dozens of generations, so many were named Lemuel that they seemed to be either stuck on replicating history or just too boring to be original. Legions of our relatives are named Robert, Archie, Adam, Max, Sam, Sarah and Susan, John, Jon, Jody, Jamie, Jessie, Jacob, Joshua, and so on.

THIS DRAFT AND "THE DRAFT"

Like a daily newspaper, this series of essays is a first rough draft of history. However, a different kind of draft, that darned military draft, is central to the Russian stories, as well as the Simmons and Gordick essays that encompass the French-and-Indian, Revolutionary, and American Civil Wars as well as WWII.

A dozen Krulevitzky boys vanished from what sarcastically might be called metropolitan Kapulia in Belarus (then a part of Russia). The 1897 census tallied 2,671 Jews in Kapulia out of a total population of 4,463. That is about 60 percent. The young men's names survive online because they were wanted by the Tsar's police as draft dodgers. More about that in a Kapulia essay.

Sam Kroloff my grandfather, had a Russian accent. The last words I remember from him, as he sat in a rocker on the porch of an old person's home in Sioux City, were "Save your seed." Fifty years later, I learned he was talking about masturbation and quoting from the Bible.

Sam was unforgettable. I see him in the mirror every time I shave. Because Kapulia was the location of several sometimes humorous stories by a couple of the most famous Yiddish writers around the turn of the last century, I have included a fair amount of those stories (or links to them) in the Appendix after the Kapulia essays. They portray the day-to-day lives of our ancestors that got lost over the years. Picture is an old Russian print https://pmeyer.faculty.wesleyan.edu/russian-206-a-matter-of-life-and-death/206images/206pobed/

For instance, in that appendix, you will learn even more about Finke the candlemaker, as well as the Police Commissioner, "Sheriff Zdroyevsky" who ruled over the realm and the Tsar's "ever-more-oppressive decrees."

You will also learn about some of the scams at German fumigation facilities. Many emigrants from Russia and Central Europe had to endure them before boarding ships to England and beyond.

Our family stories are not ours alone. Others have them. For instance, the percentage of Jewish residents attacked in pogroms before 1900 was very small. Nonetheless, there was rampant fear of a deadly pogrom (riot) with its looting, killing, raping and maiming of Jews waiting around every corner. Nightmares floated across Jewish settlements like a flock of dark crows swarming overhead, seeking preferred places to peck and poop. Picture: The fear of death flies over the land.

That's why so many descendants of Eastern European Jews contain stories about pogroms, or fear of attack, in their family's oral history. They truly were scary and deadly.

Most Jews were forbidden to emigrate, so almost everyone who worked their way out of the Pale had yet another tale to tell. Unfortunately, most didn't tell them. More about the Pale later. And there is more about the tortuous trials of getting out of Europe and finding a home in a very different society.

At the same time, in the late 1800s, Chinese and African American workers and Native Indians were facing equally deadly mobs in the USA. The ultimate results for many were like the results dumped upon the Russian controlled Jews. As you will read later, the Russians were equal opportunity oppressors. The Polish Catholics, for instance, had serious troubles when the partition of Poland made many of them Russian subjects. The Gordick/Gordiczuks of the Austro-Hungarian Empire were severely persecuted by their rulers in part because they didn't part with their Orthodox Catholic religion.

In South Asia, ethnic debasement was occurring between Hindus and Muslims. White-skinned Boers vs. British vs. dark skinned natives and similar perversities spread across Africa, Central and South America.

Today's skin-color politics in industrialized and "Third World" countries alike are branches of the deeply rooted tree of intolerance. It seems that fear and oppression are ingrained in the human condition.

While the Jews in The Pale of Russia arguably were the most put-upon minority, Mennonites, Catholics and other religious groups who would not convert to the Russian Orthodox Church also were seriously discriminated against. The centuries-long Inquisition started in France and was carried to an even more hysterical extreme by the then evil Spanish priest Torquemada. Jews were tortured unless they converted to Roman Catholicism. Muslims also were pressured by the Inquisition and the Iberian royalty.

In some places, not having any religion at all was a call for even worse punishment.

So, these essays try to explain how one-or-two sentence family myths ("They left because of the Tsars' oppression!") might be correct, but they aren't more than a headline, not the full story.

The mass emigration (1845 and onward) of the Irish after the potato famine has a religious (Catholic vs. Protestant) backstory. There also is a scientific corollary that proves messing with Mother Nature is not always a good idea. In this case, European potato farm owners thought they knew more about growing the tuber than the people who grew potatoes in Central and South America, where varieties of potatoes with different genetic makeups were planted side by side. They were wrong, and the European potato plants, all of the same variety, "caught" a virus and died. (From fascinating book 1493 Uncovering The New World Columbus Created by Charles C. Mann)

I don't know if it is appropriate to compare our family histories and our genes with the seemingly infinite variety of potatoes, but we sure are genetically diverse.

Put another way, these essays also attempt to give a "feel" for what the lives of the immigrants were like in the hard times, as well as the good.

They are a tribute to those strong souls who worked and sometimes died in an effort to better themselves and their families and eventually benefit you and me. They left the "Old Country."

They were optimistic, or at least hopeful that their new world would be better than the old. The introduction above is but a smattering of their lives and the pressures they withstood.

Of course, there are ironies. One involves the Simmons family members fighting on both sides of the US Civil War. What was their concept of the "Old Country?" Or of "A House Divided."

Nevertheless, whatever and whoever they were … as said before, today, you are what they were.

MY FAMILY HIT THE SHORES OF NORTH AMERICA ... 255 YEARS AFTER SUSAN'S

The Pale of Russia needs more explanation. According to the 1897 Russian census, nearly five million Jews lived within the Pale. That was about 95 percent of Russia's Jewish population, but it was less than 12 percent of the Pale's total population.

While some of Pale's Jewish residents might have had roots in their communities going back to the 1400s or even earlier, most of them probably were forced into their small town shtetls or city ghettos in the 1800s.

The map at right gives some idea of recorded movements, including mass expulsions of Jews. Think about being told to leave your residence at 10 am tomorrow with no place to go and no supplies other than what you could carry.

We have no clue how or when the Krulevitskys arrived in Kapulia. Or when the Helfets arrived in the town they called Chernush in Poltava, Ukraine. One unverified legend is the Helfgott-Helfet clan came from Holland, where, allegedly, they settled after being kicked out of Spain or Portugal because of The 1492 Inquisition. Illustration from https://mapsontheweb.zoom-maps.com/post/142230137907/the-pale-of-settlement-a-region-in-western

OUR DNA TOOK A GREAT CIRCLE ROUTE

Historically, any group with legends, or any "people," claim to have had problems.

Shards of our Jewish DNA traveled from ancient and dusty dunes and opulent oases in the Mideast. According to the Old Testament, they left Egypt to wander around a desert for 40 years. Over centuries, our genetic helixes roughly ricocheted across all the inhabited continents. Some took a twisty path, like when they were expelled from Spain and Portugal or forced to leave England. Much of that DNA landed in Russia's notorious Pale of Settlement. Illustration from https://commons.wikimedia.org/wiki/File:Beni_Hassan_(Lepsius,_BH_3)_04.jpg

Some of Susan's ancestors can be traced to Medieval England and Ireland. They sailed across the Atlantic pretty early in white America's history. Bob Simmons (Susan's birth father) seems to be descended from a Simoms who landed in Virginia around 1610. The family of Edith Marks (Susan's mother) first set foot in the New World in Canada and New England many years later. Our son-in-law Glenn Galloway's family traces back to the famous Mayflower, in which Puritans were fleeing the English Monarchy and landed in what is now Massachusetts. Galloway's ancestor was a businessman named Warren, who was on the voyage to make money. He was successful.

As explained later, the Mayflower/Plymouth passengers and the earlier Jamestown, Virginia settlers were afraid of the Inquisition and Spanish for other reasons. Susan's adoptive father, John Gordick's mother, was Slovak, and his father was from an area once ruled by the Ottomans, now in Ukraine. As previously mentioned, our family genes are quite diverse.

In any event, Christians and Jews trace their roots to ancient areas of Israel and Muslims to Mecca and Medina, about 750 miles west of Jerusalem. All of us, no matter what our religion or race, trace our roots even further back to some obscure place in Africa.

For over 2,500 years, millions of Jews refused to give up their religion in the face of withering antisemitism, which caused them to be kicked out of their homes and left to wander from place to place, seeking a new life. Many converted to whatever religion was dominant at the time.

Others died during their journeys to some unknown exile haven or hell. Most of those deaths were in Europe at the hands of the Crusaders, the Russians, the Catholic Inquisition and the Nazis. An unknown number were wiped out by plagues, hunger and unfortunate circumstances like being caught between two warring armies or in a land conquered by "the bad guys."

Transferring the standard used by segregationists that one drop of "negro" blood made a person black, it is conceivable that, going back far enough, nearly all Nazis were Jews, as were all the early Christians.

ANTISEMITISM VISUALIZED

The Jewish part of our family suffered from antisemitism, and most still do, although in many cases it is not overt or even realized. These examples illustrate a few probably trivial personal examples, although this is a short list.

A sweet African-American ex-school teacher driving an Uber in Chicago kept referring to Jew Town (Maxwell Street). My grandmother lived there, near Maxwell Street, in the late 1880s. I actually was offended. As minor as that might have been, it's no different than saying something about a restaurant in China Town.

A lady at our dinner table on a very long cruise kept talking about "Jewing Down" people. When told that was offensive, she turned beet red and said it had never occurred to her. Minor, not life and death. Nor was my annual beating by a gang of Catholic kids when in grammar school because I killed Christ.

In the 1970s, a coworker in the PR department of The Washington Post, and eventually one of my very dearest and definitely smartest friends, was an African American from New York. He went on to have a much more important role in shaping a better America than I ever did. I desperately miss our regular lunches over dozens of years. One day, we were in a very posh New Jersey country club to hear a speech by our boss, Katharine Graham, The Post's owner. I jestingly said, "You know, if Katharine wasn't here, you probably wouldn't be allowed into this club. He replied, "Nor you!" It, too, was minor and appropriate, we both laughed.

Fifty years later, Susan and I live in a very large multi-ethnic building. I am sure the guy who lived across the hall from us in apartment 911 was a spy. I had taken him out for a drink and we were in the lobby headed home. As he left for reassignment to Europe, his last words to me were, "George, why does everybody hate the Jews?" I only had nine floors in the elevator to respond to him.

If there was time, my answer would have been like this. The globalization of ideas about "the others" is old, probably 2000 years older than when the Viking's long-boats brought information to "foreigners," sometimes in peace, sometimes with brutal force. All religions have a checkered past. All religions, at one time or another, suffered discrimination and death. The first Christians, including Jesus, were dark skinned Jews. Islam recognizes early Jewish prophets, like Abraham, as their own.

Most of the seeds from which antisemitism grew were planted in the Middle East. They were gathered, replanted, and matured in Europe.

The illustration to the right illustrates a common theme where "the Jew" was in control and holding the world in his hands. "Rothschild," by C. Léandre; France, 1890s. Additional information about this image and the the Holocaust is at https://collections.ushmm.org/search/catalog/pa1041697
\

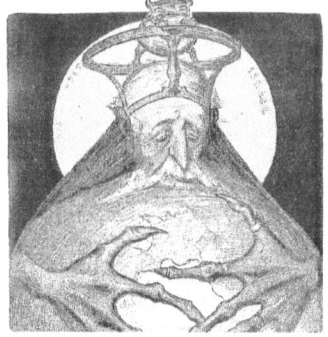

A recent incarnation of the ancient myth of ritual murder still being spread is from a 1983 book, "The Matzoh of Zion," claiming Jews sought human blood to make matzoh eaten at Passover. How red blood could make white matzoh remains a mystery, but people believe what politicians and preachers preach. This particular screed about blood and matzos was written by Syria's Minister of Defense, Mustafa Tlass.

The picture right below commemorates 1239, when Pope Gregory ordered the Talmud to be put on trial because it allegedly contained lies about the life of Christ and the Blessed Virgin. The Talmud actually contains the teachings and opinions of many ancient rabbis on a vast array of topics. Talmuds were confiscated and burned. The Talmud remains a target of suspicion into the 21st century.

More about this later, but one of the more recent (Middle Ages) reasons has to do with the nobility of Europe, who didn't want to deal with their subjects. They hired Jews to manage their lands and/or be the tax collectors for the peasants ... who despised the taxes and couldn't get to the land owners, so they took out their anger on the Jews, all the Jews. Like most of history in a paragraph, it was more complicated. But, essentially, that's what I told the spy who took his prejudices in his backpack wherever he went.

Every once in a while, I will throw in an almost relevant aside to break up the seriousness of some of these essays. It's unclear how many spies or retired spies live in our tall complex of almost 500 "units." Maybe it's because I ran into a few during my quirky career inside and outside of the US government, if I talk with one long enough, sometimes I can guess their other life.

So, one day in a gym, after several conversations with a retired American military officer who I figured had more than one life in several countries, I asked a question that I'd wondered about for years. "How can you suddenly show up in a country where you have no contacts other than those in the embassy and figure out how to discover useful information for our government?" I love his answer ... "Well, the first task is to find the right girlfriend (who knows the right people.)"

THE MOSTLY DARK ROAD TO THE PALE

The Jews never really morphed into anything like the Thundering Hordes of the Huns or the mythic conquering heroes of other cultures until the ugly 2023-4 episode in Gaza. Although, the one-off story of Moses parting the Red Sea was somewhat dramatic. (Illustration from deviantart.com.)

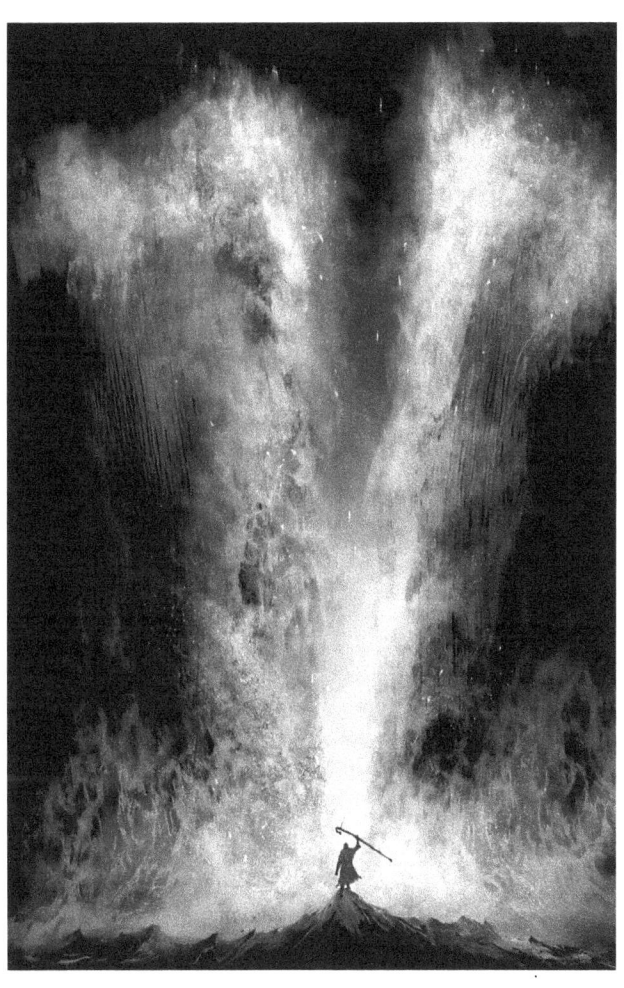

There are not many tales of conquests by Jews except for a few Bible stories, the Khazar Empire (more about that in another essay, and recently, the Israeli wars. Mostly, they are tales of Jewish submission, expulsion, fleeing, fasting, and death most notably the Inquisition and Holocaust. Nonetheless, sprinkled through history were periods of great art, science, philosophy, and contentment.

Reflecting on The Chaos Theory … patterns direct what we see as chaos in business, politics, life, and even our universe. One pattern that runs through most episodes of the Jewish narrative is a steadfast desire by many not to convert to another religion. That's what some of the oppressors claimed was "all" they wanted the Jews to do.

It wasn't quite that simple, of course, but loyalty to its religion and religious teachings was much of what held the "Chosen People" together.

That doesn't mean they were free from fear. They wanted, believed, and felt they had to be different. That is one reason they were persecuted … because they were different and not afraid to flaunt their difference. Certainly, many did convert or claimed they converted.

Fear and chaos, all too often, are the twin towers of fate and death. Those who escaped the Russian Tzars' difficult rules and made their way to the USA, struggled to recreate themselves as loyal Americans and solid family members. Those who remained in my grandfather's Kapulia and their children were savagely exterminated by the Russians and Germans.

Even if they had wealth in the old country, most of our ancestors came to America dirt-poor in the late 1800s. For many, "dirt-poor" was a step up the social ladder. Contemporary descriptions of Kapulia tell of a very hard life.

MEANWHILE, 300 MILES SOUTH OF KAPULIA, TWO ORTHODOX CATHOLIC PEASANTS IN THE AUSTRO-HUNGARIAN EMPIRE LANDS CALLED GALICIA TAKE FRONT AND CENTER STAGE IN HAZELTON, PENNSYLVANIA

THEIR MIDDLE SON WAS JOHN

This is my photo of my father-in-law, John Calvin Gordick, taken in 1969. He was in his early 50s and retired from a long US Air Force career. John Calvin was a patriotic American family man. Born in Hazelton in 1916, he died in 1978 in Lowell, Massachusetts.

John lived through the great flu epidemic of 1918-20, the highs of the Roaring Twenties, the depths of the 1930s Depression, World War II, the Korean War, and a fairly busy retirement. His duty stations were around the world: the US, Africa, Europe, and along the southern and eastern edges of Asia.

Based on discussions with John Calvin's children and hours of searching online, his life remains as much an enigma as this photo. His kids, including my wife Susan, know nearly nothing about his upbringing nor about his life experiences.

This essay examines his relevant record and the outside forces on his family and upon him during his youth and some of his military career. Like the other essays in this collection, I try to provide context to the questions, WHY DID OUR FAMILIES DO THAT?. Note that in the late 1800s, Central European Orthodox Jewish and Orthodox Catholic relatives were afflicted with similar pressures. Different nuances, but in the big picture, they were the same. Susan's birth father (Bob Simmons) died just after WWII. Several months later, Edith, Susan's mother, remarried. She became Edith Gordick. Susan Simmons and her brother Bob were adopted into what appeared to be a very small Gordick universe. I discovered it was pretty big.

THE BIG PICTURE

The most obvious decision our European ancestors made was to leave home. If they stayed in Europe, most of the people mentioned herein would never have been born. Picture from Wikimedia Commons, the free media repository depicts immigrants entering New York's harbor and getting their first glimpse of the Statue of Liberty.

Most came to America in the 1800s. But not the Simmons of Blue Mountain Mississippi. They were the family of Robert (Bob) Simmons, the birth father of Susan and Bob Gordick. The long Simmons essays provide a sketch of how white English adventurers came to Virginia in the 1600s (even before the Pilgrims) and surged westward. If the innumerable family trees I researched online are right, the first surviving Simmons in America was William. (An earlier, probably unrelated one died.) Most likely, Susan's ancestor was an indentured servant ... as were most English men and women who immigrated into what became the United States until the mid-1700s. He landed in Jamestown in 1608. Being indentured was a form of slavery for a specific length, such as ten years, during which a person could be bought and sold. At the end of a contract, they might get some clothes and a plot of land.

Susan's father, Robert Bernard Simmons died in a tragic accident on his way home from being discharged from the US Navy after World War II. His widow, Edith, later married John Calvin Gordick, who adopted Susan and her brother Bob. In a few years, there were three other children, John Michael, Jody, and Shelley. (Edith Marks Simmons Gordick's family was also from the British Isles. They were in New England and Canada by the early 1800s.)

Just about everybody has a story.
But our Gordicks don't.

Most families have a set of legends or myths that are passed along from generation to generation. They get shorter over time and eventually are condensed into a paragraph or sentence. They disappear if the histories are not talked about, as with John Calvin Gordick.

Each family probably claims its situation was special. Its suffering (of which there was plenty) certainly seemed special. In the late 1800s, pressures upon most poor central Europeans of every denomination led many to find a new home. My grandfather, Sam Kroloff, and his siblings arrived in the USA about the same time as John Calvin's father, Elek, and his mother, Anna's parents, who were named Wassil and Susan. Note there are too many Susans to keep track of. However, my sister Susan and my wife Susan are special.

The Kroloffs (not their given names) lived about 700 miles north of where the Gordicks (not their given names) lived. Both families saw intense religious discrimination and cruelty from their rulers, along with a lack of income. There were many differences, but the main one was that the Orthodox Catholic Gordicks apparently were serfs or peasants who probably worked on farms controlled by the nobles. The Kroloffs, because they were Jewish, by law, were not allowed to become farmers or participate in most other trades. So they often became the middlemen who sold the farmers' products. A few flourished, but not the majority. Some were in trades, like being a blacksmith or shoemaker.

That is a huge oversimplification but basically is correct.

John Calvin's parents and my grandparents came to North America because their world was changing rapidly. The quick got out.

The Jews who stayed wound up in the gas chambers of Auschwitz. The Slovak and other Orthodox Catholics who stayed in the region were caught between powerful armies and modern killing machines with few options.

The ones who left earned an A for their effort. They became Americans, Australians, and South Africans. They arrived in the A countries because that's where there were jobs.

In the USA and Canada, free land was a draw for the former serfs who were "sure" they could be farmers, like the Gordicks who settled in Canada. Meanwhile, there were millions of other new jobs being created for three main reasons.

Regarding the Northwestern RR Poster. See how a small town in South Dakota grew through the eyes of a young mother who moved from Webster City, Iowa. https://www.sdpb.org/rural-life-and-history/2023-09-11/small-town-survival-on-the-great-plains-miller-dakota-territory-in-the-1880s

First, in the USA, it was a time when the children of US Civil War soldiers would be entering the job market. But, the workers did not exist. Their potential fathers were killed or maimed. Almost a whole generation of American young men was lost.

Second, the job market was changing because of new technology.

Third, the American Dream. It was the Manifest Destiny of the US to be ever-expanding. To the emigrants, it was a dream or aspiration of a better life, a reason to live. "Work hard and be rewarded.

Or, after being asked why his family came to the USA, my pharmacist shouted out as he slammed his hand on a table so that all in the supermarket could hear, OPPORTUNITY!!! He is of South Asian heritage. Some things about the way some people think of America seem to still be viable.

PRESSURES CRUSHED JOHN CALVIN'S FAMILY IN EUROPE IN ABOUT 1880

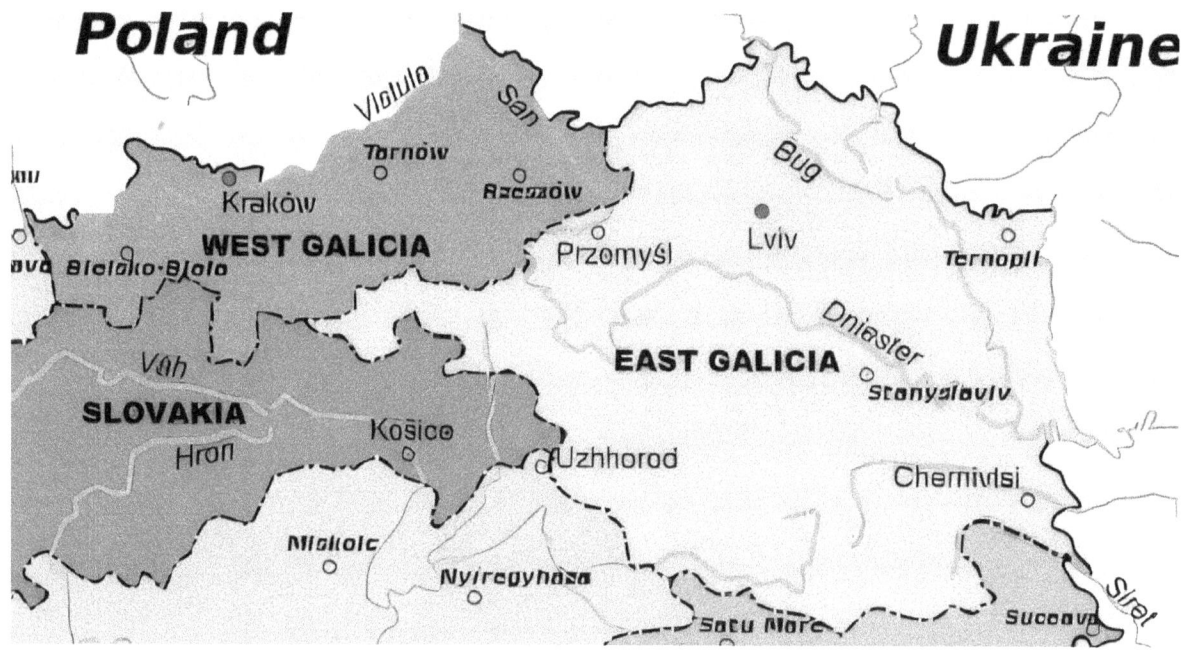

When I first questioned a couple of John Calvin Gordick's kids about where his family came from, there was confusion about whether it was Slovenia or Slovakia. Turns out his mother's family was from Slovakia, and his father was from what today is Ukraine.

They came from areas many miles away in the aforementioned Galicia, which included much of Slovakia.

The feudal barons probably shaped their early lives and destinies more than anyone else. The barons of The Austro-Hungarian Empire owned the lands the Delnaks and Gordicks inhabited. Because John Calvin's grandparents probably were serfs and/or peasants, they did not go to school, so they were pretty much illiterate. (While the serfs in the Austro-Hungarian Empire were freed about 1850, their lives weren't changed dramatically.) Not having "schooling" was, as you will see, an advantage for some of the immigrants to Hazleton. (For the map above and background, search alchetron.com/Wikipedia)

Once in America, the Wall Street Barons, the so-called Robber Barons, were in charge of the Delnaks and Gordicks.

Just as a furious thunderstorm is but a tiny cell in a bigger weather system, each family was a cell fighting furious high and low pressures, raging winds pushing them hither-and-yon, and the loud cracking of lightning, along with soaking cold rainwater causing apprehension about the future. It was like all the forces on earth were enveloping them.

Young men tended to be the first to leave.

In my view, at least, ten main big-picture forces were hitting them from all sides as noted in the beginning of this book.

- **Weather change.**
- **Mechanization**
- **Medical advancements and overpopulation**
- **The money economy replaced barter**
- **Wars, the draft, egos, and taxes**
- **Transportation**
- **Education and unions**
- **Information and Communication**
- **Crushing cultures**
- **Mass Marketing**

Meanwhile, in the 1800s companies and states or provinces in the New World were sending agents throughout Europe, including Slovakia and Ukraine, to encourage people to emigrate to North America and Canada. They had deals, intriguing deals. Free land in America. Jobs in America. The postal services were improving. Letters from relatives and friends in America were actually being delivered. Sometimes, with prepaid tickets inside.

Here and there, and then almost everywhere in central Europe, the poor, downtrodden were waking up to their version of the American Dream. Emma Lazarus' poem, which was part of the Statue of Liberty, The "Mother of Exiles," read in part…

"Give me your tired, your poor,
Your huddled masses yearning to breathe free,
The wretched refuse of your teeming shore.
Send these, the homeless, tempest-tost to me,
I lift my lamp beside the golden door!"

Most people knew that the streets of America were not paved with gold, the concept of a "golden door," however, was quite appealing. Even rural Slovaks who were not literate understood what their hands could do. Setting big-picture goals, like learning complex skills and musing about the morality of daily life, was the purview of the priests and nobles.

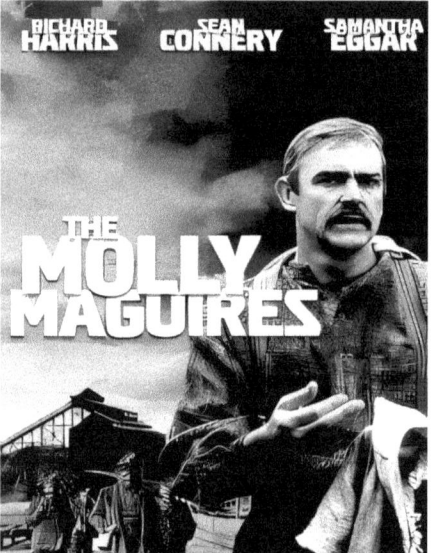

Typically, the people who came from the lands of John Calvin's parents were perfect for mining. The New York Robber Barons lording over northeast Pennsylvania owned the mines below ground and the land above them. They owned the canals and railroads, the reservoirs, the banks, and the politicians.

An advantage of hiring strong hard-working people with no previous skills in mining meant they could be trained the "right" way and led to believe their training was the "only way." At least, that's what the owners thought. Of course, they didn't want people who were dumb. Teddy Roosevelt photo from https://commons.wikimedia.org/ public domain

Not being literate didn't mean they were not quick. The owners wanted quick learners. The people from central Europe were quick learners and desperate.

Hazleton, in the center of the anthracite coal fields of northeast Pennsylvania became an important center of the union movement in America. That had to influence John Calvin. The movie, THE MOLLY MAGUIRES depicts the situation. It is about just one of the high-profile local "massacres" of union and non-union demonstrators wanting better wages and working conditions.

The Molly Maguires movie poster is used in the family website posted to the public at https://familynibbles.com/2022/10/19/243-molly-maguires/ The large genealogical website for a couple of families appears to be well researched that shows how information about the lives our forefathers and foremothers lived can make for interesting, informative reading and great fodder for grammar school assignments to write an essay about a student's family.

Hazleton also was a Big Time mill town. The Robber Barons welcomed the silk mills, which employed women and children. And didn't pay much. Employees worked very long hours with dangerous machinery to supplement the low wages of their miner husbands, fathers, and brothers.

Women in John Calvin's large family were silk weavers. His mother and sisters worked at the huge one-million-square-foot Duplan mill. There, machines unstrung millions of silk worms' cocoons, many imported from Asia, into thousands of tons of silk thread. It was woven into cloth which would be sewn by hand and machine in New York sweatshops and the wretched tenements of Chicago, where my Polish grandmother Mary and family lived.

The picture (right) from the Hazletown Museum web site is a "prettified" visualization of the massive Duplan company mill.

In large part, the barons kept wages low by encouraging chain immigration, where an early arrival would contact those still in the old country. Their invitations were reinforced by the agents hired to further encourage immigration by the ship lines that made a ton of money filling their holds with poor people in steerage, including the future miners and weavers. Of course, some of the Robber Barons invested in the ship lines.

The idea of attracting more potential miners than jobs available in Hazleton meant that any miner who was sick, physically incapacitated, or just didn't like the bosses, knew they would be unemployed. Healthier men or boys would be hungry to grab onto an opening in the mines.

So, for one or more of the reasons above, a flock of John Calvin's family arrived in and around Hazleton starting in the 1890s. Maybe the first in our family were his mother's parents, Wassil and Susan Dalina/Danelak (eventually Delaney). Wassil was a miner and, along with his wife Susan, started producing children right away. Their oldest was Anna (1895), the mother of John Calvin.

As earlier mentioned, both sides of John Calvin's family came from Galicia … both sides of Galicia. Not the Spanish Galicia, but the area of the Austro-Hungarian Empire that included Slovakia to the west and lands to the east that extended far into what today is Ukraine.

I remember once being told that John Calvin was a Slovak. Well, his grandmother, was from Slovakia. John Calvin was surrounded, almost smothered, by his mom's family, and apparently, he had few contacts with his dad's family. The only recorded one I could find with new information is below.

John Calvin's father Elek/Alex was from eastern Galicia, near today's Ukrainian city of Chernivtsi, hundreds of miles away from Slovakia. (Chernivtsi is located furthest right in yellow, just above Bukovinia, the former Ottoman-Byzantine State.)

Life isn't long enough, at least for me, to learn the ins and outs of Central European history and the various ethnicities. Alexander/Elek is a perfect example.

It is hard to read the card below. It says his dad lived in Ustrezko, a village in Eastern Galicia, several miles north of Chernivtsi. Over many years the residents had been called Austrians, Hungarians, Slavs, Galicians, Romanians, Poles, or Byzantines, among other ethnicities, as their rulers changed.

Elek reported that he came to New York in November of 1902 on a ship named Rotterdam. By 1909, he was married to Anna and living with his herd of in-laws at 221 S. Cedar St. in Hazleton.

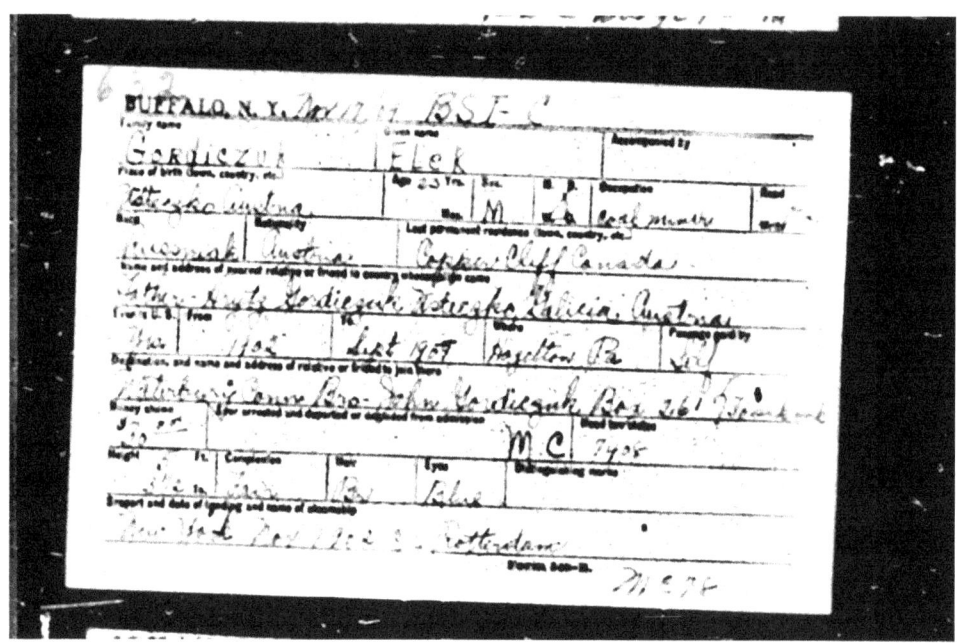

Elek, about 23, and 18-year-old Anna, along with Elek's 21-year-old cousin William visited a small mining town in northern Ontario, Canada. I couldn't find out why. The card was filled out at a border crossing. There also is a border record of them coming the other way.

The one above also said Elek's father was named Hyrtz, and the family came from the village of Usteczko, which is several miles north of Chernivtsi. His cousin's last name is indecipherable on the document. It says he was staying in Waterbury, Connecticut, where Elek's brother, John the Blacksmith, lived. The village where William lived before arriving in America was near the village where Elek's father, Hyrtz, lived.

I assume, all were Orthodox Catholics, of which there were many variations. John Calvin, born in Hazleton, seemed to have been a Slovak Orthodox. One of the first two Slovak Orthodox churches in America was in Hazleton. In its cemetery are John Calvin's mother, Anna, and her father, Wassil, some in-laws, at least one of his brothers, and other relatives. The Orthodox Catholics and the Roman Catholics are the same thing but different, with many similar beliefs and many dissimilarities, like whether priests could marry or not.

Not all Catholics got along, nor did the other Europeans who settled in smallish Hazleton or a big city like Chicago or New York unless they had to get along, like when unions were organized.

In the Hazleton mines, the Irish and Germans were often supervisors. Polish, Slovaks, and other central Europeans were lower down in the pecking order.

Elek, like many immigrants, must have been like a chameleon. He left the mines to take a job in the insurance game. Elek must have displayed his European ethnicity when necessary, and his American veneer when necessary, and wore any other cloak when needed. I assume his background of several ethnicities didn't hurt in dealing with his current or potential Metropolitan Life insurance clients in the 1920s.

HAZLETON

It certainly was a mill town, but underneath it all, literally and figuratively, it was a coal town. Just about everybody and everything in Hazleton happened because of the solid river of black anthracite gold frozen under the Gordiczuk's feet. I don't remember where I read it, but there were several entrances to mines within the city limits. One entrance reportedly still visible, is next to the present CVS pharmacy relatively close to where the Gordiczuks lived. Everybody, from baby sitters to barbers, to bar maids eventually could be traced back to the avarice of the Barons.

Next to the mines were the breaker buildings and other structures as well as the rails necessary for processing and transporting coal. A "colliery" (mine and support buildings) is pictured in the distance, across town.

Sioux City was dependent on farming and the cattle/hog and meat packing economy, but it wanted to be a Second Chicago (see Corn Palaces essay P22). Chicago was big, boisterous and, generally BOOMING (see "What Mary Saw.") Apparently, Hazleton, just wanted to be.

Hazleton was caught up in the Gilded Age and Roaring Twenties where there were the super rich and the supposedly supine super poor. Mark Twain, author and humorist said the Gilded Age was glittering on the surface but corrupt underneath. There were a few highs in Hazleton, like when water and electricity became available to homes, when strikes were considered successful, a local ball team did well, or when the local movie theater was open.

John Calvin's brother Peter's lifetime job was at the theater. Another brother William also kept a lifetime job in Hazleton working for an ice cream company. Michael moved to Chicago and Alfred worked for Bethlehem Steel.

Hazleton looked like any typical Coal Belt or industrial town of that time. As elsewhere, Hazleton took a huge hit from deaths and sickness during the massive flu pandemic as World War I was ending. Many streets remained unpaved.

ONE FINAL LOOK AT OLD VS. NEW COUNTRY

Travel from central Europe to the USA in steerage is covered in other essays and appendixes. As are the realities of life in small villages in central Europe. What happened to the Jews in Kapulia is similar to what Elek and the Catholic Wassil saw and lived in Galicia even if the run-up to the pressures they strived to survive were different. The picture on the left is from website (mostly Italian stories), https://prinzessirene.com/ Center is one Hazelton Colliary from https://upthewoods.net/anthracite-coal/collieries-and-coal-breakers.html#top Right is an Austrian coat of arms at https://simple.m.wikipedia.org/wiki/File:Austria_Bundesadler_1919-1934.svg

It was tough to decide to leave, gather the will and resources to get to America and deal with those who would be left behind.

If the eagle on the Austro-Hungarian coat of arms flew directly from Chernivtsi to Hazleton, it would travel well over 4,400 miles. Elek's land and sea route would not have been as direct so it would have been longer. In terms of technology and the so-called progress of Western Civilization … in a few weeks, Elek would have traveled at least 440 years.

WHY ANTHRACITE COAL?

There are two kinds of coal used in America. Hard anthracite burns hotter, longer and cleaner than soft smog-producing bituminous. In Pennsylvania, much of the hard coal is in the northeast around Hazelton and Scranton. Soft coal is in the southwest, around Pittsburgh.

It was difficult to get anthracite to burn until Judge Jesse Fell installed a simple metal grate into the fireplace in a tavern he owned north of Hazleton. In 1808, he took some of the dense black coal rocks lying around the area, put them on the top of the grate, and lit some kindling below. The little kindling fire separated a few inches below the coal caused a hot upward draft and lit the coal sitting on the grate. It burned unexpectedly long, through the whole night. Picture from Plymouth Historical Society - Luzerne County https://www.facebook.com/permalink.php/?story_fbid=1651936801520998&id=182329111815115

Suddenly, there was an industry to be created, not just because the hard coal was cleaner for soot-covered cities but also because it was better for machinery like railroad locomotives. But it was buried deep in the ground. That's where the Robber Barons came in. It took a long time, but they had the money to get people, dynamite, and whatever else was needed to find and extract the coal. Picture and more about canals at https://canals.org/learn/the-canal-era/

Early on, they built canals that were expensive, slow, and couldn't carry anywhere near the amount of coal that could be sold. This was a big deal for a lot of economic reasons. For instance, from the Mississippi and Missouri Rivers all the way east to the Atlantic Ocean, forests were being decimated as wood was needed not only for buildings and fences but also for keeping fires going day and night.

Then, the Barons built railroads. Expensive but able to carry massive amounts of coal.

The Vanderbilts, Harrimans, Rockefellers, and their crowd, sold stocks, built up fortunes, and then funded the railroads. They financed efforts to get cheap labor from abroad and backed the bigger and faster ocean liners and cargo ships, as well as the businesses to make the products that an emerging middle class wanted, like Coca-Cola.

MINES

John Calvin Gordiczuk's early life was directly connected to the dangerous mines under his feet in Hazeltown. (Different spelling of his last name, same person. He married Edith Marks Simmons, adopted Susan, and brother Bob, changing their last names to Gordick.)

Miners regularly were maimed and died from poisonous gasses, explosions that broke up the solid veins of coal, or collapsing walls and ceilings in the tunnels below ground. There is a long litany of other dangers. There were floods, collapses, and serious accidents. Mines had rudimentary medical staff in the dark, cramped areas. There was heavy traffic getting the coal out of the "seams" and up the steep ramps to the ground.

The phrase "canary in the coal mine" evolved because canaries were brought into the mines in little cages (right). If the bird became sick or dropped dead, there was poison in the air. Miners fled as fast as possible.

Fires often were lit as metal pick-axes threw sparks while hitting stone, igniting gas escaping from the underground caverns, some millions of years in the making. Explosives that were used to loosen the seams of coal sometimes caused deadly fires.

Next to the mines were gigantic buildings like the one pictured earlier and just above. They were eight or more stories high, made of wood, and called "breakers" among other things.

Pictures above and more background on mines at https://explorepahistory.com/displayimage.php?imgId=1-2-18D And https://journal.sciencemuseum.ac.uk/ And https://www.wikiwand.com/en/articles/Coal_mining_in_Plymouth_Pennsylvania And https://www.appalachiabare.com/coal-creek-part-3-cross-mountain/

Dangerous devices cranked big chunks of coal up to the top floor, then it flowed down through a series of slides passing humans armed with hammers and machines to break big rocks of coal down to smaller pieces, small enough to be shoveled into a furnace or fireplace on Park Avenue in New York.

Near the bottom of the tall buildings were the breaker boys. John Calvin and his brothers may have been breaker boys on and off as they grew up, maybe at summer breaks (pun intended). Breaker boys were eliminated by the 1930s.

The bloodied breaker boys worked without gloves but with full bladders and bowels. They picked out the non-coal bits and pieces so customers would receive only coal and not the slate and shale and other rocks that also rose from the mines. They worked ten hours a day, six days a week. Some older men, half broken by their days as miners, were working alongside the boys, making a pittance. The man with the stick kept the kids alert.

#12

UNIONS, JOHN GOES TO WAR, MARRIES EDITH, THE FAMILY EXPANDS

By the 1880s, the coal fields in and around Hazleton were hotbeds of the union movement. Until the fall of coal and the rise of oil and gas, the United Mine Workers was one of the most powerful unions in America. Later, Mother Jones was a prominent miners union spokesperson.

Typically clad in a black dress, her face framed by a lace collar and black hat, the barely five-foot-tall Mother Jones was a forceful fighter for workers' rights—once labeled "the most dangerous woman in America" by a U.S. district attorney. Mary Harris "Mother" Jones rose to prominence as a fiery orator and fearless organizer for the Mine Workers during the first two decades of the 20th century. Her voice had great carrying power. Her energy and passion inspired men half her age into action and compelled their wives and daughters to join in the struggle. If that didn't work, she would embarrass men to action. "I have been in jail more than once, and I expect to go again. If you are too cowardly to fight, I will fight," she told them. Mother Jones' organizing methods were unique for her time. She welcomed African-American

workers and involved women and children in strikes. She organized miners' wives into teams armed with mops and brooms to guard the mines against scabs. She staged parades with children carrying signs that read, "We Want to Go to School and Not to the Mines." (AFL/CIO website) Breaker boys at work and more about mining from https://www.citizensvoice.com/lifestyles/coal-a-shared-heritage/article_4c433ded-c0e8-5544-81be-f9bb0efffdba.html

Thousands, probably millions, of Americans were involved. John Calvin couldn't have been isolated from the strikes and violence of the workers in Hazleton. The miners' sons worked in the mines even after child labor laws were enacted. The wives and daughters and a few young boys worked in the silk mills. As mentioned, John Calvin's mother, Anna, plus her mom and siblings, were "weavers" caught up in the silk mill strikes.

While growing up, John Calvin saw and heard about the murders and "massacres" of mine workers seeking better wages and working conditions. He saw when the whole town shut down and demonstrated or conducted a parade down the main street in support of the strikers. Picture and background information https://www.articonog.com/2019/12/child-labour-in-industrial-revolution.html

He knew of the almost daily reports about friction between the workers and management. And he knew about the big brouhaha's at the mills, which had to have involved his family.

The strikes at mines in and around Hazleton were so serious that President Teddy Roosevelt intervened. He was the first American president to publicly mediate between big business and labor. There was fear that the strike would rage into the winter and New York apartment dwellers and mansion owners would freeze.

The railroads controlled the mines, and JP Morgan, the king of Wall Street, controlled the railroads. Much to Roosevelt's relief, JP "convinced" the railroad presidents to negotiate. Roosevelt, according to a 2020 Washington Post book review, thought this was among his greatest achievements.

That strike was one of many legends Anna's family must have talked about because the strike was very hard on the citizens of Hazleton. Not just the miners but all other businesses.

As of this writing, it is unclear how much influence the union movement and other frictions in his teenage years pushed John Calvin into a military career.

Interestingly, Edith Marks Simmons Gordick's first husband (Bob Simmons) joined the Navy on the west coast about the same time as John Calvin joined what became the Army Air Corps on the east coast. Bob Simmons wanted direction and to learn a trade. It is unclear what John Calvin wanted. Maybe he just wanted out.

There is way more to my father-in-law's story that I haven't discovered. Why was his middle name, Calvin? Certainly, that is not a Catholic-Orthodox name. Why, around the time his dad disappeared in 1929, did the family take the same Americanized name of so many of their relatives, Gordick? Why did his mother Anna's family, about the same time, change their name from Danelak to the Irish-sounding Delaney? Anna then called herself Anna Delaney Gordick.

And why did John Calvin not tell his kids about his youth and their extended family?

Not discussing their past is not that unusual. One of my favorite Kroloff/Kauffman family stories involves a young man who married a midwestern cousin. He came from a fairly modest family, joined the Marines, and eventually obtained an Ivy League law degree. On his way home from law school, he decided to detour and visit New York Harbor to see the Statue of Liberty and Ellis Island and drink in what his father must have seen and felt when first arriving from Europe.

In the middle of emotionally recounting the experience, his father put his warm hand upon his son's even warmer hand and interrupted in the thick Central European accent he never lost … he said, "But son, we came in through Canada."

Not much is known about what made John Calvin tick. His youngest son, John Michael, told me he and his siblings "were like in a witness protection plan. We knew nothing about his background."

We do know that by the 1930s, coal from deep mines was less important to the economy. Oil and gas were taking their place in diesel railroad engines and furnaces in buildings. Strip mining was beginning to be the most efficient and least labor-intensive way to get the coal out of the ground. The Depression was killing jobs right and left. Hazleton was still mulling over the big hit it took 15 years earlier, with an estimated 1,000 deaths from the Spanish Flu pandemic just after WWI.

Like small towns all across the country, young men and women were drifting off to larger cities. (My dad left Sioux City, Iowa, to find a job in Chicago.) In John Calvin's case, Philadelphia is where his enlistment papers say he lived for about two years. He entered the Army in late 1936 and reported for duty in 1937. That was before WWII, which started with Germany invading Poland on Sept 1, 1939.

The most information I could find about John Calvin's life came from a deep dive into a shallow pool of information online (like the census and news articles) and Xeroxed page-upon-page of his military records. Those are the bureaucratic forms that showed every time he got a vaccine shot or a lecture on sexually transmitted diseases, where he was stationed, and in which town he would lay over between assignments, near Asian airfields, for instance. When I was in the active US Army Reserves, a couple of weeks a year, my so-called summer camp training was writing press releases like this one about Sgt. Gordick, that would be reprinted word for word in local papers.

IS CREW CHIEF ON HELICOPTER PLANES

Master Sergeant John C. Gordick, son of Mrs. Anna Gordick, of New Coxeville on the Hazleton-Beaver Meadows, road is serving as crew chief for helicopter maintenance with the 62nd AAF Base Unit, Air Rescue Service, March Field, Riverside, California. Two projects in which the helicopters are being used and which require expert maintenance to be performed, are tests of the plane in forest firefighting and other forestry work in cooperation with the United States Forest Service, and the forthcoming tests to determine the feasibility of using helicopters to deliver mail to post offices in metropolitan areas. Sergeant Gordick came to March Field in April 1945, after attending a special Army school for helicopter mechanics. Previous to that time, he had served overseas in both the European and Asiatic-Pacific theaters. Serving with the 33rd Fighting Group as flight chief in the North African, Sicilian, and Italian campaigns, he was wounded June 6, 1942. In January 1943 he went to the China-Burma-India theater for six months duty, returning to the United States, March 25, 1945.

Sergeant Gordick wears the Purple Heart and the Good Conduct Ribbon. His campaign ribbons include the ETO ribbon with five battle stars, and the Bronze Arrowhead for the African campaign; the Asiatic-Pacific ribbon with three battle stars, the American theater, the American Defense, and the Victory Ribbon.

Here is some of the little I learned.

Not too long after high school graduation, he left town, apparently finding work as a ticket taker in a Philadelphia movie house and a truck driver.

John Calvin probably went through some kind of basic training in New Jersey and was sent to Langley Air Field near Hampton Roads in Virginia. Eventually, Private Gordick rose to the rank of Master Sergeant after being shipped to several posts in Africa, Europe and Asia during WWII and the Korean War.

Robert Mitchell Gordick, the oldest son of John Calvin (This Bob is Susan's brother), became a Master Sergeant in the US Air Force and was stationed at Langley a generation later.

Edith and John's middle son, John Michael Gordick, enlisted in the Air Force to see the world. He had lived much of his life at home in Lowell, Massachusetts. John Michael left the Air Force when his initial enlistment was over. He never was sent by the military out of the state of Massachusetts, so much for seeing the world. By coincidence, his unit was the same one his dad had served in many years earlier.

The news article summarizes John Calvin's military career up until a few months before he married Edith in 1946. The family then lived in San Bernardino, a 15-mile commute to March Field, where he was stationed.

Based on my conversations with his children, John Calvin must have cut off most family relationships, rarely acknowledging or seeing his siblings. And, nary a word was spoken about his parents and their large families. To this day, the hundreds of US and Canadian cousins are unknown to the Gordick kids. Nor, as this is written, do they know the names of their grandparents, Anna and Elek.

The blurry picture is Edith and John Calvin, probably taken in 1946/47.

A new adventure began in 1951. During the Korean War, John Calvin was again stationed in Asia. Edith, Susan, Bob, and toddler John Michael took a troop ship to live with him at Johnson Air Force Base in Japan. Under a Japanese name, it had been the headquarters airfield for the Japanese Air Force during WWII. Their house on the base came with a still-usable foxhole in the yard. And a maid to keep the small property clean.

Upon returning to the USA on another troop ship in December 1952, the family followed John Calvin as he was stationed in Kansas, Nebraska, Massachusetts, then near Chicago, Illinois, and finally retired in Massachusetts. Along the way, Jody and Shelley were born. Those stories are for someone else to relate.

The Gordick children had abundant contact with their mom's New England family. Bob and Susan remember, as youngsters, only one short visit to their father's Hazleton. The highlight apparently was watching John Calvin's brother Peter changing reels of film in the projector room of the movie theater.

John Calvin and Edith would retire to Lowell, Mass., a decaying mill town not unlike the decaying Hazleton he wanted to leave 30 years earlier. They would live in a big old house that reminded me of the home of the TV Addams Family. It had a truly spooky basement with a mostly mud floor. The basement walls holding up the house were stacks of rocks, vaguely reminiscent of the walls of a mine. My father-in-law bragged about the many tools strewn around the basement that he had "liberated" from the garbage piles at the armory he had been hired to guard against people like thieves.

The photo (right) was taken in 1966. The Gordick Lowell Mass. home featured a sprawling side and back yard, a gathering place for an expanding family that included several more grandkids and husbands than the photo. It shows five children, my wife (Susan), one girlfriend, three grandchildren, plus John Calvin and Edith. Susan is the hot chick at the bottom right with our two oldest kids, Amy and Adam.

Back row (l-r) Edith, Bob, Carol, John Michael Gordick. Seated are John Calvin, Jean and Rob Gordick (on lap), Susan Kroloff, Abby and Adam Kroloff (on lap). Seated in front, Shelley and Jody Gordick

The undated picture below is believed to be Elek's hometown in Galicia

It is a few miles northwest of where the borders of Ukraine, Moldova, and Romania meet. Ustechko (a current spelling) is on the Dnister River northeast of Horodenka. It is also known as Uścieczko, Us'tsechko, Usechko, and, as mentioned above, it is near Chenivitsi, Ukraine.

The one story I could find about the village, or shtetl, indicated it was much like Kapulia (now Kopyl or Kopil) in Belarus. That's where the Kroloff's came from. The only information about the town that I could find in English comes from the website JewishGen. Most residents in Galacia probably couldn't write, but members of the Jewish shtetls could write and provide some history. They wrote in Hebrew, Yiddish, or maybe Hungarian or Ukrainian. Remember that Shtetls tended to be part of larger communities that contained Russians, Poles, Tatars, Muslims, Catholics, Orthodox, or other ethnicities and religions.

Meanwhile up north in Kapulia the Kroloff clan was experiencing a somewhat similar pre-Industrial Age life.

A SMART ELEK?

- John's mother was Anna Delnak Gordiczok. Well, that was one version of her name when he was born. I suspect she was the biggest influence on his life. When Anna died in 1975, she was living in an institution often labeled as an insane asylum. Her mother and father were from different regions of Galicia in the Austro-Hungarian Empire.

- When John was born in 1916, his father was a miner known as Alexander or Elek Gordiczok or by similar names. Elek/Alex disappeared in 1929, the year of the Wall Street Crash that brought on the Great Depression. This is the Hazleton, PA, house in which John Calvin lived. It is 221-223 South Cedar St. (Picture from Google.)

- John was born there. His parents lived there with his mother's family which appeared to be dominated by women.

- Anna, in 1929, suddenly a single mom with a flock of kids, declared she was a widow. I could not figure out where Elek went or why he left. By chance, I found online that in 1942 Alex reported to his draft board. He said he was 57 years of age, unemployed, and living in New York City's Lower East Side at the edge of "Little Ukraine," then the largest settlement of Ukrainians in the USA. Elek's hometown in the old country because of moving borders was in The Ukraine, a part of the Soviet Union. Elek/Alex died in 1944, according to Anna's obit in a Hazleton paper,

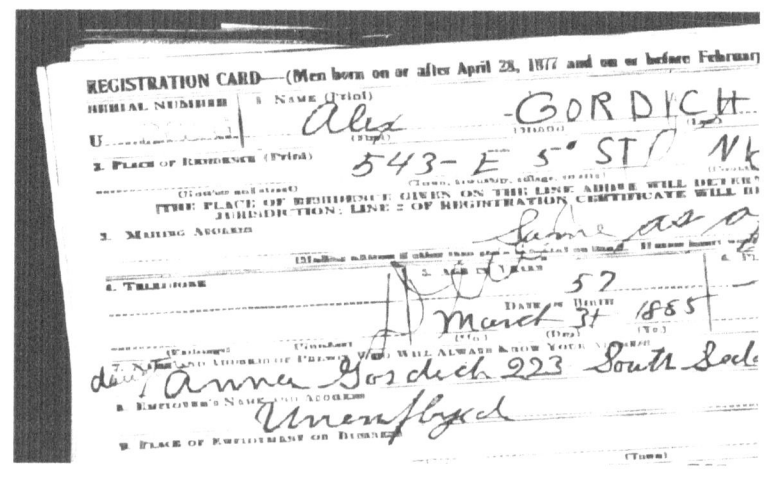

although there is no evidence I could find that she knew he was alive after 1929. The penciled note on this WWII draft card says, Deceased 3/26/44.

- From birth to about 1935, John Calvin and eight or ten first cousins, his parents, grandparents, and siblings, lived in the 221-223 Cedar St. duplex. In 1935, he left for Philadelphia. The building had two doorways and two apartments. One was occupied by the family, then named Gordick. By January 1937, he had joined the Army Air Corps and was soon to see the world. His military papers said he graduated high school in 1934. At least a couple of his four brothers also went to war. His sister Jean outlasted them all. The Gordick presence stayed in Hazleton for many years. Checking in with Google Earth, the building and neighborhood today still look like those built by coal mining companies for employees. Exterior brick walls may have been added later.

- Susan's stepfather had cousins throughout the USA and Canada, including his uncle John the Blacksmith in Waterbury, Connecticut … and untold dozens of cousins on his mother's side of the family. He lost contact with all of them. A Gordick clan that settled in Missouri claims to have come from Russia, but the Gordicks in western Canada seem to have come from the same area that Elek lived in Galicia. The Canadian Gordicks and the Pennsylvania Gordicks may be the same family.

- John's mother was a Delnak (there were several spellings in English). Census reports said Anna's mother never learned English. Her father was a miner. It's unclear how John Calvin got along with the Delnaks. Wassil, his father-in-law, owned the duplex in which he, his wife Anna, and their kids lived. Around 1917 Elek, Anna Delnak Gordichuk (John's mother), and their growing family moved from 221 S. Cedar, just a couple of feet next door where they raised their family in the other half of the duplex at 223 S. Cedar St. My guess is it was around the time Elek left the mine and took a job with MetLife.

Some of this may not make sense at this point. By the time you finish this essay, it may be clearer. Maybe not.

UNCLE JAKE'S DRAMATIC ESCAPE FROM UKRAINE

One hundred years ago, like today, millions of people feared for their lives and wanted to flee somewhere safe. For many emigrants, their destination was America. Often, the trips were dangerous, not direct, and very scary. (Some things just don't change.)

A large number from Europe's rural areas crossed 5,500 miles and about 500 years in just a few weeks … from the Dark Ages to the Industrial Age, from candles to electric lights.

That generation has died off, and with them, the back stories of their adventures, good and bad, and even why most Americans today are Americans.

Their travels and travails tend to be reduced to a sentence or paragraph. For example, I often heard "He came to America to avoid the Russian draft and a long, probably deadly, term in the Tsar's army." (From the late 1700s Russia and almost all other European nations were continuously fighting wars. Whether winning or losing, military men died and rulers were ever more fearing the next war and enforcing drafts. As the modernization of guns and tactics of war progressed killing power increased and more men were needed to fill the ranks of those dead, wounded and captured.

This series of essays, WHY DID OUR FAMILIES DO THAT? is designed to provide context to those six words, which are both a question and a statement as well as provide you with hints on what might make your family stories more compelling.

Here, I introduce Uncle Jake. He married my great-aunt Esther Helfet.

THE UNUSUAL PART OF THE BACK STORY

By 1899, a Helfet family from a place they called Chernush (later Chornucky) emigrated to Liverpool, England. Separately, a family named Dobrofsky traveled from Mena and were living in Liverpool. Mena and Chernush are many miles apart in what today is named Ukraine. The families met, and in a few years, most left and married in the U.S. and South Africa. Also from Chernush were our Helfgott relatives and a few others whose names begin with "He."

But this is about my Uncle Jake Dobrofsky, who fell in love with Esther Helfet. In late September 1904, Jake entered America at the port of Philadelphia. Later, he reunited with Esther in Sioux City, Iowa, where four Helfet siblings had gathered in 1903. One of them was my grandmother, Sarah Helfet, who later married Sam Kroloff. I lost track of how many Sarahs are in our family.

Jake jokingly wrote in his memoir that "his feet never touched the ground" until he was about ten years old. Jacob was the youngest child of a family that had wealth, servants, a profitable business and a good life ... or as good as it can get while paying off the authorities and making all the sacrifices necessary to "get along" in the Pale ruled by a tyrannical Russian Tsar. Tyrannical sounds trite, yet it was true.

The abundant Dobrofsky wealth apparently was something of a rarity for Jews in the small towns of The Pale. The word Pale comes from England and translates to "boundary." The boundary encircled much of what later was called Eastern Europe. That's where the Russian rulers had herded almost all of the country's Jews. The Pale was peppered with thousands of rural settlements and fewer towns and cities. Villages that housed at least a few Jewish families were called shtetls.

All shtetls had unpaved streets and wood houses. Every generation or two, a candle at night, a stray ember from a cooking fire, or a bolt of lightning would set off raging fires that quickly leveled the community. If a community had relatively large buildings "downtown" it probably was a small to large city rather than a rural shtetl.

The 1916 scene is from a shtetl named Iwanowo. It shows troughs like small canals alongside the houses to prevent flooding. Usually, some sewage and garbage could be found in the streets. The shtetls were full of smells, flavorful cooking, sweet odors of flowers, outhouses, and rotting unused parts of butchered animals.

Some houses had a large section of roof that could be propped up in good weather, airing out the entire building. Those with thatched roofs became homes for birds and bugs.

But not all sthetl homes and residents were destitute. And not all were tiny. Pictured right, 1902, is Panska Street in Mielic, South Poland population of 5,500, about half Jews.

Uncle Jake wrote in his memoir that the Dobrofsky house in Mena seemed like a mansion. The town, northeast of Kiev, was home to 1,659 Jews (26 percent of the total population), according to the 1897 census. Jacob reported that his father bought smoked and packed fish by the trainload from the Volga River and sold the catches far and wide. The business had its own fisheries and warehouses. Below are fishermen on the Volga about 1890.

As a pre-teen, Jake was less interested in becoming a religious scholar as his father wanted and more interested in the business, for which he had a flair. The youngster became active in the enterprise.

Unfortunately, one day in the 1890s, instead of taking several months of the company's cash to a bank, an employee, who was a relative, took the money and his girlfriend to America. Without cash, the high-flying family crashed.

For purposes of this essay, his "flight" to Liverpool (actually on land and sea because there were no airplanes) illustrates the difficulties of escaping from The Pale and then crossing national borders with armed guards staked out along the way. Those guards often wanted to see official papers with their eyes and feel bribes in their hands before allowing people to pass west toward the oceans.

The context is important. The fear of Programs (bloody mob riots aimed at killing, defiling and robbing Jews) was sweeping across the Pale. That fear was felt in Mena. Right is a Russian policeman.

As this excerpt begins, Jake's uncle, David Dobrofsky, was living in England. David was wanted by the Mena authorities. Several years earlier, he had been hiding at Jake's house to escape the Russian draft. Jake's father had bribed officials and others to sneak David out of the country.

Each year, the officials would come back to demand further bribes and threaten to turn in Jake's father if he didn't pay. Below are some of Jakes's own words.

EXCERPTS FROM JAKE'S AUTOBIOGRAPHY

"Uncle David... corresponded with Father regularly and told him that he was doing fairly well. By that time, he had already brought some of his wife's relatives to England from Russia, and they were in the furniture manufacturing business ...

One day there was much excitement because we received a letter from England. Of course, no one ever opened any mail except Father, and we did not learn what was actually in the letter until one Friday night, after the late Shabos dinner. Father called us into the Szall, the living room, and told us the secret and the big surprise: That he had decided to go to England and see what it looks like: that if he liked it and could get settled there and find a business, he would send for us; if not, he would come back.

Another surprise was that he had decided not to go alone, but to take Uncle Nathan with him, as he was absolutely useless in the small business that we conducted at home. (This was after the money had been stolen and they were trying to make a living selling fish retail from stalls, like the fishmonger pictured below.)

He also decided to take Auntie Broche with him; in the six months previous she had been taking up dressmaking, and Father figured that she and Uncle Nathan could get jobs temporarily until Father could find a business of some sort, and perhaps they would remain there, even if Father did return to Russia... it was a bolt out of the blue... Since the entire family, both the boys and girls, were growing up without any trade or profession to depend on, he made a very wise decision in deciding that we should try our luck in a foreign land...

(Without that decision) there probably would not be any of us here right now. No doubt we would not have been able to escape the horrible catastrophe that struck the millions of Jews that stayed in any part of Europe…

As soon as the initial excitement and surprise of Father's announcement wore off, complications began to pile up. According to the Government regulations… the oldest one in the family was responsible for anyone escaping and avoiding military service.

Since Father was responsible to the Government for the disappearance of Uncle David from the military service, he was not eligible to get a Government passport or permission to leave Russia. The only thing left to do was to try to cross the borders or frontiers through the illegal agents who were established throughout Europe.

Ninety per cent of all the Jews that left Russia in those days were not eligible to get regular permission to emigrate and had to get across the borders by paying fees to these agents.

(Left above shows Austria/Ukraine border town of Brody. This Jewish market, similar to many others at the edge of The Pale, was the last place to buy before trying to get across border. The border gate on the first page of this essay was at Brody. Right is Libau on the Southwest Latvian coast, now Liepaja, see red arrow. Below is Libau port.)

We had some relatives living in the town of Libau, which at that time belonged to Russia, but had at one time been part of Curland Or Latvia. Libau was on the border of Germany, and it was possible to cross over into Germany either by boat or by land. The Agents charged terrific prices, not only because of the risk involved, because they knew the frightened Jews had no alternative and would pay whatever price was asked. There was no other way out for Father. He finally made the arrangements, through his relatives in Libau, to try to get across the border with Uncle Nathan and Auntie Broche.

We were unaware of all the hardships they encountered until two years later when the rest of the family followed to England. They told us that they had tried to cross the border so many times and had to return to the town of Libau that they finally lost track … eventually, they succeeded in crossing the border and got a boat for England from the town of Yutkin (I can't find it on a map GK).

The rest of us were left in Mena to shift for ourselves and it was no picnic. We all had to work from morning until night and plan constantly in order to make ends meet, but somehow or other, we managed (for 15 months, mostly by selling fish retail in stalls in the surrounding territory.)

Father left for England in March of 1897. (Jake left in late 1898.)

When the time came for us to make arrangements to leave, we wanted to get Guvernaterski passports for the three of us so we would not have to go through the dangers of crossing the border with the agent. It was getting more and more dangerous and many, many times lives were lost in the attempt. In order to get the Government passport, it was necessary to make up some papers signed by Father, stating that he gave us permission to go to England for a visit. We could not tell them that Father was already in England, because he had left illegally, and was supposed to pay up the fine that had been levied against him for allowing his brother to escape from his military service.

We went to a shyster attorney (they had them, even in those days) to draw up the permit, but it was necessary that we have Father's signature. Instead of sending the paper to England to get it signed, the attorney suggested that I should sign it, as the chances were the Government officials would not know who had signed it.

I went down to the County Seat by myself, and my heart was pounding so I could hardly get the words out. I told him that my father was very sick with asthma, and could not leave his bed; and that the reason my signature was exactly the same as my father's was because I never went to school, that my father taught me everything I knew, writing as well as other studies, and that I learned to copy my father's handwriting exactly.

I don't know whether they believed me or not, but through some miracle, they told me to come back in the afternoon.

I was scared stiff that they would find out the whole story, so I went to the Kashone Rov, who is the official Government Rabbi appointed to handle all affairs between Jewish people and the Government, and to act as their emissary or representative with the Government. When I look back on it now, I don't know how I happened to have the good judgment to do that; I guess it was because I was too scared to go back alone. I imagined all sorts of dire consequences, including being sent to Siberia; even though I had so much responsibility put upon me, I was still a child in my imaginings.

I told the Rabbi the whole story and he went in with me and told me sit down and wait. He went into different room than I had been in, and in less than ten minutes he was back with the papers. He told me that I would have to pay ten rubles to one of the clerks for it, and I had the money on me, I lost no time in paying the money and, believe me, I got out of there fast, with my heart pounding all the time.

The Rabbi told me that he had got the passport from a different man entirely than I had dealt with; and that is the way all Government affairs were conducted in those days in Russia. You could not accomplish anything without bribing some minor official, even if it was only ten rubles.

I was still too scared to even go down to the depot to get my ticket and asked the Rabbi to do that for me, which he did. When the time came, I did not go to the depot until the last minute before the train left – I kept expecting them to discover the error they made by giving me the passport, and my heart was in my mouth until the train started to move.

I remember the simcha (rejoicing) there was when I finally got home and I showed them the passports; and when I told them what had happened they could not believe that a boy of my age could think fast enough and outwit the Government officials, which was always the prime ambition of every Jew in Russia at that time ...

I don't recall any of the details of disposing of our property or our furniture and only remember how exciting it all was ...

We had to go almost all the way across Russia to get to the place where we would take the boat, and then after several days on the boat we landed in Libau, Kurland, where our relatives were, and took the boat from there to go to England. (Jake and family probably traveled northwest out of the present Ukraine, through Belarus and Latvia, a trip of about 500 miles, as the crow flies, but they weren't crows. They were cowed. As noted above. Libau today is Liepaja, the westernmost point in Latvia.)

"The examination of our papers, with our permission to leave Russia, was when we boarded the boat, and up to the last second that the boat started - and all the way across Russia I had a terrible premonition that we would be stopped because I had forged the signature on the passport.

(In Libau, Jake marveled at the big buildings and electricity.) "I used to wait around to watch someone turn lights on and off."

"… in those days the boats were mostly combined freight and passenger ships, and I guess our boat was mostly for freight."

They landed in Hull, England, most likely at Victoria Pier, and probably went to the emigrant holding building, which abutted the RR and took a train to London. Right is the entirely unimposing holding building.

London was "like being on a different planet, surrounded by strange looking people, the likes of which I had never seen before. The tall buildings, Tramways rushing so fast and the brightly lit streets astonished me. And the people were so different from the Russian people that I was tongue-tied with wonder." Cartoon depicts a crowded London RR platform.

And then, another train and finally…."OUR DESTINATION." … Liverpool

The Terminal Hotel of the London and Northwestern Railway. The station is at the rear of the building.

LIVERPOOL, MID-1890s HELFETS AND DOBROFSKYS

The Helfets reportedly traveled from Chernush, Ukraine, as a family unit and portable support system. They were not split up as the Dobrofskys were to be. Yet, their collective brains must have been swirling like a whipped omelet being bombarded with new onions.

As they moved west, the family was exposed to electric lights, foreign smells, incomprehensible languages, big buildings, big ships, and indoor plumbing.

Below is Liverpool's "L," the elevated railway.

Liverpool boasted the first overhead elevated railway. It supposedly just preceded the Chicago "L," the Sioux City mini-version of an elevated RR, and the NY Transit. That was the same year as the Chicago Columbian Exposition, the World's Fair. More about the importance of 1893 to our families in other essays.

In the late 1890s, Liverpool housed nearly 700,000 permanent residents, of whom about 5,000 were Jews. Again, the Helfets and Dobrovskys were living among a small minority. They settled around Brownlow Hill, Pembroke Place and Islington near the town centre.

For five of Jacob and Leah Helfet's children, like almost all their neighbors, Liverpool turned out to be only a stopping-off place, not their final destination. The city was a major cog in a massive infrastructure set up to funnel millions of people from all parts of Europe into the booming economies in South Africa and the Americas. The "Immigrant Trade" was devoted to shoving an unending line of travelers onto railroads and ships. It was a big business run by people who saw the emigrants as commodities.

The picture purports to be a doctor examining steerage passengers on a ship called The Wisconsin in Liverpool's port before departing for America. It was important for the shipping companies to be transporting healthy people … that would be people who would probably not be a burden on American society. The main reason the commodities (passengers) had to be in reasonably good shape was that the shipping companies would be forced to pay for the return of their commodities if the American authorities thought they were damaged goods. Thus, Aunt Minnie Helfet's "low-eye" diagnosis by a doctor at Ellis Island could have been a disaster for the Helfets.

As the flow of Jews escaping The Pale in the late 1800s became a torrent, several fairly well-funded Jewish organizations were set up to keep their co-religionists alive during the trip to a port … and to keep them from setting roots in towns along the route where they would become wards of the more affluent local Jews.

Something similar, but on a smaller scale, happened in the USA, particularly in New York, where rich German Jews funded an effort to funnel poor Russian Jews to the port in Galveston, Texas. My sister Susan married into an Iowa family from Texas named Silverstein, who probably were part of the Galveston Project.

The same phenomenon occurred in Liverpool, although the Jews were only a small part of the mix. For years, millions of emigrants from mainland Europe landed on the east coast of England in Hull and a few other ports and took a train to the west coast, usually Liverpool, which faces Ireland and North America.

During the 1840s Potato Famine, it was estimated that over one million poor Irish passed through the port. Essentially, the Liverpool mantra seemed to be, get them in, make as much money as you could without being obviously illegally greedy, and help them ship off to America where they won't be Liverpool's problem. Of course, there were some illegal activities along the way.

For the record: The Irish immigration to the USA after the Potato Famine is at least as tragic as the Jewish passage. Proportionately, more Irish died along the way, and the conditions were just a step or two above slave ships. That's why they were called "coffin ships." The business side of Irish immigration is interesting. In the beginning, ships with New England or Canadian lumber sailed east, and their empty cargo areas, still with lumber scraps and vermin, were filled with departing Irish going west, with little human comforts available.

On arrival, the anti-Catholicism among the English colonies rained down upon the Irish like blacksmith hammers hitting an anvil. This continued throughout American history and abated somewhat during the John F. Kennedy presidency. Throughout former American history, Italian Catholics felt the brunt of discrimination along with blacks, native Americans, Asians, and Jews, which raises the eternal question. Was man created in some god's image, or was that god created in some man's image?

Jacob, the Helfet patriarch from Chernuch, Russia (now Ukraine), had transferable skills. He was a kosher butcher who settled in a neighborhood with Orthodox Jews. Some of his provisions likely wound up in kosher meals for Jews waiting to be loaded on ships to America, Argentina, or Africa at the busy port. THE PICTURE OF A BUTCHER WAS COMPOSED BY MARC CHAGALL IN 1910.

Jacob Helfet's children went to school and worked in Liverpool. The antisemitism they faced was tame compared to that in the old country.

The first Helfet to leave Liverpool was teenage Leon. He went to South Africa and prospered. His siblings saved money and became, rather English … as in Victorian English. The girls, as adults, reportedly were "Strait-laced." The family myth is that son Harry was a bit of a loose cannon, not playing by the rules. This was stated as a fact but not explained to me.

Cousin Arnie Levin stayed with my grandparents in Sioux City for several weeks as a kid. Years later, he told me that Sarah Helfet Kroloff was a very strict Victorian-Era disciplinarian.

Unfortunately, around the turn of the century, the high hopes of Liverpool's Helfet and Dobrofsky clans were clouded by the rotten economic climate. Along with that, the Helfet children faced a family dilemma. Within 18 months, their mother, Leah, died, and Jacob soon remarried. Then he suddenly died, and the stepmother left the kids to fend for themselves.

There were too few jobs open, too many people to fill them, and it was too depressing to stay. The good news was they felt reasonably comfortable about leaving their extended family in Liverpool. Only one sibling stayed.

Leon, in South Africa, never again saw his brother Harry (Isaac) and sisters Sarah, Esther and Minna. They moved on to Sioux City. Harry was there first, a few months before a Cunard Line ship carried the three Helfet "girls" to the USA in February 1903. The Ivernia was among the most modern and faster ships catering to the immigrant trade with a better environment for the poorer passengers. The tragic Titanic was another one. The majority of Titanic's passengers were "below deck" in steerage.

As always, the world was in chaos. The butterfly wings in the Tsar's gardens (as predicted by Chaos Theory mentioned earlier) continued to propel the Helfets onward. The ships in Liverpool went where jobs and a better life beckoned.

There are solid parallels to the stories of Helfet siblings, Leon, Esther, Sarah, Minnie, and both Jacob Dobrofsky and Sam Kroloff. They married two of the Helfet sisters.

Each of their stories began in The Pale, an area of west Russia into which Jews were herded. Each concluded thousands of miles away in Los Angeles, Sioux City, Chicago, Cape Town and in Calvinia, a god-forsaken "dorp" (small town) on the dry high altitude Great Karoo Desert in colonial South Africa. And each was the same and, at the same time, amazingly different.

But those are stories for other essays. Pictures: The Cunard passenger ship Ivernia at sea and an old photo of passengers seeing the Statue of Liberty emerge from the mists for the first time.

THE HELFET SISTERS HAD TWO BROTHERS, ONE WAS LEON

Leon's son Arnold wrote a biography of the adventurous Leon, who experienced an interesting life in South Africa. Much more about Leon is in other essays. Here is an excerpt from the early years.

Afrikaners, Jews and Calvinia

by Arnold Helfet

He was a small, stocky man with a heart of gold and respected and loved by all. One of the early business (and later also farmer) pioneers in the North Western districts of the then Cape Colony, his name and memory were stamped into the history of Calvinia and its enormous district.

I have chosen him to be the chief protagonist in this story as I knew him better than any of the others. He was my father.

Leon Helfet was born in the shtetl Chernuck, Poltava, in Ukraine, on June 6th, 1879. Within the first eighteen years of his life, his saga took him from the Ukraine to Liverpool, England, at the age of 13, to Cape Town 5 years later in 1897 and then to Worcester, Ceres and finally to another shtetl or "dorp", Calvinia, shortly after his nineteenth birthday. And he dwelt in Calvinia for most of the rest of his life. (Map, see red circle. Calvinia is about 260 miles north of Cape Town on smooth modern roads. Much longer by oxcart on steep rutted roads.)

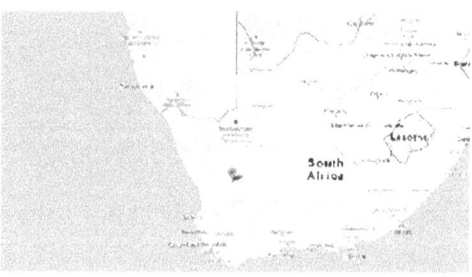

To begin at the beginning. Chernuck was a small town with a proportionately large Jewish community. Leon's father, Jacob, was an impressive man with a strong black beard trimmed to beneath his Adam's apple, as was the fashion. He was a man of standing in the very religious Jewish community, as he owned an essential institution, the main kosher butchery. Like many others of his generation and faith, he was also a man of learning.

His beautiful wife, Leah, bore him a large family comprising six daughters and two sons, of whom Leon was the elder. And, as the government school systems in Russia and her satellite countries were restricted against Jews, the two boys attended the congregational religious school, the Yeshiva. The girls received their education at home through private teachers.

At school, they studied the Old Testament, the Torah, the Talmud and all the daily and festival prayers, all of which were taught exclusively in Hebrew. Classes commenced at 8 o'clock in the morning in the pitch dark for more than half of the year and ended also in the dark as late as 9 in the evenings. Commencing school at the age of five, Leon and brother Harry were very educated young men by the time they reached their Bar Mitzvahs (confirmations) at the age of thirteen.

Years later, his intimate knowledge of the Bible and the fact that he was a Man of the Book brought him profound admiration and respect from his Afrikaaner friends, most of whom were Boere (farmers).

In the early 1890s, renewed anti-Jewish pogroms once again made life intolerable, and hence, those families who could afford to "buy" exit visas from corrupt bureaucrats emigrated mainly to England and America in the hope of starting new lives in the freedom offered by the West. As they were obliged to leave behind all but carryable possessions, their new lives commenced with little or no available capital. Thus, after the boys attained their Bar Mitzvahs but were still too young to be drafted into the hated army, Jacob Helfet arranged for his family to emigrate to England.

The first stage of what was to be nearly a month-long uncomfortable, hungry and exhausting journey in a covered wagon drawn by horses, which took them across the Polish border. Thereafter, they traveled on slow, crowded trains to the coast of Germany. The last lap on an even more crowded and unsavory ship took them finally to Liverpool in Lancashire, England.

There, the already settled English Jewish communities, in collaboration with committees that included earlier immigrants, welcomed the new arrivals. They assisted the bewildered newcomers in finding accommodation and jobs where possible or in starting small businesses. Also, where and how to learn to read and speak English. In essence, they were taught how to discard the unhappiness of Russian oppression of their previous lives and to establish a new existence under the hospitable Union Jack.

The new life was far from easy. In fact, it took a few years before the Helfet family was reasonably comfortably established. With financial assistance from the Liverpool Jewish committee, Jacob opened a business for which he had had years of experience, a Kosher butchery, in an area inhabited by many of the orthodox immigrants. He was obliged to trade with great caution as he had to pay cash for his meat supplies while supplying his struggling customers on credit. Some paid weekly, some monthly, and some just could not pay at all. Enough money had to be earned by the business to provide for the needs of his large family.

After a few moves from very cramped accommodation to slightly better and still better until eventually, the family moved to a suitable house which they could afford. The six young daughters assisted in the home and attended school and extra English classes. The boys worked in their father's business and, on weekends, earned extra pittances by doing house-to-house collections of weekly payments for small merchants.

They, too, were naturally eager to learn English, the lack of which frustrated them during their early Liverpool years. Leon joined an evening class where very young "pupil teachers" from a Jewish public school gained their early professional experience. And fate decreed happily for him that he had enrolled in a class which not only made him proficient in English but was instrumental in providing him with a charming and beautiful wife who became his life-long partner. This romance was triggered by his admiration and respect for the young teacher, Sara Levin, who, though not yet sixteen, was very beautiful and talented and who spoke and wrote English like a post-graduate college scholar.

Attending her classes four nights a week for nearly two years, Leon's feelings for her changed from admiration to love. She, in turn, found him to be an excellent student, friendly and gentle. After he had plucked up the courage to invite her for meetings, walks and inevitably to meet his family, Sara found herself returning his love and affection. Leon, like his classmates and other friends, espired almost desperately to acquire the mannerisms, culture, lifestyles, and dreams of their settled Anglicised acquaintances.

It was in his seventeenth year that this budding young lover found himself faced with circumstances that required the making of momentous decisions. The first was to propose betrothal to beautiful Sara, and he prayed to be accepted. The next was where they could settle and establish a home if she agreed to become his wife.

Conditions in Liverpool in the 1890s were depressing, and future prospects were even more depressing. Five of his sisters and brother Harry had decided to apply for emigration to America. But for two "good" reasons, Leon decided to seek his fortune in South Africa. Firstly, the steamship ticket to Cape Town was cheaper than to New York and could be obtained weekly, while it would have taken months to obtain one to New York. In 1897, six of the Helfet offspring chose to abide the months of waiting for tickets to America. Leon found a berth destined for Cape Town within weeks at a cheaper fare than his siblings had to pay and thus began what in later years became known in his family as "the Carmel Villa Saga." (Carmel Villa was the house he had built for his wife-to-be.)

Although her admiration had also developed into affection and then love, Sara, at the tender age of fifteen, found it very difficult to make up her mind on such vital questions. But Leon was not only head-over-heels in love but also charmingly persuasive. After many hours of discussions between themselves and their families, the suitor won the day, and he won over her family, who shuddered at the prospect of their young daughter facing unknown dangers and isolation by burying herself in "darkest Africa".

Hurdle number one was thus successfully crossed when Sara accepted his proposal. And number two, when he persuaded her to believe his promise that he would make his fortune in South Africa, build a beautiful home, and finish it to her in a few years' time. She, in turn, agreed that her betrothal promise was final and that she would accept no other offers of marriage and would wait eagerly for the great embarkation date and her arrival at her faraway home-to-be. Never did either of them dream that she would have to wait faithfully for over seven years.

Sara's background was similar, yet very different from Leon's. She was born in Switslotz, Kovno, Porosova, Belarus, on May 1, 1881, as one of three sons and three daughters to Aaron and Gertrude Levin. (Note from George Kroloff … "I could not find this location online.")

One son and one daughter were born in Liverpool, where the family had settled in 1884 when Sara was almost three. As a result, she remembered little of her birthplace and grew up as an English-speaking child immersed in the lifestyle and culture of her adopted land. She was enrolled in a good school before her fifth birthday, where she proved to be exceptionally bright. At the tender age of twelve, she was chosen to join a pupil teachers class preemptory to becoming a teacher of English after completion of her schooling.

With farewell parcels from family and friends and the rest of his worldly goods in a trunk and a blanket roll, Leon paid the 12 pounds for a third-class ticket, bade farewell to people, most of whom he would never see again, and commenced a journey into the unknown. In his purse were 26 pounds, "capital" to be used in his search for the "fortune" he was confident he would make in his "new world."

Note: The Avondale Castle had four classes of passage. Steerage was the lowest. The shipping line had a contract with the British government to deliver mail to Cape Town, and the passenger rates on its ships were lower than on ships without the contract. Typically, the Castle Line ships at that time were capable of carrying between 100 and 150 third-class passengers like Leon in addition to several hundred steerage passengers. Because sails were used when the wind was "right," less fuel for the steam engines was needed, with more room for passengers and cargo.

The twenty-one-day voyage in the "Avondale Castle' was a great adventure and a vast improvement on the shorter but dismal voyage to Liverpool made six years earlier. Although the cabin accommodation with three other passengers was very cramped, his bunk hard, and the food poor compared to his mother's excellent home cooking, he enjoyed every hour of this, his first glorious holiday. Being easy-going and friendly, he made many shipboard friends. Almost too soon, on a glorious morning, the majestic bulk of Table Mountain materialized "out of the sea". And below it, the small, beautiful city of Cape Town. Thus began the new life for the shtetl-born, nineteen-year-old South-African-to-be!

Note: The Helfets and Helfgotts from the province of Poltava in today's Ukraine may have settled there after being forced out of Spain (the Inquisition) with stops in Holland, Poland, and maybe Oettinger in today's Austria. The Helfet name may have been Etten (as in someone who came from Oettinger). Helfgott may be a reference to "son of God." This comes from a conversation recorded in my home during the 1970s with Jay Leon Helfgott, a Washington ophthalmologist whose father, Max, also a doctor, was a leader of the Jewish community in Sioux City, Iowa, during the early 1900s. (George Kroloff, 2020)

(Table Mountain is seen from the sea in the 21st century. When the clouds lower to cover the top, they are called the Table Cloth.)

CAPE TOWN AND CALVINIA ... A LITTLE MORE CONTEXT

During the 1800s, recessions were called panics. When people panic, they want out. Liverpool couldn't quickly shake off the festering panic of 1893. By 1897, Leon really wanted out. Even though the panics had spread worldwide. Optimism about the possibility of better lives in the Americas and South Africa did not decline. Leon was 17 years old and already betrothed (engaged) to Sarah Levin, his 15-year-old English-as-a-Second-Language (ESOL) teacher. He went out on his own to seek his fortune.

A ticket to Cape Town was cheaper than one to New York and available any week. Four of Leon's siblings later sailed to New York and then took a train to Iowa. But they needed a few more years to save enough money.

There may have been another reason for choosing Cape Town. Sarah had come from an area in Lithuania, around Kovno, that was home to a surprisingly large number of Jews who had already emigrated to South Africa. So, she might have felt more comfortable with the decision. (Because of borders changing over the years I believe her birthplace might have been Belarus, Latvia, and Lithuania.)

The impatient Leon had 26 British Pounds in his pocket when he landed in South Africa (1897). That would be about $3,000 in 2014. He had taken the long, pleasant ride on a new ship, the Avondale Castle, and he was ready to make his fortune. (See ship's postcard above.) Where, when, and how his fortune might appear would somehow be determined. His wish list included building a dream house for his bride-to-be. It turned out that he eventually would settle and prosper far to the north in a small town named Calvinia. Several years later, Sarah arrived.

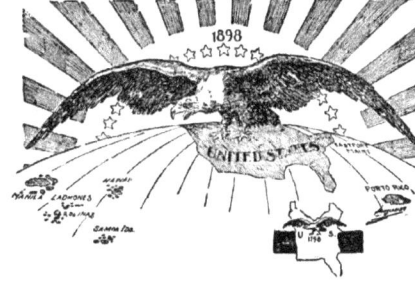

Walking down the Cape Town gangplank of that ship must have been a truly gutsy decision. His bride-to-be would have known about the concentration camps, atrocities and pent-up anger among all classes in South Africa because the British papers had correspondents on the spot. One of those reporters was Winston Churchill, who had been jailed while covering what we in the USA call the Boer War. And it was the war that delayed Sarah from going to South Africa. Actually, most of the action was far from Calvinia … Until it arrived on the dorp's door-stoop.

Here is some background. Between 1898 and 1905, three wars dramatically changed history.

The first (1898) was the Spanish-America War. That's the one in which Teddy Roosevelt led his Rough Riders up Cuba's San Juan Hill. By the war's end, the USA had become ruler of Cuba, Puerto Rico and various other islands, including The Philippines. Suddenly, America had become a big-time Pacific power.

Second came the Anglo-Boer War (1899-1902). That was Leon's local war. Both the British soldiers and the Boer commandos were brutal fighters who did very bad things to each other. They did even worse to civilians. Both sides practiced "scorched earth" tactics. Sympathizers of the other side were tortured, especially by the Boers. And especially if they were of color. Everything they had was burned.

The conflict was the first major war of the 1900s. It changed centuries-old European tactics. Previously, it was not unusual for lines of men with rifles to shoot at the opposing lines of soldiers. After the first rank of men was hit by bullets and fell, the second rank moved forward. The remaining soldiers either fled or advanced up to the enemy and engaged in hand-to-hand combat (knives, pistols, fingernails and teeth). There were cavalry and cannons, but European armies often just lined up and shot at each other rather than looking for shelter, like behind rocks where the Boers were. The British were still wearing red coats, making them easy-to-spot targets.

The Boer commandos usually were relatively small bands of guerrillas, B-level warriors. They were interested in showing the British, the Brown, and the Black populations that they were going to crush them. England was desperately trying to hold onto an empire that was soon to be a shadow of its former self. It is claimed that the sun never set on the British Empire.

Actually, it began to set during the Anglo-Boer War. In part because, at home, British citizens were asking an age-old question. "Is it worth the blood and taxes to maintain an Empire?"

The Boers were wild game hunters since they were kids. They were better marksmen (shooters) than the British, who tended to come from working class neighborhoods. Riding on horses, Boers would sneak up on the British infantry and ambush them. They also had a few cannon and machine guns, wagons with supplies and Blacks and other people of color (colour) who, essentially, were slaves. Picture of Boers attacking the British.

With their husbands and fathers "on commando," British troops burned Boer farms, usually without a fight. Boer women and children were herded into concentration camps where conditions were awful, and many died. Thousands of Black, Coloured and White jobs, homes, and marriages perished along with the dead soldiers. On top of that, there were more and more and even more British soldiers' stomachs and horse's bellies to be filled. Meanwhile, not everything either side needed and seized was paid for.

The third war was the Russo-Japanese War (1904–05). It was on the other side of the world from Calvinia, Chicago and Kapulia. And, as we will read about, from Mississippi. It was a much colder, bloody mess. At its end, Japan was established as another heavy-duty military power in the Pacific Ocean. China, obviously, was wary. The Asian super-state has long been nervous about the USA. The fact that the end of the Russo-Japanese War was brokered by Teddy Roosevelt is a key part of history we have forgotten.

Russia's loss put a weighty chip on the Tsar's shoulder. Japan was the first Asian power in modern times to defeat a European power. Numerous seeds for World Wars I and II were sown during those years. That's the big picture.

Back in tiny Calvinia, before Sarah arrived, Leon was doing quite well for a very young man. A big project was building a substantial home for his bride-to-be. Another was opening a store. Trust had developed between Leon and many of the Boer farmers he had visited on his peddling route, and he worked to keep that up. He hired a Boer helper to mind the store, who became very close to the family. Leon periodically would get on horse and cart and go back on his peddling route to the farms. Eventually, young Mr. Helfet went into other successful businesses, but this essay reflects on the years before 1909.

From afar, the situation Leon faced during the Anglo-Boer War was what his counterparts in the American South had faced during the Civil War, "The War Between The States."

The American conflict had similar Black and White issues. Servants and slaves were usually considered to be a form of animal purchased to do the master's work. By not paying them, the owners could profit. Like Leon, peddlers in the American South and the South of Africa would have seen and heard the sound of a whip and felt the emotional baggage the sound carried with it.

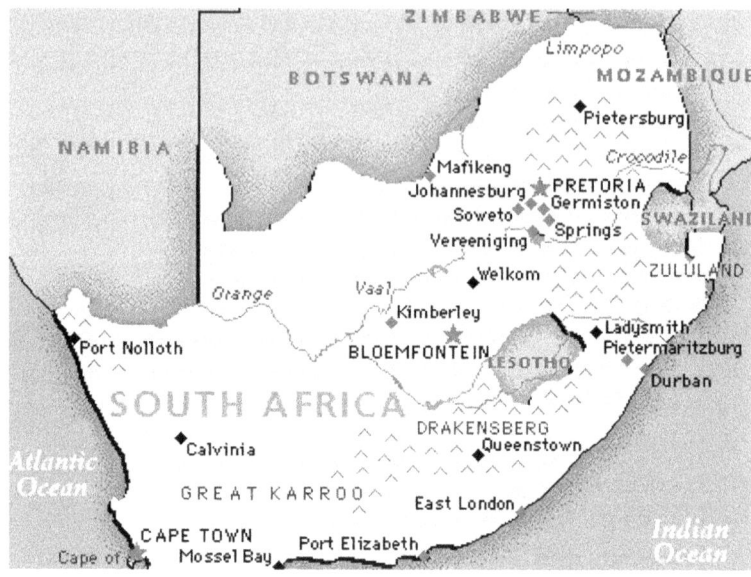

Leon, it seems, was able to navigate the conflicting winds and stress swirling around everyone in Calvinia. There were many people of colour. Not a lot were black skinned (they lived further north and east). Most were mixed-blood and Bushmen whose skin had a light brown tone. Overall, the Coloured Africans were thought to be British supporters.

Even though English authorities had freed the South African slaves in 1834, when Leon arrived at the colony 53 years later, he found Boers' attitudes and actions regarding people of color had not changed much at all.

To put this in another context, the Apartheid Laws of 1948 were enacted after South Africa became independent and the Boers took over the government. Those laws forced Black and Coloured classes out of cities, and most were herded into abjectly poor ghettos or slums called Townships.

On the map, you can find Calvinia under the U in SOUTH AFRICA. The country is about twice the size of Texas.

The segregation was as severe as forcing Jews into European ghettos. In some ways, more so. For more background, click the links under Appendix #2. While up-country, I did not get outside of the town of Calvinia with its estimated 1,000 population who, as far as I could see, were White. One or more areas outside the town were populated, I was told, by over 10,000 people of colour.

Down south, I spent several hours in and out of homes in a coloured township with a population of over one million located a few miles from Cape Town. It is far enough to be almost impossible to get to the city where the jobs were. But close enough so that young girls would line an entrance willing to sell their bodies because prostitution was a relatively well paying job. It wasn't pretty ... although, with such a large population, there was money to be made on their poverty, like selling food and drugs, I was told that the drug trade was controlled by the Israeli and Brazilian Mafia.

There are townships closer to the city of Cape Town that house thousands of families with lighter skin ... typically of Asian heritage, not African. These are the working class and merchants of Cape Town who reluctantly built what might be called a reasonable middle class life, or better after they had been forcibly uprooted from their Cape Town homes at the implementation of Apartheid in 1948.

As mentioned before, around 1900, when Leon left Cape Town to go north to Calvinia, the Boer farmers did not want to enter the money-based economy championed by the British. They preferred to barter the products they harvested and the animals they raised. A few years before Leon arrived, however, gold and diamonds were discovered on land the Boers claimed far northeast of Calvinia. So, on their list of grievances that led them to war was a pretty big one. They wanted to get a piece of the action on mine property they thought should be theirs.

Apparently, because the gold and gems were about 750 miles away, getting that piece of action wasn't a high priority for the Calvinia Boers, who were Leon's customers. They just wanted to go back to the good old days when they reigned supreme. Leon's previous history with Boers proved that he would not cheat.

He must have had more than a hint of a British accent. Thus, any bias against him around 1900 probably wasn't anti-Semitic, rather, it was anti-British. Back in Liverpool, Leon's father had become a naturalized British citizen, which, according to Leon's son Arnold, made Leon a citizen, too.

He also would have been a middle man between people of color and whites, at least in the hiring of "help" and selling products. In Calvinia, like small towns everywhere, people knew more than in big cities about what their neighbors were doing and thinking. Above: Family photo of Leon. Upper Right: Scorched Earth.

The Calvinia area, surrounded by Boer farmers, became a British garrison town, but the army was not always around. There would have been a brisk business supplying the troops. "The Calvinia village itself was left almost unscarred although a number of farmers suffered damage and losses," Arnold Helfet wrote. See Appendix #2.

Many Afrikaner 'rebels' who were technically subjects of the British Cape Colony left their homes and farms in the care of their families and joined the Boer forces in the Orange Free State and the Transvaal Republic, where the gold and gems were. A few joined the local civilian garrison as part time 'home guards.' Apparently, it was an all white assemblage that included Brits and Boers.

THE BRUTAL TORTURE OF ABRAHAM ESAU

On the surface, at least, it appeared the healthy relationship between Leon and the Boers continued.

Beyond his control, Leon, the middle man, was being sucked into the middle of an expanding Boer War zone. As Boer raids moved closer, gossiping neighbors became spies... for both sides. White people were armed, wary, and waiting for trouble. Most people of color were unarmed, trying to keep out of trouble and simply survive.

There was a report of Calvinia windows being sandbagged, awaiting a Boer raid, and there was news of Boer commando activity in towns within the Calvinia trading area.

And then there was Abraham Esau (Left). He emerged as another bit player, albeit a tragic one, who characterized the brutality of the war. Esau was a rare, educated, Coloured businessman in Calvinia. Reportedly, he was an "admirable" orator and the center of a group of his kinsmen and women who supported the British. There is a report of the Esau group meeting in basement hideouts, including the basement of a store owned by a man named Cohen, for a while.

Unless a letter from Leon to Sarah or a hidden note in a diary shows up, there is no way to know of Leon's relationship with Esau. Since both were businessmen in a small community and both were British supporters, there is little possibility they didn't talk. Right: Boer Masiphumeleler camp.

JANUARY 7, 1901, LEON'S AND ABRAHAM'S FATES WERE SEALED

About 600 Boer commandos took over Calvinia, declared martial law, and confiscated everything they wanted, including Coloured children for slaves.

British supporters and officials (like the police) who had not fled were imprisoned. Leon was nowhere to be seen. His store was broken into, and everything disappeared, according to what Leon's brother-in-law, Jake Dobrofsky, later heard in Liverpool. That fact is reported in Uncle Jake's biography. Leon, by then, probably had evacuated the area and set up business in another small town with a British garrison, where he became the equivalent of a quartermaster supplying the troops.

Abraham Esau was captured, imprisoned and repeatedly taken out of his downtown cell, chained to a gum tree surrounded by the public, stripped naked, whipped and kicked, and spat upon until he collapsed. On his last day, Esau either was made to walk out of town encircled by Boers on horseback or dragged behind the horses in chains. He was shot three times and left in the desert to rot. Esau's was not the only Calvinia atrocity; it was just the most famous. On February 5, just before a column of British marched into Calvinia, the Boer commandos exited. See articles by Bill Nasson and his book "Abraham Esau's War: A Black South African War in the Cape, 1899- 1902." It centers on Calvinia.

The British, as mentioned, were not angels. They had already begun the scorched earth policy that included a war on women and children who were captured and placed in concentration camps. It is not clear how that policy played out around Calvinia, but elsewhere, the "Red Coats" burned farms, spread salt on fields, and confiscated food.

Camps also were created for people of colour who were coerced into working for the British at wages that just paid for their meager meals, for which they were charged.

Camp conditions were scandalous. Records are inaccurate, but out of a Boer population of maybe three million, at least 150,000 Whites were held prisoner in 45 tented camps. Of them, about 28,000 died, 1,700 men, mainly those too old to be "on commando," 4,177 women and 22,074 children under sixteen. Photo: Whites only tented concentration camp.

The 64 Black/Brown concentration camps appear to have held a similar number. About 20,000 died, 81% were children. http://www.sahistory.org.za/topic/black-concentration-camps-during-anglo-boer-war-2-1900-1902

Of the 28,000 Boer men captured as prisoners of war, 25,630 were sent overseas to at least a half dozen islands and countries. The eventual return to their homeland was very difficult, if not impossible.

So, Leon joined up with the British army, became a "civilian Master of Provisions," and "After the war was over, the English Government paid him thousands and thousands of pounds as reimbursement for the losses that he had suffered." At least, that is what Jake Dobrofsky wrote in his memoir. Jake was getting his information from Leon's sister Esther, whom he followed from Liverpool to Sioux City, Iowa and married.

The Helfets of Calvinia produced a large, successful family. Sarah and Leon lived there until Nazi sympathizers settled nearby and made life uncomfortable for the small Jewish community.

Their desert community was no longer an oasis. They all moved away. Leon and Sarah resettled in the lush, more hospitable seaside climes of Cape Town.

The beautiful home Leon built for Sarah is where they raised their family and where I slept in my great uncle's bed. Standing in front of it are Linda Helfet, her husband Bill Hilliker, and the owner of the building, who lived inside and rented out bedrooms (a B&B). I am on the left in 2014.

Note: The Helfets and Helfgotts from the province of Poltava in today's Ukraine may have settled there after being forced out of Spain (the Inquisition) with stops in Holland, Poland and maybe Oettinger in today's Austria. At one time, the Helfet name may have been Etten (as in someone who came from Oettinger). Helfgott may be a reference to "son of God." This comes from a conversation recorded in my home during the 1970s with cousin Jay Leon Helfgott, a Washington ophthalmologist whose father Max, also a doctor, was a leader of the Jewish community in Sioux City, Iowa, during the early 1900s. (George Kroloff, 2020)

APPENDIX #1

UKRAINE AND SOUTH AFRICA

1. History of the Jews in Ukraine http://www.berdichev.org/history_of_the_jews_in_ukraine.html

2. Excerpt from, Arthur Conan Doyle's book on the Anglo Boer War with other references. http://www.pinetreeweb.com/conan-doyle-chapter-32.htm

3. Excellent videos, documentaries and background on youtube.com and Facebook.com. Search for Boer War. You might start with these on YouTube: VIDEO OF BOER WAR AND CONCENTRATION CAMPS IN AFRIKAANS

4. https://www.youtube.com/watch?feature=player_embedded&v=RQRzNuaW

   VIDEO OF BOER WAR SHOWING BOTH SIDES, MOSTLY BOER

   https://www.youtube.com/watch?v=LPJXPp5TsQQ

   And these on Facebook:

   https://www.facebook.com/pages/Second-Boer-War/103733446332162#

   Click on "Continue Reading" at the end of the first paragraph.

   also

   https://www.facebook.com/pages/Boer-Wars/103100186397559#

Memorial for the Jews who fought and died on Boer side

This posting is a mini-history of South Africa from the beginning of the Boer Wars to the early 21st century.

5. Arnold Helfet's biography of his father Leon has rich detail about Calvinia is available as a PDF see: https://www.dropbox.com/s/4r4b7vjbznh298v/Butterflies%20Leon%20Helfet%20Story%206.28.14.pdf?dl=0

6. Writings of Prof. Bill Nasson. Several mention Calvinia. Start with:

http://www.jstor.org/discover/10.2307/ 722402?uid=3739704&uid=2129&uid=2&uid=70&uid=4&uid=3739256&sid=21104925360207

Then check his book titled THE WAR OF ABRAHAM ESAU 1899 - 1901: MARTYRDOM, MYTH AND FOLK MEMORY IN CALVINIA, SOUTH AFRICA. Look for excerpts at:

http://books.google.com/books?id=e2gBuJJpJK4C&pg=PA133&lpg=PA133&dq=the+death+of+abraham+esau+in+calvinia&source=bl&ots=fP65naFhGG&sig=vRgq8EBFe1_OteP2s54B9tCxhVk&hl=en&sa=X&ei=8khNVNmcM8ONsQTA94DACQ&ved=0CCYQ6AEwAQ#v=onepage&q=the%20death%20of%20abraham%20esau%20in%20calvinia&f=false

In your search box, type in Calvinia and Esau. Many references will pop up.

7. Geopolitics … The Russians and the Anglo-Boer War http://www.dangoor.com/70005.html

8. Stories of Jews in the Boer Wars http://talesofawanderingjew.blogspot.com/2006/12/jews-of-anglo-boer-war.html

9. Antisemitism … there can't be a war without at least one well researched article that concludes the Jews were to blame. This article is of that nature. http://www.ihr.org/jhr/v18/v18n3p14_Weber.html

10. To understand the dozens of arcane classifications of racial differences under Apartheid, click the links below. One of the tests South African citizens of color had to endure was sticking a pencil through their hair to help determine the kinkiness of it, and that would help classify an individual. http://en.wikipedia.org/wiki/Population_Registration_Act,_1950 also see

http://books.google.com/books?id=yXYKAgAAQBAJ&pg=PA115&lpg=PA115&dq=How+many+subcategories+were+in+the+South+African+law+of+racial+categories&source=bl&ots=2JN8Iycrjo&sig=WxTJgZ9a7V_EGntQpFDaPB3PcF0&hl=en&sa=X&ei=qLVSVIn6FtPnsATt34KQBw&ved=0CDEQ6AEwAg#v=onepage&q=How%20many%20subcategories%20were%20in%20the%20South%20African%20law%20of%20racial%20categories&f=false

11. "Trains and Shelters and Ships © Aubrey Newman" is an interesting paper on the business aspects of moving emigrants from The Pale to England. See insights on the further movement to South Africa. https://www.jewishroots.uct.ac.za/trains.htm

WARMED OVER HASH GOING BACK 2600 YEARS

Both my sister Susan and I were assigned to write a short essay about our family's history in fourth or fifth grade. I don't remember what our parents told us, but whatever it was today it would have sounded like cold corned beef hash.

Corned beef because they both were raised in Sioux City, Iowa, surrounded by corn being grown to feed farm animals about to be sold for body parts in the sprawling nearby stockyards and meat packing houses and then across the Eastern USA. In those bloody factories, the cows, pigs and sheep were sliced and diced into separate parts like a tongue, steak, leg, or chop, and neatly packaged for meat markets near and far away. (photo of hash from Simply Recipes)

It would take a genius to figure out where a Chuck Eye Delmonico steak fits into a real live animal or what the animal might have looked like.

And that is what genealogy and history is all about. A farm here. A painting there. Births and deaths over several years, etc. But not the way all separate parts fit together. Few people realize that the bits and pieces of their lives fit into larger patterns, just as a small passing downpour is part of a massive weather system.

For example, hash. Each individual part might be a bit interesting, even savory, but we had no idea how the bits of beef or the kernels of corn fit into the ecology of humans or how French fried potatoes help explain the worldwide population explosion.

It has to do with something called the Columbian Exchange. Wikipedia says that was the transfer of plants, animals, and diseases between the Old World of Europe and Africa and the New World of the Americas after 1492. Somebody may have investigated how the Columbian Exchange changed the world for Jews, Japanese, and Jesuits. (A good idea for a thesis?)

I symbolically began reheating a bowl of warmed-over hash when I first thought of writing something for my grandkids about why they were born and where they were born. And what pushed our ancestors to make the decisions that affect us to this very day?

One ingredient was Kapulia. Today, it is called Kopil, a town in Belarus. Every relative who lived there is dead. The Russians, Germans, Cossacks, and crooks who wanted our relative's belongings or beautiful daughters took care of them in the worst possible way.

There were droughts, government changes, and marauding armies. Not all life, but much in our few family myths and legends, was best described by my friend Fred Freeman as a "sock full of Diarrhea."

I hardly knew my grandfather, Sam Kroloff. Yet, whenever we were together, it seemed his home village of Kapulia, Belorussia, came up. I thought that might be a first stop in explaining our family's voyage to wherever you are. Amazingly to me, life for my despondent, trodden Orthodox Jews in what now is Belarus wasn't that different from life experienced by my wife Susan's Catholic Orthodox relatives in the Austro-Hungarian Empire at the same time (late 1800s) just before they escaped and arrived on the USA east coast.

When Sam was growing up, nearby was the decrepit hulk of a castle. It was one of several owned by a Polish family named Radziwill. Jackie Kennedy, the wife of US President John F. Kennedy, had a sister who married a Polish nobleman named Radziwill … Same family.

It is impossible to learn how or why so many of this extended family originally settled in the Byelorussia-White Russia-Pale of Settlements. But there are hints.

In about 600 BCE, an estimated 10,000 of Jerusalem's most important Jews … professionals, priests, craftsmen, and the wealthy … were exiled and forced to settle in Babylonia.

About 60 years later, they were freed. An unknown number moved north into what eventually became the powerful empire known as Khazaria, where a part of the population retained some of their Jewish traditions. For political and military reasons, the Khazar rulers converted (some might say reverted) to Judaism in the late 8th and early 9th centuries. That theory comes from a few scholars who are now looking into Khazaria. See http://www.khazaria.com/

The Khazar empire was west of the Caspian Sea, which even today is known by millions as the Khazar Sea. A few descendants of red haired Khazar Jews survive in Azerbaijan, where many are part of the political and business class. As of 2018, that country was the source of much of Israel's oil, and it imported a huge amount of other products from Israel. http://althistory.wikia.com/wiki/File:Khazar_Empire_%28Celtic_Rules%29.png

Around 970 AD, the Khazar kingdom was overthrown by the Rus prince Sviatoslav I of Kiev. He was from what today is northern Ukraine. An untold number of Jewish Khazarians remained there. A type of cloth named Astrakhan (probably lamb wool) was woven and sold in Kapulia in the 1800s. Yes, the humans of the world have long been interconnected.

Anyhow, about 130 years ago, some of our family emigrated from Ukraine, Belarus, Poland and other parts of Europe to the USA. Before that, our distant past is as if it never was.

Evidence has turned up of a few Jews in Lithuania and Belarus as early as the 8th century. They may have come from Babylonia and the Byzantine Empire and later from the persecution of the German Jews by the Crusaders. Off and on, the Jews were left alone. Occasionally, they were ousted from their homes and sent fleeing.

Some were encouraged to settle in border areas between empires as rulers let up on the harsh methods used to convert Jews and allowed them to live in underpopulated lands as a way to extend their claims to contested territory.

At times, Jews in various places had a measure of self-government. The elite were active in social and government affairs and as advisors to non-Jewish businesses. Often, they were middlemen between the aristocratic land owners and the peasants because that was a job Jews were allowed to perform. They collected the taxes, for instance, which was a two-edged sword. When the economy tanked, the Jews were blamed. Economies often tank, and for better, but usually worse, the Jews still are blamed.

Elsewhere, I have written about the European chap who lived across the hall from us. It was pretty clear he was a spy. A few hours before he left the USA for a new assignment, I took him to a nearby bar for a going-away drink. As we approached the apartment building's elevator, his last words with me were, "George, why does everyone hate the Jews?" I had nine floors to give him a rational answer. Pretty sure it wasn't helpful.

Meanwhile, there is one element of European history that rarely is mentioned but is part of the jig-saw puzzle that illustrates the environment of our family's ancestors ... a jig-saw puzzle with many missing pieces.

Jewish males usually knew how to read and write Hebrew and later Yiddish, Ladino, or any of the other local dialects that had a lot of Hebrew in them. Before 1600, hardly any white Europeans, other than clergy and some elite, could read or write. Picture (right) Jewish scribes Wikipedia.

As reported earlier and later, my wife's Orthodox Catholic ancestors from Galicia (now Slovakia and Ukraine) were illiterate peasants or peons. The Robber Barons of New York's Wall Street sought strong illiterates from the Austro-Hungarian Empire to come to the Pennsylvania coal mines so they could be taught the "right" way to work. Just because they were illiterate didn't mean they were ignorant.

In some societies, literacy skills were valued. Rarely mentioned is that European Jews were raised speaking Yiddish or other Hebrew-infused languages they could communicate with fellow religionists if traveling outside their home areas. (The languages of our history are not deeply investigated in this series of essays, but languages were a big deal.)

Studies based on DNA sampling indicate there were only 50,000 Jews in all of Europe in the Middle Ages (600 to 1600 AD). After that, there was a population explosion. (Newsweek: June 3, 2010)

In 1290, England's 16,000 Jews were expelled by King Edward I. Earlier, the king had banned usury (lending money at high rates) and forced Jews over the age of seven to wear an identifying badge. Some Jews managed to remain in England by hiding their religious identity. (Years earlier, King Henry III forced Jews to pay half the value of their property in taxes and ordered Jewish worship in synagogues to be held quietly so that Christians would not have to hear it.) Following Edward's expulsion, Jews would not return to England for 350 years. The policy was reversed by Oliver Cromwell in 1655.

Back in the 1300s, thousands of Jews were massacred because they were blamed for, among other things, the Black Death pandemic, which had killed tens of millions of people, an estimated one-third of Europe's population. *Left above: black plague doctors wore masks filled with scents, like flowers, to ward off the smell of disease and the dying and dead. See plague doctors' masks, at the wikipedia website.*

The quality of Jews' lives further deteriorated with accusations that they were unfair competition in trade and crafts, which led to their being banned from even more occupations. In 1495, soon after the Jews and Muslims were expelled from Spain, Jews were booted from Lithuania for eight years. Some went back to their former places of residence. Some died.

Returning to hats. A 1566 statute reads as if it came from Hitler (or maybe Hitler's ideas came from it). The edict said Jews in Lithuania and today's Belarus would "wear yellow caps, and their wives wear kerchiefs of yellow linen, in order that all may be enabled to distinguish Jews from Christians."

IMMIGRATION TO POLAND-LITHUANIA UNTIL 1600; JEWISH COMMUNITIES IN THE 17TH CENTURY

As the situation for Jews in Western Europe deteriorated during the 14th century, many moved eastward. Communities were found rapidly. By the year 1600, between 20,000 and 30,000 Jews lived in 60 communities. After the Mongol invasion in the 13th century brought death and destruction to Poland, Polish princes invited settlers from Germany in the hope of stimulating the economy. Map: https://www.pinterest.com/pin/186125397093306811/

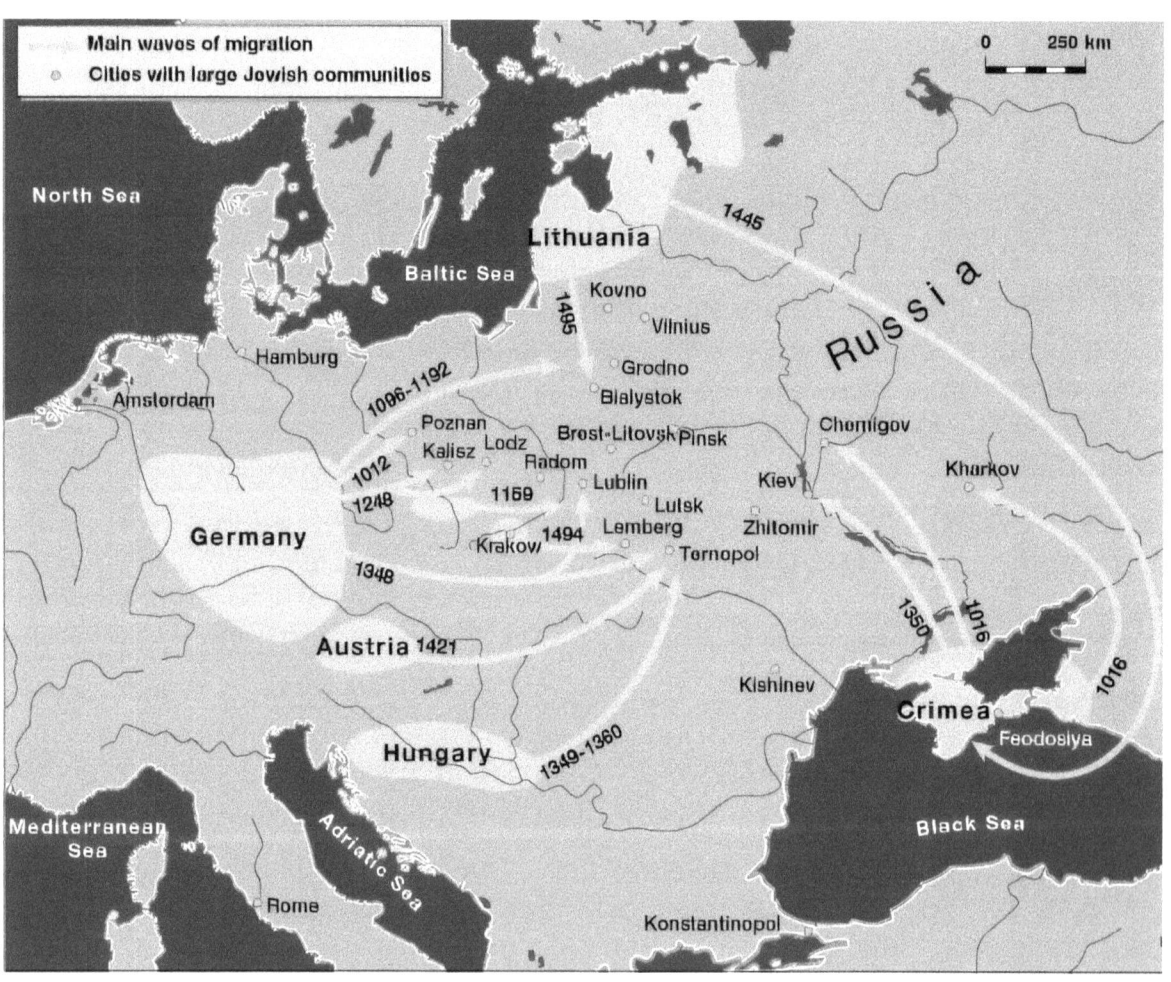

The picture depicts the "Expulsion of the Jews from Frankfurt, Germany on August 23, 1614, after Vincent Fettmilch led riots in the "Jews Street." According to the text, *"1380 persons old and young were counted at the exit of the gate"* and herded onto ships on the river Main. Jews were connected in business to the city's wealthy merchants. Fettmilch led the group of craftsmen and traders opposed to the Jewish presence (their economic competition). Picture and background are at https://en.wikipedia.org/wiki/Fettmilch_uprising#

From 1569 to 1795, the Polish-Lithuanian Commonwealth controlled a huge swath of Eastern Europe. For many of those years, Jews were guaranteed the right to become moneylenders and businessmen. There was freedom of worship and assembly. But, elsewhere, things were "dicey."

After occasional expulsions from England, France, Spain, and other Western European countries, it was not surprising that eventually, Jews moved east toward Russia and Poland.

Antisemitism in Russia and areas it dominated then ratcheted up. In the mid-1500s, Ivan the Terrible reportedly drowned 300 Jews who would not convert.

Nonetheless, by 1600, Kiev City and Chernigov in today's Ukraine had thriving Jewish populations. At that time, they probably still were culturally and religiously under the sway of Jewish thinking of the Babylonians, Byzantines, and Palestinians … far to their south. Maybe that was the influence of the Khazars. Later, the Kiev Jews were either murdered or expelled and then welcomed back always, of course, with restrictions.

Unlike in North America at that time, where Native Americans were taller and led a healthier lifestyle, Europeans, overall, were short, and death by 40 was not unusual. European life was hard. Pockmarked faces, bad teeth, and worse breath were the norm. Shoes were crude, and overseers rude. Unlike almost all other Europeans, Jews bathed once a week, mostly for religious reasons.

No matter what their physical condition, being expelled from a city in the brutal European winter was dramatic, traumatic, and often catastrophic. Dates of some Jewish expulsions. Many other examples on Wikipedia.

Place	Year	Place	Year	Place	Year	Place	Year
Carthage	250	Zurich	1424	Naples	1541	Wurtemburg	1738
Alexandria	415	Cologne	1424	Prague & Bohemia	1542	W Russia Belarus	1740
Clement France	554	Savoy	1432	Genoa	1550	Prague, Bohemia	1744
Uzzes France	561	Mainz	1438	Bavaria	1551	Slovakia	1744
Visigoth Spain	612	Augsburg	1439	Pesaro	1555	Livonia	1744
Visigoth Empire	642	Netherlands	1442	Prague	1557	Moravia	1745
Italy	855	Netherlands	1444	Austria	1559	Kovad Lithuania	1753
Sens	876	Bavaria	1446	Prague	1561	Bordeaux	1761
Mainz	1012	France	1453	Wurzburg	1567	Depor Pale Russia	1772
France	1182	Breslau	1453	Papal States	1569	Warsaw	1775
Germany	1182	Wurzburg	1454	Brandenburg	1571	Alsace	1789
Upper Bavaria	1276	Mainz	1462	Netherlands	1582	Villages in Russia	1804
England	1290	Mainz	1483	Hungary	1582	Countrysid Russia	1808
France	1306	Warsaw	1484	Brandenberg Austria	1593	Lubeck & Bremen	1815
France (again)	1322	Vincenza (Italy)	1485	Cremona, Pavia	1597	Franconia, Swabia	1815
Switzerland	1348	Spain	1492	Frankfort	1614	Bremen	1820
Hielbronn Germany	1349	Italy	1492	Worms	1615	Austria & Prussia	1843
Saxony	1349	Lithuania	1495	Kiev	1619	Areas US (Grant)	1862
Hungary	1349	Naples	1496	Ukraine	1648	Galatz, Romania	1866
Hungary	1360	Portugal	1496	Poland	1648	Russia	1884
Belgium	1370	Nuremburg	1498	Hamburg	1649	Moscow	1891
Slovakia	1380	Navarre	1498	Little Russia	1654	Bavaria Foreign b.	1919
Strasbourg	1388	Brandenburg	1510	Lithuania	1656	N.S. Germany	1939-
Germany	1394	Prussia	1510	Oran (North Africa)	1669		1945
France	1394	Strasbourg	1514	Vienna	1669	Arab Countries	1948
Lyons	1420	Genoa	1515	Vienna	1670		
Austria	1421	Regensburg	1519	Sandomir	1712		
Fribourg	1424	Naples	1533	Russia	1727		

SEPARATE AND UNEQUAL, WITH A COMMON HERITAGE AND LANGUAGE ... SORT OF

Around the world today, even if they live in integrated communities, Orthodox Jews tend to follow Eastern European traditions that mostly evolved in a closed European society... The Russian Pale of Settlement. There are many obvious exceptions to that statement.

One historian wrote the Jews in the Pale either lived in separate sections of cities (often ghettos) with "a unique set of religious beliefs and practices, as well as an ethnically unique economic role" ... or they lived in small rural villages called shtetls. Most shtetls were not just Jews. One writer reported that Jews in Kapulia lived on one part of the main hill, while Muslims and Orthodox Catholics lived in other areas. He did not call them ghettos, but, in effect, they were.

As a rule, except for business purposes or when the government knocked on their door, they did not interact with non-Jewish neighbors. Their role was forced upon them to survive. Most were poor. The photo above shows a "Market Day" where people of all religions and backgrounds gathered to barter. https://usdin.dumes.net/shtetld.html Translating from Italian, it appears this market picture was taken in the Polish city of Auschwitz around 1900.

Customs of Jews living in the south of Europe, in Asia, the Middle East, and across North Africa were different. For example, the painting on the left shows a Jewish Festival in Tetuan, Morocco, by Alfred Dehodencq in 1865. (Paris Museum of Jewish Art and History)

The northerners had a special language of their own, called Yiddish. It had a high percentage of German mixed in with Hebrew. Southern Europeans often spoke Ladino, a version of Spanish used before the expulsion from Spain in 1492. It also includes Hebrew. Neither Yiddish nor Ladino are robust languages now, although there is a small push to re-teach them. Other groups of Jews spoke different versions of Yiddish or Ladino, which mixed Hebrew with local tongues.

The unique languages and strong reliance on The Torah (the first five books of modern Christian Bibles) and the thousands of pages regarding every aspect of life in The Talmud were two of the strongest glues holding Judaism together. Think about it. For thousands of years, there were large and small groups of people milling around the world … being pushed out of here and being pulled there. And, one way or another, they found co-religionists with whom they could communicate and commiserate and do business.

WHY SO FEW JEWISH FARMERS

A few years ago I tripped over an article from a Reformed Jewish magazine that my computer now warns me not to open because the site is suspected of being overtaken by the bad guys. So I'll not mention the address but will mention some items I jotted down.

A few Jews became money lenders because the Catholic Church banned the lending of money at interest. It was a way to survive. Yet, Catholic individuals and institutions wanted lent money for various reasons, like building a church. It is hard to estimate, but probably throughout history most Jews were far from rich. Sometimes Jewish populations were kicked out of a jurisdiction so the ruling class wouldn't have to pay off their debts. But, of course persecution of any kind tends to have a diverse DNA.

The article noted something new to me. Judaism, it claimed, changed after destruction of the Second Temple in 70CE. The religion went from being farm-based to education and skills based. And that is why in many areas of Europe, and other parts of the world, Jews were among the few who could read, write and handle numbers.

So, after destruction of the Second Temple priorities of Jewish leadership changed dramatically. This caused a large number of Jewish farmers to convert to other religions. The new priorities centered upon education and literacy. In the reformatting, there was an emphasis on Jewish men learning to read and write. And that is why they were able to communicate with fellow Jews they met in places where they did not speak the language ... like in a foreign land ... using Hebrew, Yiddish, Ladino, etc. In a subsistence farming economy learning those skills was a waste of time and energy. Of course,, Jews were not allowed to farm in much of Europe.

Even if Jews were not liked and often kicked-out of a place, there was a tendency to realized their skills were needed. And often that's why they were allowed back. Once mass communications tools evolved, like the printing press, the situation was different. Picture above is an edited version of The Scribe by Arthur Szyk from Wikimedia Commons.

COMING TO AMERICA

This is based on my Eastern European ancestors' experience, not unlike those of yours if they were European ... be they from Bergen, or Bukovinia, or Berlin, or Britain, or Bulgaria, or Bologna

In 1961, millions of Americans listened to their radios and sang along with the loopy lyrics of a pop song titled "Love Makes the World Go Round."

While many memorized the song, other millions were memorizing the very funny lines of "The 2000-Year-Old Man." Carl Reiner played an astounded interviewer, asking questions of Mel Brooks, the very old Jewish guy who knew Christ, Joan of Arc, and all the other biggies. "What did he use for transportation?" Mr. Reiner asked the 2000-Year-Old Man.

"Fear" was the answer. "You see, an animal would growl at you, and you would go two miles a minute," he replied. I interpret that as fear makes the world go round.

Not surprisingly, countries and their rulers often take on the images of feared animals and reptiles. Pharaohs were depicted in hieroglyphics with heads of ferocious animals or reptiles. Sobek was an ancient Egyptian crocodile god.

Later, the threatening Russian Bear was around every corner of the Pale, where millions of Jews were confined in the 1800s. My relatives feared the bear. Others did too. Remember the Cold War?

The Russian Bear was central in Nazi propaganda. Nazis claimed the only hope of saving Europe from Russian Bolshevism was the German army. "The Russian bear is about to devour Europe."

A 1943 cover of the humor magazine SIMPLICISSIMUS shows Winston Churchill of England saying about Europe: "You can devour it only when I say you can. And be careful not to take a bite out of me." My modern relatives remain confused about who to support or hate as Presidents and other "leaders" change their minds about who is on "our" side and who (or what) is not. For instance, during World War II, Russia, the USA, and England were allies. Then they weren't.

Notice the Great Seal of the United States. Fear and arrows are on one side, and an olive branch means peace on the other.

Fear and growling empty stomachs were top of the minds of many people in the 1800s, not just residents of the Pale. In Ireland, for example. The potato famine in the 1840s was the impetus for nearly 5 million dirt-poor Irish immigrants into the US. Their harrowing trips over the Atlantic were in ships that became floating lice and typhus-filled coffins.

Across the poorer sections of European cities and impoverished rural territories, scared, starving, and unsuccessful job seekers were working through the agony of deciding to leave. That meant somehow gathering enough money for transportation and food, paying whatever bribes were necessary, and still having a few precious trinkets or coins in their pockets or sewn into cuffs of shirts when arriving.

Vast numbers of immigrants had no one to guide them at each stop along their way safely. Although, at any emigrant processing center in Europe, like Bremen or Liverpool, or a pier in New York or Philadelphia, there were plenty of Sharpies. Usually, with bad advice.

There also were plenty of "Sharpies" pitching ideas and schemes to get the "greenhorns" jobs, food, housing, and whatever. The costs tended to be about as much cash as the immigrant still had.

Before January 1925, when the "doors to the USA were closed," immigrants needed little US government paperwork to enter the country. Most paperwork came from their home countries or ports of embarkation.

Thus, the stories about names being changed as people were processed at Ellis Island or other USA ports of entry are usually wrong. The names were changed on the paperwork prepared by the ship crews in Europe or wherever they came from. I think my Kauffman relatives were named Secoy or something similar in Europe. When asked his name in Europe, my great-grandfather must have thought the question was about his occupation. Kauffman means merchant or maybe trader in German/Yiddish.

JUDGE MAGAZINE

An anti-Italian cartoon from the June 6, 1903, edition of Judge Magazine.

Hopefully, I'll have the time in my old age to investigate and report on the not-for-profit "do-gooders" organizations set up to aid the wandering Jews as they journeyed from central Europe to a shipping port during the great wave of immigration from Europe to America (1880-1920). Some of the do-gooders were honest, but a key impetus was to keep the line moving west to the Atlantic and across the ocean away from Europe. They didn't want impoverished travelers to decide to stay in a friendly town. Locals were frightened that the fleeing horde would sink roots and be in long-term need.

Although some Jewish "agencies" assisted them, much of the burden was carried on travelers' backs. Even before they began their journey out of the old country, there were plenty of people wanting to fleece them of any money, jewelry, or even clothing. See the story of Uncle Jake's harrowing journey from Mena, a small town in Ukraine, to Liverpool.

In the USA, the thoughts about immigrants, even as this is written, were illuminated by century-old cartoons from Judge Magazine expressing concerns about Italians and others.

Anti-Catholic feelings in what became the United States of America already existed when the first settlers arrived from England in the 1600s. There was a strong "strain" of anti-Catholicism in England. The bitter result of years of wars between Protestant and Catholic kings and their followers. This antipathy festered among immigrants from England, including many of the US Founding Fathers. I think it is fair to say that until John F. Kennedy's election in 1960, the USA was pretty anti-Catholic. In some parts of the country, it probably still is.

Illustrations from https://hti.osu.edu/opper/lesson-plans/immigration/images/the-immigrant and century old newspapers.

Notice to Contractors. —The whitewashing and papering of Hackett & Keefe's Saloon will be given to the lowest bidder. Bids to be in sealed proposals and not to exceed $13—the balance in whisky. No Irish need apply.

HACKETT & KEEFE.

BUFFALO EVENING NEWS, FRIDAY, JUNE 3, 1892.

WANTED—Girl for general housework; no Irish need apply. 121 West Mohawk street.

BUFFALO EVENING NEWS, MONDAY, AUGUST 3, 1914.

WANTED—A night maid at 139 Oak st.; no colored woman need apply.

BUFFALO EVENING NEWS, TUESDAY, SEPTEMBER 16, 1913.

WANTED—Girl or middle-aged woman for housework; no Polish need apply. 'Phone Howard 1768-R.

WANTED—General girl...

BUFFALO EVENING NEWS, TUESDAY, MAY 10, 1892.

WANTED—25 laborers, $1.00 per day, for salt works 45 miles from Buffalo; inside work, steady employment year round; no Italians need apply. M. Drill & Sons Employment Bureau, 100 Pearl street.

ENTERING THE USA AT NEW YORK CITY

Before Ellis Island opened in the early 1890s, many immigrants were processed at the foot of Manhattan in a building called Castle Gardens. Over 12 million immigrants entered the United States through the portal of Ellis Island. Between 1880 and 1930, over 27 million people entered America … 44.44% of them came through Ellis Island. Overall, about 8 million came into the US at other ports during that period. More about the processing of immigrants in other essays but first…

Steerage was the lowest class on a ship. Broadway stars were in First Class. They slept on the upper decks. Others who could afford it were in Second Class. At the Manhattan dock, steerage passengers and their luggage were segregated and placed on shuttle ships to Ellis Island. First or second-class cabin occupants could get off the ship and go anywhere.

At Ellis Island, all steerage emigrants were scrutinized by at least two doctors. There was a detention pen for suspects needing closer inspection and hospital wards for the sick. One doctor looked for diseases, the second for deformities.

My grandmother's sister Minnie Helfet had a "low eye," according to an Ellis Island report. Imagine how she must have trembled during the examination. Not being considered "whole" could mean being sent back to Europe at the shipping line's cost and just dumped on the dock upon arrival. (She passed the inspection). Minnie met her husband Joe in Sioux City. They moved to Chicago. Joe was a furniture mover. When he aged and weakened, he was "promoted" to driver. Unfortunately, he had very bad eyes. I always worried about him because he had such a nice family in Chicago when I was a kid. But, I was afraid to be in the neighborhood where he drove.

Importantly, ship doctors examined people at the European port before sailing to America. A family member could accompany a youngster sent back to Europe. (I could never find out who paid the family member's ticket if they went back to America.)

Most Ellis Island immigrants did not set foot in New York City. Millions left the island on ferry boats that took them a few minutes away to railroad stations in New Jersey to board immigrant trains for Atlanta, Chicago, Boston, and hundreds of other cities. Some rode immigrant cars attached to regularly scheduled trains. More about this in a few pages.

The basic anti-immigration arguments in the Americas for the last 150 years have been pretty much the same. It was worse for blacks and other people of color. An old mournful song that still rings true in parts of the US and other countries includes, "If you're white, you're alright, if you're brown, stick around, but if you're black, get back." Those who arrived in chains, of course, were powerless to go back. The North American history of Asians, indigenous tribes and First Nations is as wrenching as others described herein.

As always, the most basic human instinct is not love but fear, and anything not perfect is someone else's fault.

FEAR AND FLEEING, KEEP COMING UP

"Fear," no question. Fear for their future. Fear about leaving the devil they knew for the devil they didn't know. Fear they couldn't get across the borders in Europe or make it through the gauntlet of Ellis Island where the "idiots," lame, and halt were sent back … to what?

Why did they want to come to the USA? Because one dominant fear overcame another. And often, they thought there may not be a devil on the other side of the Atlantic but maybe some kind of an angel. Many, if not most, had faith in themselves and their future.

For some, it was about another kind of faith. Possibly America was the heaven their religion told them was ahead if they worked hard and led good lives. It didn't matter if they were Lutheran or Catholic or Jewish, Anglican or Orthodox. They were driven by fears and faith … even if they knew there would be bumps in the road and some Americans would not welcome them. Yes, some came to make a quick buck and return home with a pocket full of cash.

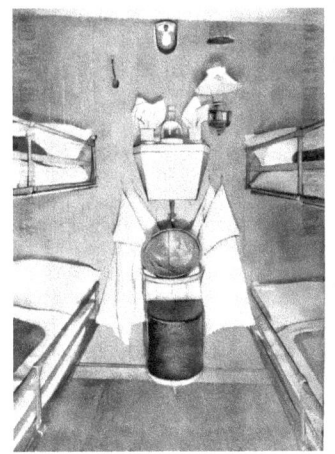

So, each immigrant had his or her own vision or hope to go on and devils to get away from. For each, the trip was a life-changing adventure or torture. The stories that follow range from happy to horrific. Imagine being a single woman sailing solo or crossing a border without protection. Or a child accidentally separated from his or her family.

Meanwhile, even though the trips of our forefathers and foremothers from the old country to the New World are often shrouded in mystery, there are clues.

For instance, early in the morning February 10, 1903, most passengers aboard the Cunard Line's Ivernia began to leave the ship at a New York City dock to board a ferry to take them to Ellis Island, New York. Three Helfet sisters from Liverpool, England, were among the passengers. Sarah (my grandmother), Minnie, and Esther.

Photos above show an Ivernia steerage sleeping room and the steerage dining room. As railroad magnates and shipping barons realized they could make money by moving immigrants faster and safer, the "market economy" evolved into a "money economy," and there was competition for the immigrants' money, and conditions improved.

The Ivernia and her sister ship, the Saxonia, were heavily promoted. The Ivernia had beds for about 2,000 paying passengers, with as many as 1700 of those in steerage.

Ivernia was relatively new, having been launched in 1899. It generally made a couple monthly round trips between Liverpool and Boston or New York. If you believe the Cunard hype, the ship was quite nice, and an April 1900 New York Times article about Ivernia's first docking at Ellis Island said the steerage berths were "good."

There were cabins for two, four, and six persons, said Cunard, so that "an entire family may be placed together in as much privacy as if they were first-class passengers." Privacy, maybe, but first class was very classy.

In 1979 I sailed down the Mississippi from St. Paul, acting as spokesperson for the Delta Queen, a vintage paddle wheeler that, ironically, spent some of its early years shuttling customers of houses of prostitution upstream from San Francisco to their destinations and back. A vacationing President Jimmy Carter and his family were on board, followed by a flock of journalists and security helicopters. My cabin was shared with a vacuous and now-forgotten former TV anchor. Our stateroom was smaller and just as basic as steerage in the Ivernia. But, we had an ensuite toilet about the size of an old-fashioned phone booth. I think the experience explains why there are no family stories about the crossing of the Atlantic to America by the Helfet sisters. Around 1900, it was tolerable.

The Ivernia was purchased by the British government in 1914 and converted to a troopship during WWI. It was torpedoed and sank off the coast of Greece in 1917 by the German sub UB-47. Over 120 of those on board lost their lives. The Captain previously had been captain of the ill-fated Lusitania, which was sunk by a German submarine in 1915. Trivia answer: The captain's name was William Thomas Turner. Separately, a scholar named Frederick Jackson Turner is famous for his work on the expanding American frontier. His "Turner Thesis" helped explain why Chicago became the second most important city in the USA. Turner went on to  declare the end of the frontier at a symposium at the Chicago World's Fair in 1893. (Everything really is connected.) Much more about the Fair later. The picture above is of a sister ship of the Ivernia at Pier 54 in New York City.

Left is an old NY Times photo of the Statue of Liberty and nearby Ellis Island.

Back at Ellis Island, the three Helfet sisters were listed as Russians, although the family had lived in Liverpool for 12 years. They arrived with pre-paid tickets to Sioux City, Iowa, where a brother they knew as Isaac was expecting them. By the time the exhausted and probably excited sisters met up with Isaac, he was calling himself Harry.

As far as I know, there are no family stories of the Helfet girls' journey from the time they entered the waters of New York City to the time they stepped off the train in Sioux City. Here is my reconstruction, with a guess that it would have taken three or four days … most of one day at Ellis Island and the New Jersey Train Station, a day to Chicago, and a day to Sioux City.

Ellis Island

- Today, over 100 million Americans - one third of the population – can trace their ancestry to the immigrants who first arrived in America at Ellis Island
- Peak year at Ellis Island was 1907, with 1,004,756 immigrants processed
- All-time daily high occurred on April 17, 1907, when 11,747 immigrants arrived
- Those immigrants who were approved spent from two to five hours at Ellis Island
- Arrivals were asked 29 questions including name, occupation, and the amount of money carried
- Those with visible health problems or diseases were sent home or held in the island's hospital facilities for long periods of time
- Some unskilled workers were rejected because they were considered "likely to become a public charge."

While still in the "quarantine area" of New York Harbor, a crew of medical inspectors would have boarded the Ivernia sometime between 7 am and 5 pm. Ships arriving after 5 pm would have to anchor overnight.

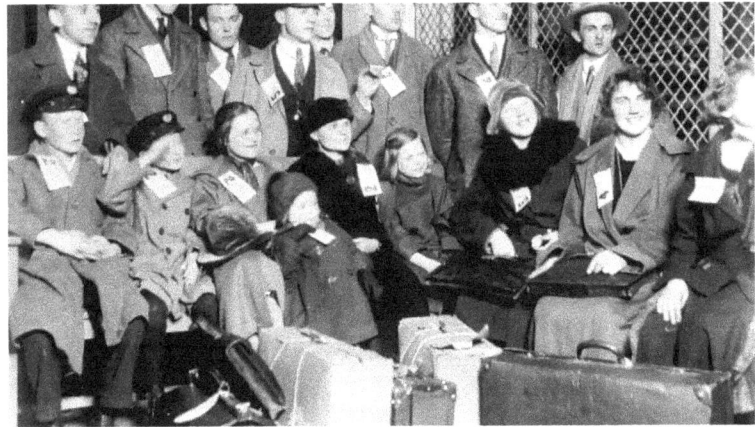

Passengers in the first and second-class cabins would be quickly checked to see if they had a contagious disease, and almost all would be cleared. A few might have to be further examined at Ellis Island.

The medical team would hasten down a ladder to board a small boat to take them to their next job on another ship. Then, the Ivernia would slowly move to a Manhattan Cunard dock.

Cabin passengers were free to depart. Steerage passengers, each with a name tag and a number attached to their clothing, were herded into a waiting area. They were divided into groups of about 30 in the same order as their names on the ship's manifest. The next step was onto the top deck of a "barge." Their luggage was put on a lower deck and then off to Ellis Island, just minutes away. The medical and mental examination, gathering baggage, dealing with train tickets, and other parts of the process lasted no more than six hours

for most. The Ellis Island website has full details. and many more photos than those shown on these pages.

The Helfet sisters were among the estimated two-thirds of people processed at Ellis Island who took ferry boats from the island directly to one of the three nearby New Jersey train stations to continue their trips.

At the train depot, the three "girls" and their luggage would have been transferred onto an immigrant train headed for Chicago or maybe onto an immigrant car attached to the regularly scheduled train.

In Chicago, they would have been off-loaded at one train station and either walked or took a horse-and-carriage to another station a few blocks away where they would "catch" a train to Sioux City.

Even today, East Coast trains headed West don't go any further than Chicago. West Coast trains still begin or end in Chicago. The photo is of the Chicago and Northwestern passenger depot around the time the Helfet sisters were traveling to meet Harry. Visible are the horse-pulled stagecoaches that shuttled between all Chicago railroad terminals.

Random note: Before speedy steamships cut voyage time in half, many immigrants spent two weeks or more seasick in their crowded bunks during rough Atlantic Ocean crossings. Upon arrival in New York City, the ships would dock at the Hudson or East River piers. First and second-class passengers would disembark, probably pass through Customs at the piers, and were free to leave. From 1892 to 1954, over twelve million immigrants entered the United States through the portal of Ellis Island on the southern shore of Manhattan.

Some names may have been changed at Ellis Island, but in most cases, this did not happen. The ship manifests were made at the port of embarkation in Europe or during the voyage, so the name on the manifest was determined before they arrived in the USA.

Ellis Island opened in the early 1890s. From mid-1855, the major New York entry point was Castle Garden at the southern tip of Manhattan. It was America's first official immigrant examining and processing center. Uncle Jake's tale reports he arrived in Philadelphia. Other family members arrived in Canada.

From 1880 to the early 1920s, about 20 million persons emigrated to America, mostly from Europe. Approximately two million were Jewish. Jews were a minority of the population in The Pale (about 10 percent). They were about 10 percent of American emigrants in that period, just before the country virtually stopped accepting emigrants.

The horrible tales about Irish potato farmers coming to America and earlier slaves being "shipped" from Africa are gruesome and well-covered elsewhere. The slave ship schematic is from the 1808 edition of The History of the Rise, Progress, and Accomplishment of the Abolition of the African Slave-trade by the British Parliament. Author was English activist Thomas Clarkson.

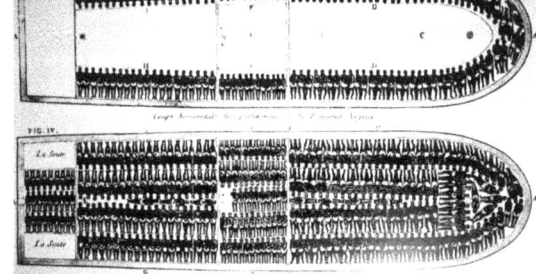

BACK TO EUROPE

In the mid-1600s, Cossacks and Ukrainians slaughtered as many as 100,000 Jews in the first modern pogroms. Other Jews were captured and often became slaves. Word quickly spread. Slaughtering mass groups of people was what many rulers hired people to do. The military campaigns of Genghis Kahn during the first half of the 1200s reportedly killed well over 50 million people.

Starting around the year 1000, the Crusaders did the same thing. Then, they were called massacres. It is estimated by some that 5 million Muslims, Jews, Heretics, and anyone the Crusaders didn't like died during over 100 years of Crusades. The human population of the entire world was about 300 million.

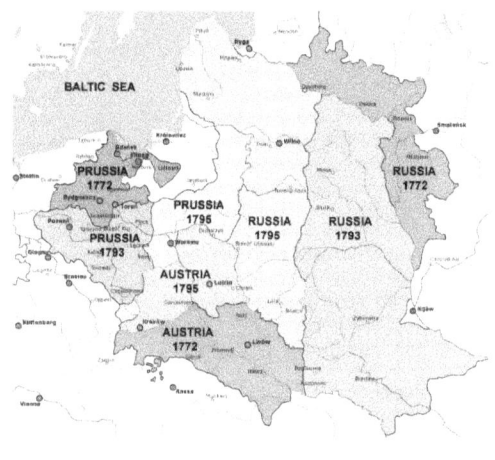

In the late 1700s, when the vast Poland-Lithuania Empire was toast, Russia, Prussia, and Austria digested the carcass, and you can imagine where the Jews came out. Catherine, the Russian empress, forced Jews to curtail travel and forced many to resettle. Left is the Lithuania/Poland Empire. The right shows Polish partitions. Partitions map from Wikipedia, Poland-Lithuania Empire and history from http://www.conflicts.rem33.com/images/Poland/decline.html

In the 1820s, Jewish military conscription began in the part of Poland the Russians controlled. Before that, Jews didn't usually serve in the Tsar's military. Often, they were subject to double taxation instead of going into the army. The drafting of Jewish boys, with quotas shooting up and then dropping down and then up again, helped convince the Kroloff relatives to

skedaddle out of The Pale and head for New York and the Missouri River Valley. Picture of train station near border to Austria.

Russian governments inflamed by what Wikipedia calls "popular antisemitism" helped provoke pogroms.

By 1885, well over 4 million Jews were living in the Pale of Settlement. Between 1820 and 1920, about 2 million of them emigrated from Russia to the United States. Among them were Kroloffs, Helfets and Kauffmans. At that time, however, the overall population of Jews was rapidly expanding. Remember, population figures cannot be expected to be exact. The photo on the previous page is a Russian train station from jewishgen.org

It was not unusual for whole Jewish families to travel as a unit. Nor was it unusual for one or two younger males to head out first, followed by the rest over a few years. For all of them, the break was permanent. An estimated one-third of the young Christian men headed to America expecting to make some money and then return. However, many who expected to return remained in the USA.

As mentioned elsewhere, the Russian government's expanding military "machines" were seeking gun fodder by drafting young men for border wars in Asia and Europe. Once conquered, the newly acquired populations, most of whom were already unhappy, were suddenly supposed to pay homage (and taxes) to whichever tsar or tsarina was in power. That was a major wind behind the backs, pushing Catholic Poles and other non-Russian Orthodox religionists to flee. Napoleon's 1812 unsuccessful invasion of Russia cost the lives of about 500,000 of his army and untold tens of thousands of Russians. Citizens were expendable.

Meanwhile, over the next century, those who wanted to escape the bureaucrats, burglars, bunglers, brigands (robbers), bandits, smugglers, police, and generally bad people used every form of transportation available to them … trains, horses, carts, and shoe leather, as long as the shoes would last. Like all international travelers, at almost every  turn, they were beset by people wanting their money. Particularly difficult was harassment for bribes.

Then, there was the railroad problem at the Russian border. Russia's railroad tracks were (and are) wider apart than those of the neighbors. Thus, rail travelers must get off one train and lug their luggage to another train station when crossing the border. During the emigration surge, individuals would pass through a passel of people with outstretched hands and sticky fingers. The picture above shows Brest-

Litovsk near the Polish-Byelorussia (Belarus) border, where wider Russian tracks ended, and Poland's closer-together rails began.

All steerage passengers in Europe were inspected for disease by the ship-line. That's because the carriers were responsible for bringing back sick people landing in North America. After cholera epidemics in the 1880s, the steerage emigrants at a few large seaports were herded into the walled-off property of shipping companies near the docks. At these medical quarantine stations, some passengers were forced to buy a new ticket or replace one that had been sold to them illegally. In a few German ports, they were required to bathe, and their clothes were washed. The picture on the previous page shows the Hamburg quarantine compound in the 1890s.

Jews had special problems making sure the food they took on the ship, or any served on the ship, was kosher (approved by rabbis). Few ships had kosher kitchens.

Keeping kosher, or not keeping kosher, could be a life or death decision and might have affected Orthodox Jews later interest in creating Conservative or Reform branches of their religion once in America.

The picture of Jewish emigrants waiting at the port of Liverpool is from Wikipedia Commons.

KAPULIA, AROUND 1850, A SENSE AND SCENT OF LIFE

Kapulia and its environs were but a pinprick on the map of the Polish-Lithuanian empire, which, for a very long time, was the largest empire in Europe. The village's recorded history begins in 1274. When, how, or why our family might have chosen or been forced to live there is a mystery. Some US census data lists Kroloffs' family birthplace as Lithuania (Litvaks, as they were known), but most said Russia, the part that now is Belarus. It was all the same place, but the borders shifted. The picture shows a spreading shtetl fire. Fires periodically devastated cities and towns like Kapulia because houses were made of wood and roofs of straw.

Some historians rate Lithuania as the area in The Pale with the lowest standard of living during the 1800s. Although it may be unrelated, a 1904 history of Jews in the State of Iowa says the Russian Jews who lived in or around Sioux City were the poorest Jews in the state. (S. Glazer: Jews of Iowa ... free on Google Books.)

For centuries, Kapulia and the surrounding territory were owned by the Polish Radziwill family. Mrs. John F. Kennedy's sister Lee married a Radziwill. But that wasn't until the mid-20th Century.

By the time the Kapulia draft dodgers were born in the 1800s, the village and Count Radziwill's decrepit fortress nearby had suffered occasional raids, rapes, sieges, and sacks. As armies Crisscrossed the territory, rulers entered "stage right" and eventually exited "stage left," but then the script and its genre were about the same, it was a tragedy. Some conquerors were Tatars from South Russia. A contingent of them stayed in Kapulia, as did White Russians. They lived on the other side of the hill in Kapulia, as discussed below.

Kapulia-Kapulie-Kapulye-Kopyl-Kopil-Kapy is about 20 miles northwest of Slutsk-Slack-Sluch. It is 55 miles south-southwest of Minsk, 12.5 miles from Snov, and on today's paved roads about 350 miles northeast of Kyiv, the capital of Ukraine.

His birth surname might have been Sekoy, Sekov, or Chekov, or something similar. Maybe, on the trip to America, Joseph's father thought an official was asking his occupation, not his name, and responded "merchant" in Yiddish, which would sound like Kauffman or Coffman.

By the 1600s, the Kapulia fair was a well-known regional marketplace, in part because of the local weaving industry. One of its popular products was a cloth called Astrakhan. That name pops up several more times in these essays in different contexts. Wikipedia puts the mid-1800s Kapulia population around 2000 inhabitants, mostly but not overwhelmingly Jewish. After being part of the Russian Empire for over a half-century, an observer said, "businesses included a brewery, two water mills, and six shops," along with three churches,  three schools, two Jewish "temples," and a prison. This is different from the colorful stories about Kapulia written by famous Yiddish writers half a century later (see Appendix #2). Most of Eastern Europe had local fairs where people exchanged products before there was money available.

By 1880, most shtetl males could read Hebrew and Yiddish and probably spoke some Russian or Byelorussian (a version of Russian). There were few, if any, government-run schools for Jewish boys or girls. Pictured above is a Yiddish typewriter. https://fsgworkinprogress.com/2012/03/20/the-archives-i-b-singer/singer5/

Books about people who weren't biblical figures were beginning to appear written in Yiddish. These were people with whom readers could identify, like Tevye of "Fiddler on the Roof." The books and newspapers were mostly read by urban middle-class Jews, but some social strivers in the hinterland, like in Kapulia, were exposed because they carried on business in cities like Slutsk, about 30 miles away, or Minsk. The printed word and word-of-mouth about the outer world were spreading. To some, it smelled like a rancid garlic meal that was not digesting well. To others, it had the sweet smell of future success. Typical small village with some Jews, thus a shtetl. From Jewishgen.org.

The Pale was a boiling cauldron of "isms" vying for attention. Among the many isms were Hasidism, socialism, the beginnings of Zionism flowing in from Minsk and Slutsk, and the ever-present antisemitism.

In the ghettos and small towns, human and animal waste odors (poopy and pee) fought to smell supreme over the garbage piles, including butchers' rotting offal (unused part of the animals), fireplace and stove smoke, and boiling cabbage. There were flies, gnats, rats, and probably bats. Nathan Feinstein, who lived in Kapulia until he was ten and eventually settled in Sioux City, recorded some of his memories. https://www.youtube.com/watch?v=lo6Wjz0LB-8 He said the first community privy appeared sometime after 1900.

A few life-saving medicines were reaching rural Europe. However, medical treatment in places like Kapulia probably still relied on the leeches collected at the nearby river and the widespread use of bleeding as a cure. Usually, the local barber was the dentist (really just a tooth puller) and the doctor.

People had missing teeth, scars, bad skin, etc. Because Jewish men and women were almost completely clothed from head to toe, except for those women seen naked by other women in the ritual mikveh bath or men seen naked by other men in a public bath, no one knew much about the neighbor's bodies.

WHAT THE KRULEVITSKYS ON-THE-LAM BROUGHT WITH THEM

And what they left behind

They were raised in a highly structured Old World Jewish shtetl. But along with the "old time" problems, like community-wide fires, suddenly there were changes for which they were totally unprepared. Forces such as industrialization were wiping out their livelihoods. (Akin to the worldwide rise of the auto, which killed the horse-drawn wagon industry, or robots and Artificial Intelligence that today are taking over many manufacturing jobs.) Picture by Lewis Wickes Hine.

The telegraph and the spread of almost instant information, of course, fed new fears. As continually mentioned in these essays, the introduction of just a few life-saving medications contributed to a huge overpopulation. There were too many people, not enough food, and, more importantly, not enough jobs.

Picture right is the Telegraph Hall, New York, 1860. A few years later, a new transatlantic cable allowed sending eight words a minute! (From PBSLearning.)

A big issue in shtetls like Kapulia was disagreement over which form of Orthodox Jewish teachings to follow. Emigrants brought their religious disagreements to America. While in Sioux City, my grandfather Sam wrote about those differences. He favored the old-time religion, not the new offsprings of Judaism like Hasidism that were popping up around Europe. When recent immigrants did not bring all their petty personal and community disagreements with them to the USA, they had to develop new petty personal disagreements in the new world.

As the Kroloffs and their ever-expanding covey of cousins were fleeing the shtetls, the old barter economy was morphing into the new cash economy. In Kapulia, many had transferable skills they could sell, having learned them in family shops or as peddlers, butchers, bakers, blacksmiths, tailors, tutors, and artisans. Some were the middlemen between those who had things to sell (like crops or Astrachan scarves) and those who had money to buy them. Picture: https://www.lzb.lt/wp-content/uploads/2017/08/mid_news_zrs_419_pen-yehuda-costurera-pintores-y-pinturas-juan-carlos-boveri.jpg

Sewing skills explain why many of the immigrants went into the "needle trades" … the making of clothes. Not just in New York's Garment District but "sweatshops" in big cities across America. See comments and photos in an essay about my grandmother, Mary, growing up in an area of Chicago where there were many sweatshops during the last quarter of the 1800s.

Faster and cheaper steamships and railroads, along with a sometimes efficient postal system, filled the Kapulia residents with ideas they had never imagined.

Therefore, it wasn't only the stereotypical explanation that "they left Russia because of the Tsar's inhumanity," which, like most stereotypes, does have some truth. It's just that there is always more to the story.

Here's a specific example of how jobs held by Jews were evaporating. Inn-keeping and distilling liquor once were mainstays of small-town Jewish economies. The murder of the Kroloff family patriarch Aaron in his Kapulia-area roadside inn and tavern is a clear example. The spreading web of railroad tracks allowed trips to be shorter and goods to be shipped more efficiently. The market for overnight roadside stays was being deflated like a leaking balloon. Old drawing of what Aaron Krulevitski's roadside inn might have looked like.

Meanwhile, the brewing and distilling of booze, a large part of rural Jewish business, was being industrialized in cities, cutting rural jobs and prices.
Booze making and selling was very important in Russia and the USA. It was a major tax generator. City factories began mass-producing shoes and other products along with liquor.
Urbanization was on the rise in The Pale as much as in the rest of Europe and America, as well as southern Africa.

For reasons mentioned many pages back, a Jewish farmer was rare. Maybe that's why only a handful of Kapulia emigrants did take up farming, and maybe that is why most of those farms failed. They not only lacked the skills but were saddled with trying to keep Kosher in an isolated environment. Cows had to be milked on the Sabbath. Kosher food was unavailable. One sad crop would lead to an even sadder outcome. That's what happened to Morris Levich in the Dakotas before he settled in Sioux City, according to his grandson Bart.

Nevertheless, posters like the free lands in Iowa and Nebraska, along with fanciful tales of streets lined with gold or the golden door mentioned in Emma Lazarus' poem on the Statue of Liberty, were effective advertising for the New World.

There were come-hither pleas from America, England and other lands where relatives and friends had flourished. These were emphasized by salesmen working on commission from railroads, steamship lines, and large businesses, encouraging residents in The Pale and all across Europe to emigrate. Even American government agencies (state and provincial) were promoting themselves and their land or manufacturing opportunities.

Without electricity, it was dark inside and outside at night, except for open flames. Not surprisingly, there were fires. Especially in dry spells, walls of wood and the thatched roofs were ready kindling. Twice in the 1800s, most of Kapulia burned down, according to contemporary sources.

Fires influenced the history of our family, not the least of which was the Great Chicago Fire of 1871. But life was not all bad. People did find time to enjoy themselves.

Homestead Act

- Federal land policy and the completion of the transcontinental railroad led to the rapid settlement of American west
- Passed in 1862 to encourage settlement of the Plains area
- Gave 160 acres of land to settlers if they improved the land and live on it

IF IT WASN'T FOR THEM, THERE WOULD BE NO US IN THE US

The fleeing Kapulia bachelors probably started on carts pulled by scrawny local ponies. There is no reason to sacrifice a really good horse that would be left behind.

Soon, with fear and trepidation, they would clamber upon the largest carriages they had ever seen, propelled by what to them were huge, thunderous iron beasts belching steam and ashes and moving slightly above ground on impossibly long metal tracks at improbable speeds. Right, is a locomotive ad for Philadelphia, Pennsylvania's Baldwin Engine Works made for export.

For the first time, they were exposed to electric lights at night, cobblestone streets, soaring buildings, teeming seaports, waters that stretched "forever," humongous metal-hulled ships, strange languages, unimagined customs, new foods, and even more fears. Somehow, they obtained the money to travel, feed themselves, and pay bribes.

Those who wanted to escape from The Pale were like iron fillings in a high school physics class, being attracted and repelled by competing magnets. The repelling or negative poles weren't just the negative Poles, but Russians, Cossacks, and others reflecting oppressive rules. The most important attracting poles were where the jobs existed. We are amazingly lucky they wanted to leave, had the guts and determination to follow through on their instincts, and that the jobs they sought were in the US, among a few other places. After all, they could have settled in Suriname or South Sudan. They also might have tried out Uganda, which some thought would be the new Palestine. Really!

Now, here is something hardly ever mentioned. The American Civil War, also known as The War Between the States, was a major factor in the burgeoning job market that lured people to the Eastern United States. Among the many people who died because of that war in the 1860s were an estimated 620,000 employable young men. For the most part, they were replaced by immigrants.

A FEW MORE CHARACTERS FROM KAPULIA

Aaron (Archie) Krulevitsky was the first "they" talked about.

On July 30, 1978, Jack Davidson wrote to his daughter Debbie: "Archie, the progenitor of us all, made the newspapers all over Europe and New York City over a century ago when he and his youngest son and daughter were brutally murdered by a gang of five who robbed them in their roadside tavern. All five were ... caught and hung." The picture is Gentiles and Jews in a tavern by G. Pillati. (Moldovan Family Collection via YIVO Encyclopedia)

Aaron had at least two other sons, Yonkel (Jacob) and Shmuel (Samuel). Jack Davidson continued, "Archie is the 'familiar' usage for Aaron. Oddly, every one of his namesakes on Yonkel's side was called Archie, and those on Shmuel's side were called Aaron. Hence, I know five Archie Kroloffs and one Archie Herzoff, plus my brother Aaron and cousins Aaron Richards & Aaron Seglis. It's mind-boggling."

In the letter, Jack said that by the 1970s, the Krulevitsky-Kroloff Klan included hundreds. Sam Kroloff, eventually of Sioux City, "had four or five brothers and three sisters, all of whom were prolific, and (Shmuel's daughter) Sara was the oldest of eight, who left in their wake a few gaggles of Richards, Rices, Allens, Zeligsons, Greenbergs, Koolishes & Davidsons, all of whom did a little begetting on their own."

Jack Davidson also reported that the Krulevitskys changed their name to Kroloff when they came to America, at least on Sam's side. Jack's mother's kids (she was one of the many Sarah Kroloffs) became Richards.

Like many emigrants, the "greenhorns" were bachelors. They wanted to be able to bring their family to America after making some money and hopefully find a bride and a more settled life. Unlike their counterparts in other ethnic groups, such as numerous Italians, the Krulevitskys had no interest in returning to their homeland.

As you will read in the Jake Dobrofsky chapter (which unfolds like a B movie thriller, some Jews were very wealthy. But not all. In the Kapulia shtetl, as far as I can discover, there were the relatively poor, the really poor, the wretched poor, and those living on alms. That carried over to America, where, at first, all were dirt poor. They relied on the small number of Jews in and near Sioux City, New York, or Chicago to help them get started in a new life. But taking that first step up from the dirt was goal #1. Several, like my grandfather Sam Kroloff, at one time or another were peddlers or salesmen whose experiences in and around small-town America were amazingly similar to that of Sam's brother-in-law, Leon Helfet, in and around Calvinia, a small town in South Africa.

CAPE TOWN SOUTH AFRICA, LATE 1800s & THE BOOTLEG SCOTTISH PASSPORT

Cousin Debbie (nee Davidson) remembers that two Davidson brothers lived in Cape Town in the 1880s and 1890s. Their names were Shmuel and Abraham, she said. They were from a town known in our family as Timkovitch. It is a very few miles from Kapulia. Her father believed their original names were a variation of Kroloff.

The brothers had a store in a Dutch (Boer) portion of Cape Town, Debbie told me. The whole block was burned down by the British during the Boer War, which led them to eventually resettle in the United States.

Coincidentally, Leon Helfet first lived in Cape Town before relocating to Calvinia a while before the Boer War. Leon was not related to the Davidson brothers and we probably will never know if they all knew each other. The stories about Leon and the Boer War begin on Page 64. They provide some details about the scorched earth activities of the British and the Dutch Boer settlers.

Debbie believes the family may have been known as Pick in Belarus and maybe in Cape Town, as well. They had a bunch of other names in the USA.

And where does the name Davidson come from? Debbie said she heard that Davidson was the name of the Scotsman from whom Abraham bought a bootlegged passport.

So, what is to be learned so far?

Try this.
We are what we are.
We are what they were.
But we probably don't understand what we are,
nor do we really know what they were.
And for most of us, it is already too late to learn.

THE PALL ON THE PALE DARKENED

Kapulia residents learned of the outside world through word of mouth. Yiddish stories about Kapulia indicate that some of the words were fact. Some fantasy. Some fake news. And, all the news became gossip, which was heated by frictions and factions. Word of Odessa's programs (organized rape, pillage, and killing of urban Jews) in 1821, 1849, 1859, and later were among the stories that led to sleepless nights and whispered plans to escape the confines of The Pale. There was fear for life, death, and even breath.

Arguably, in 1881, the pall on The Pale really darkened. Omens of the threatening Russian bear were in the threatening sky (the ominous cloud pictured looks like a bear). From https://www.freeimages.com/photo/dark-clouds-ahead-1367832

Tsar Alexander II was assassinated that year by a group that included a young Jewish woman. "The word on the street" was that Jews were responsible for his death. More programs were being reported. The reality of deadly riots getting closer must have riveted the attention of our relatives. Around 1890, about 2000 Jews were deported from St. Petersburg to the Pale, many in chains. About 750,000 Jews were evicted from Moscow, as was just about everywhere else in Russia outside the Pale. Picture, Wikimedia. Pogrom bialystok 2.jpg

By then, the first Kapulia group was in Iowa.

In some ways, though, life went on as before

As detailed in other essays, The Pale was a boiling cauldron of "isms" vying for attention. Hasidism, socialism, and many more. When the pot overflowed, the first really big wave of emigration was underway. Life was not great, but antisemitism did not appear to be virulent in Kapulia, at least not all the time.

The Kapulia author Abraham Jacob Papirna wrote, "Christians and Muslims (probably Tatars) were on the side streets on and behind the mountain."

The Jews, Paprika continued, "took the best part of the village on the highest part of the mountain where the marketplace was located. This included the street where the synagogue courtyard sat. (Even in that tiny village, there was more than one synagogue.) All the special Jewish religious and community institutions were there, he wrote. Occupying such a respected place with its large Jewish population (a few thousand) who carried on such lively commerce, Kapulia gave the impression of a clean Jewish community." (Much more about daily activities is in the works of Papirna and Mendele Mocher Sforim, another famous author, in the addenda below.)

Spending part of Friday in the bathhouse with Papirna's colorful character, "Finke," was a habit for most men. Just like in the synagogues, the richer Kapulia men sat in front. On weekdays, Finke made cheap candles in the bathhouse. Not far away, the women had their mikvah, a ritual bath tradition (see sketch by Marc Chagall 1910) that went back many centuries.

I am not sure what the writer Papirna meant by "clean," but there was a man who carried, sold, and/or bartered drinkable water in Kapulia. According to Sforim's stories, his name was Leyzer Ber. (In 1898, by one estimate, about 5,400 water carriers still were at work in the Pale's small shtetls and big cities.) Water carrier https://indeksonline.net/profesionet-qe-i-shkeli-koha-sot-jane-pjese-e-te-kaluares/

In the Appendix #2, there are excerpts from Sforim's "Those Days," discussing, among other things, schooling, the Kapulia Fair, and what he claimed was a main revenue generator for Kopyl, a thick dark green cloth known as an Astrakhan. The cloth may have been introduced by the Tatars living in Kapulia, many of their families might have originally come from the Astrakhan region of Russia near the Volga River. Astrakhan was a portion of the Kazarian Empire. It is not clear if there is a connection between the cloth and the Kazars and Kapulia.

THE LAW(S)

The Law of the Lord, The Law of Moses, and the Old Testament, otherwise known as The Torah, drove the rhythm of the daily life of the Jewish communities in and around Kapulia.

Of course, there were wildly different interpretations of what "The Law" really meant. A lot of time was spent by men and boys discussing their interpretations of ancient and current reality. For some, those discussions were part of learning that was a full-time job supported by the community, as poor as it was. Picture: https://clearlyreformed.org/jesus-doctrine-of-scripture/

While the Law of the Lord was delivered by scroll and mouth, the Law of the Russian Tsar was delivered by mouth, hands and feet. One hard hand was a gloved fist. The other hand, often held out for bribes, sometimes was soft and reassuring and supposedly protecting. The feet were heavily booted and had the severe force of the state behind them.

Though not always carried out in full, the restrictions on Kapulia's Jews could be quite specific, ranging from limitations on education, clothing, and haircutting for men (no peyes or side curls) and for women (no shaving of heads or wearing wigs). There also were restrictions on travel.

Above is a picture, allegedly about 1865, of Joseph Afroinow and his wife or sister Sora in Kapulia ... likely neighbors of the Krulevitskys. Their hairstyles would be changed by decree. Right is the document that allowed a member of their family to leave The Pale for one year. Eventually, the Afroinows moved to Wisconsin, where several other Kapulia residents settled. I have no proof, but suspect the piece of paper Uncle Jake sought that he thought might save or end his life looked like this.

In shtetls across The Pale, it was not unusual for the rabbis to try to ease the pressure of the Tsar's lieutenants. They often were the designated intermediaries between the Jews and Christians, Jews and Muslim Tatars and the Tsar's other minions. How they worked (often with fees and bribes) is clearly illustrated in the essay previously mentioned "A DRAMATIC ESCAPE FROM UKRAINE" P51. It relies on excepts from Uncle Jake Dobrovsky's nearly 200-page memoir.

Even though there is evidence the people of Kapulia more or less got along with each other, there was petty crime and the usual commercial and personal differences. Some of the "cases," according to the stories told by writers about Kapulia, fell under the "jurisdiction" of the authorities. It must have been like a small claims court. Others were taken to rabbis, who were supposed to figure out how they should be resolved.

Then there was the police commissioner. Papirna characterized him as "Sheriff Zdroyevsky." He ruled over Kopyl and the Tsar's ever-more-oppressive edicts. "These were not good times, the era of Tsar Nicholai's evil decrees, one after the other, terrifying and unbearable."

The picture shows Jewish soldiers on a rare 1887 holiday in Troitskossovsk (modern name unclear). Jewish soldiers were not allowed to spend their leave where they were stationed but had to return to the Pale of Settlement.

THE LABORS, NEIGHBORS AND TRADES

Abraham Jacob Papirna was born about the same time as my great-grandparents. He said of one year (likely before 1850), "there were about 3,000 people in Kopyl from three different populations, beliefs and groups: Jews (the majority), White Russians (Russian Orthodox) and Tatars (Muslims). The three groups were different from each other in language, customs, and beliefs. Even their history represented three different worlds, and still, they lived a peaceful, quiet life together," he wrote. (Population figures from different sources differ.)

Photo right: Old Tatar mosque, http://cosmopolitanreview.com/kresy-first-the-forest/ located about 70 miles northwest of Kapulia. Photo below: Tatar family circa 1885.

Each ethnic group had its role, Papirna wrote. The White Russians worked in the fields and as weavers. A few Tatar families were gardeners. Jewish storekeepers and peddlers baked and sold bread, as well as wood, flax, and products bought from peasants.

Not surprisingly, a large number of our relatives in Sioux City and its environs became bakery, grocery, and general store owners. Several started as peddlers. Few, including Morris Levich (Yankelevich), unsuccessfully tried farming in South Dakota. Some of the Yankelevich family also settled in or near Omaha, Nebraska.

While the Jewish residents did not farm, many were gardeners with very small plots of land to nurture and harvest for their own food. So posters announcing free land in Canada and the US were appealing, as were reports by a scattering of Jewish groups promoting the very few successful emigrant farmers from The Pale. Meanwhile, as noted in the coverage of the Gordick family in these essays, Orthodox Christians from the Austro-Hungarian Empire had some experience on farms, even as serfs or peasants. The free land in western Canada was a huge draw, and the Gordicks apparently farmed successfully.

Meanwhile, in 1882, Julius Schwarz wrote: "It is with much satisfaction and justifiable pride that I pronounce the agricultural colony of the Rocky Mountains a full and complete success and the question whether Jews are fit to be farmers, solved and answered in the affirmative."

https://www.loc.gov/exhibits/haventohome/haven-century.html That didn't change the fact that history records very few successful Jewish farmers in the USA.

Kapulia had a reputation for horse trading … figuratively and literally. Horses pulling, pooping, and procreating played a part in The Pale's past as well as all northern hemisphere cities of that era. Since the1600s the Kopyl fair, had reportedly been well-known. The Fair, like similar ones in similar shtetls, served several purposes, not the least of which was providing welcomed tax revenues. It is important to record that many shtetl stories about market days describe the scene from a Jewish point of view, but the non-Jews might have been more numerous. Photo of typical shtetl market day.

"Kopylites were most proud of … their struggle and defense against Hasidism," a popular form of orthodoxy based, in part, on mysticism and an inner drive to be more observant than other Jews," Papirna wrote.

They survive today with their dark clothing, black hats and determination to keep their separate "ways" in New York, Israel and around the world.

Sforim's Kapulia narratives in the addendum below involve the usual complement of town characters. Among them was the man he called "Yudel Shul-Klapper," who knocked on doors and windows to announce it was time to go to the synagogue or that someone had died. There were drunks, shysters, pious and impious, and the gypsies who came to town to bilk the bumpkins.

(Same job, different name.) "On Friday evenings, he knocks on the shutters, announcing the beginning of the Sabbath."

That picture from the 1920s is an example of how some things didn't change with modernity.
Pictured is someone like Sforim's.

AND THEN IT ENDED

Alas, the last word on the Kapulia shtetl comes from my friend, the late Alan Kulakow, who visited Kopyl-Kapulia in the mid-1990s, the town of his and my forefathers and foremothers. He reported at that time, there was no physical evidence of Jews ever living there. The Jewish cemetery lay deep beneath the high school soccer field.

A more chilling revelation, he said, came from a local woman who tugged at his sleeve while the visiting dignitaries in his group were looking at a possible riverside site for a cultural center. The woman claimed that she witnessed the Nazis in early February of 1943 herding the area's 2,325 surviving Jews down to the Komenka River and shooting them all.

"The river ran red," Kulakow was told.

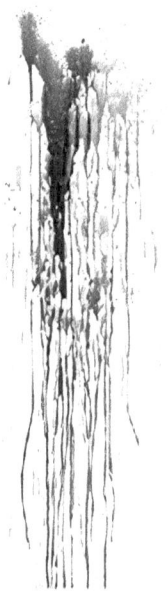

That was our family's blood.

I discovered a reference to the village of about 300 people where my paternal grandmother, Sarah Helfet Kroloff, was born in the late 1800s. It said in September 1941, the Nazis occupied Chernukhi (Chernush or Chornucky), and 132 Jews were shot by local police in the county park.

APPENDIX #2

THIS IS LONG WITH FEW PICTURES

It depicts the life they lived before crossing the Atlantic Ocean.

The following stories are found on JewishGen.org and/or http://www.jewishgen.org/yizkor/slutsk/slu473.html some have copyright restrictions.

The stories below are:

- What were Shtetls
- Two observations
- From the Newspapers … Fire
- Occupations in Kopyl
- The Kopyl Market Place
- The Decree of the Schools
- The Kopyl Fair
- Sources of Livelihood in Kopyl
- Kopyl, memories
- Religious and Community Institutions
- The Men of the Kloyz (religious school)
- The "Kloyz" Youngsters
- Community and Private Libraries
- The Shul-Klapper, the Bathhouse, and Finke the Bath Attendant
- The Administration
- Kahal, Tributes, Monopoly, Excommunication

- The Rabbis of Kopyl
- From Kapulie to Slutsk
- Kopyl Gets Other Faces
- Folklore
- Writers who were Natives of Kopyl Draft dodgers list of 2 Krulevetskys and 10 Krulevitskys is at http://www.jewishgen.org/belarus/surname_list.htm

Occupations of Jews in the Pale. Interesting stuff: http://yannayspitzer.net/2012/09/30/jewish-occupations-in-the-pale-of-settlement/ This is nothing like what you might have thought about the occupations of Jews in the Pale of Russia.

A concise history of The Pale can be found here. Most of this is lifted from https://www.globalsecurity.org/military/world/russia/pale-of-settlement.htm

What Were Shtetls? Clearing up myths about these Eastern European villages where Jews lived. In many the Jews were minorities, in some majorities. https://www.myjewishlearning.com/article/shtetl-in-jewish-history-and-memory/

Much of the following was Translated by Judie Ostroff Goldstein see Kopyl files on JewishGen.org

Observations

Kopyl – a shtetl near the Komenka River. Together with Slutsk, Kopyl was made a special principality during the era of Lithuanian rule. At the beginning of the 17th century, the land was given to Prince Radziwill.

At one point there were 41 courts (whatever that means?), a Russian Orthodox Church, a Catholic Church, a Reform Church, two Jewish prayer houses, a public school and two besmedresh, synagogue, or study houses, a brewery, two water mills and two stores. (According to Brockhaus-Efrons Encyclopedia)

Slutsk, the largest nearby community was less than 30 miles away … about 43 kilometers.

From the Newspapers … Fire 1886 http://www.jewishgen.org/yizkor/slutsk/slu246.html

On April 11th, a fire broke out in one barn and consumed the city. Approximately 300 houses, 4 Beis Midrashes and the Great Synagogue that had been standing for about 300 years and had been recently renovated were all consumed by the fire within two hours. The residents were not able to save the treasures and valuables from the Beis Midrashes and the synagogues. Thirty-seven Torah scrolls were burnt in the Great Synagogue, over and above the

Torah scrolls and the many books and other items that were consumed in the Beis Midrashes. Kopyl became a ruin. Only 20 houses in the higher points of the city remained. On April 13th, the fire returned to consume that which remained. It destroyed fifteen of the remaining houses, including one Jewish house. We are hereby publicizing our great sorrow to the public, and requesting assistance and kindness from the neighboring towns, that they should have mercy upon the poor people of Kopyl, and offer them support so that they can rebuild, and a city among the Jewish people shall not be wiped out. (How much of the desire to leave Kopyl for Sioux City and other locations was fired by the catastrophe in 1886??)

An upright man, a resident of Kopyl.

From "Hakarmel," Volume 8, Tammuz 2, 5626 – 1866. Printed in mid 1870s.

Occupations in Kopyl and differing views of the same story by Sforim.

Mendele Moyhker Sforim (1836-1917), Sholem Jacob Abramovich, was the grandfather of modern Yiddish literature. Born in Kopyl, a town which was part of Poland until the partition of Poland in 1793, when it became part of the Russian empire. As a young man he studied in the Yeshivas of Slutsk and Vilna. At first he wrote in modern Hebrew. Wanting to reach the Jewish masses, he later wrote primarily in Yiddish. from YIVO Archives.

Great Yiddish authors (r-l) Sholom Aleichem, Ben-Ami, Bialik and Mendel Mocher Sforim. Sforim from Kapulia. Picture allegedly from Odessa, 1910. http://www.berdichev.org/great_yiddish_writers.htm

Mendele Mocher Sforim (Extracts from Shlomo, Reb Chaim's)

One of the main occupations that made Kapulie different from all the other towns in Lithuania was "astrohonke" and especially "woven articles." "Astrohonke" – this was a sort of linen, dyed dark green, and laid together in pieces from a certain number of arshin [a measure of length formerly used in Russia, equal to 28 inches] that would be used mainly as linings and also for caftans for the poor. (Astrakhan an area in South Russia once part of the Kazarian Empire. It might be assumed that the Tatars who lived in Kopyl-Kapulia had roots in that region going back several hundred years. Maybe not. GK.)

Why was this linen called "astrohonke?" This was never explained in the history of the shtetl. A bleached piece of linen, long and narrow like a towel was called a veil, also made by the shtetl weavers. With the look of a towel, the women wound them around their heads, over their bonnets, tying them behind at the nape, leaving two large corners hanging in the shape of a windmill and two smaller ones on the sides that were called "fans." The veiled head was like a hoop wrapped in a folded shawl, twisted, with a knot on the forehead and the corners of the shawl tucked in or pinned, one on each side of the head. Old, pious women and those of the middle-class wore the knot in the front of the head, like a " shel rosh" [phylactery, a small leather box worn by men when praying worn on the head an arms by men]. Young, modern women, shoved the knot a little to the side. On the Sabbath and holidays they wore silk, cashmere or Turkish shawls and during the week, woolen ones with large flowers – apple shawls. Both these types of shawls were given to brides as wedding gifts from the groom's parents. The bride's parents gave the groom a shtreimel [fur edged hat worn by Orthodox Jews on Sabbaths and holidays].

This is what our grandmothers looked liked in a veil, Sforim wrote. The veil had to be white as snow, starched and rolled. Rolling the veil flat was a job for two women and one held the corners with both hands at one end and at the other end the other woman did the same. In this way the veil stayed stretched out between the women like a long, narrow gutter in which a large, round, smooth glass or iron ball was placed. One of the women raised her hands a little and the ball ran in the veil from her side to the other. The woman on the other end raised her hands a little and the ball ran back. The ball ran back and forth until the veil was smooth as a turner's lathe. To look at the women, they seem so earnest. They stand far apart, raising their hands with a shake of the shoulder, pushing out their bellies, laying their heads on the side as if to bend, twisting their noses, watching with their eyes and sending from one to other sweet, poisonous smiles, good conversation with stinging barbs. To see this, one would think there is nothing more beautiful in the world.

This veil as well as the "astrokhonke" gave work to gentile weavers in the shtetl. Several had their own workrooms at home. The Jews took away the merchandise they had paid for. Each one dealt with his own weavers. Those involved in this trade were children after kest [room and board provided to a son-in-law so he could continue his Torah studies], or just finishing kest, or who still had dowry money. Reb Chaim's children already given in marriage were also involved and made a living from this trade. The merchandise was bought up by large merchants and sent to all the Lithuanian cities where it always sold well.

Everyone praised Kopyl veils. This was the profession in the shtetl and a lot of Jews made their living from this trade.

And suddenly an evil decree was issued. The evil decree concerned clothing – women were not allowed to shave their heads and Jews had to dress like everyone else! No more veils, no more commerce, no more income! It was as if the town had been killed. Everyone felt the blow, the weavers and spinners, small and large buyers. The tavern keepers also felt it as the weavers did not have money to even buy bread and certainly were not drinking. These were sorrowful times for the storekeepers. The artisans and everybody was touched. As fate would have it, more bad luck was in the offing. Suddenly one beautiful summer day, the season when fires break out in Jewish towns, there was a fire, a hellish fire in Kopyl. More than half the houses were lost. Among those lost to the fire was Fradel's parents' house. There were hills of ash where once there were houses. Naked chimneys stuck up from the ash heaps like gravestones in a cemetery. Hungry, displaced, scrawny, pale people, really living corpses, wandered in the streets. Some rummaged and searched in the handful of garbage that was their homes. They searched, as is said, for the horseshoes from a dead horse. They were searching for a trace of their household goods. And what joy when somebody found these valuable things under the ashes, such as a nail, a pot or several roasted potatoes.

The Kopyl Market Place. (Note: similar to the Ukrainian market near where Elek Gordick grew up. See The Smart Elek essay. Jews wrote glorious stories about the town fairs, making them seem unique, but the one near where Susan's ancestors grew up in Catholic Orthodox Austrian Empire territory seemed just as interesting. The Jewish Gen stories were stories about the many local fairs are from Jews who could write, while the other religious families in the Empire were illiterate and any oral stories have been lost, as far as I know. GK.)

The shtetl Kopyl, as some know, lies … Far from the beaten path, there is no mail, no bells are heard, aside from one; the ringing of the assessor's bell on his carriage.

But still it is not a foolish town. The Jewish population reportedly was quiet, calm and law-abiding, concerned mainly with studying Torah [Five Books of Moses, the Bible], praying and important work. The Torah students labor in the kloyiz [house of study] in the besmedresh [synagogue, house of study, meeting hall] spending time, giving their hearts to studying and discussions. And, of course, making a living.

Important work refers to the work of small taverns, small shops, small stores-these are called businesses. Not racing, not making a great uproar, or hoo-ha, not cracking the whip in far off places like Moscow, Leipzig, Krakow or Lemberg [Lvov], God forbid! Only small taverns, small stores for their own people or for townsmen or peasants from the surrounding villages. The peasant usually comes to town on Sundays riding on oxen with sacks of potatoes, beets, cabbage heads, also with a game rooster, an already smoked old fool. During the autumn, around Chanukah, a fellow brings geese, sheepskins and the like. He gets a drink of liquor at the tavern, one drink, several drinks, snacks on an old baked bagel and leaves to roam, a little tipsy, among the shops, to buy salt, matches, cheap tobacco; one man buys a red shawl with large flowers for his wife a crimson ribbon to tie his daughter's braids – short and sweet. A shtetl it is called, and it conducts its trade, alone, between its inhabitants, quietly, slowly, and so smoothly, nothing for a rooster to crow about!... That is with the exception of several summer fairs where trade is a little broader and tumultuous. Shoes, smelly, thickly smeared heavy shoes of the village peasants with ugly wives.

There one truly sees all sorts of new faces: Here is the small town simpleton, with his head to side, a crazy, backward hat, caps, clothes of strange, wild styles. And there one sees hands, tapping something in the wagon, beady little eyes and twisted noses, that thing pretends to be doing nothing; also lots of hair, new fur caps. Squeaking basket of beads hung around naked necks, and coarse linen embroidered shirts. The majority of folks are sitting, not touching.

Among spring onions and small baskets of eggs, is a recently born calf with all four legs tied up, yearning for the breast. The calf is strong, languishing in a loaded wagon, to which a cow stands tied by its horns. The cow is the mother, poor thing, and she is led out to sell, her milk to go elsewhere. This child of hers – this calf – is to be slaughtered.

Suddenly a hound runs from under the mountain of animals and humanity, lifting its wagging tail, kicking its hind legs and raising its back end. Now the drove of horses scream, an uproar, and hooligans crack their whips, lashing their sides. The horses will be exhibited at the horse market. Contractors (horse dealers) are the big experts. They look at the horses' teeth, treasures, and haggle and wrangle, all the while as they slap each horse on the flank. There walking about very excited is Grishka, the gypsy with his horse which is tall with a fat round belly, glossy brown hide and fiery eyes.

Leyzer Ber, the town's water carrier, upon discovering this merchandise, this lovely horse, is trembling, almost epileptic. But he laughs – a horse yet, a horse! Oy, pauper, pauper! Leyzer-Ber pauper, this you should not desire. This is not for your pocket. Well, as the gemore (observer) says, one must try. No – no, and maybe yes? Hey, Grishka! Tell me brother! How much?

A word here, a word there, the point is – a good man, Grishka the gypsy!

Where is the stomach? This horse is old, scrawny, skin and bones. See what a gypsy is capable of! He blew up the horse under its skin. He also filed the teeth and gave him some herbs – sneeze-wort in liquor. These herbs warmed up the horse enabling it to stand upright, start its fee – a fire burning!

Now a circle of people forms around a newly arrived person with an accordion, an important person, a musician, who gives a concert! He moves the accordion and it plays songs. A small monkey all dressed up in human clothes dances on its hind legs, a small girl in pants jumps through a hoop, and a pale, mute young boy walks around on his hands with his feet in the air. The crowd quivers, mad about this amazing display – they have never seen or heard such artistry!

Meanwhile time does not stand still. Hour after hour is passing until, little by little, afternoon shadows are spreading. The market place says a song of praise! Somewhere in a wagon, a tied pig squeals. He is hungry, tired of lying the entire day without food. From a distance his is answered by the cow, tied by the horns, who is also weary of standing such a long time. Fettered roosters wait in the wagons, crowing in anger – such a long time to be separated from their wives!

Now all the animals start complaining. A chorus of calves lying stretched out, with a bleat, coarse and rough voices, chimes in. The sun is going down to rest. And the people begin to leave – no more fair!

Hens are walking about the market place searching only for a morsel to put in their mouths. Village cows, voracious eaters, constantly hungry, while walking, grab a handful of straw, a small bit of hay.

And young boys with sticks, sent from home expressly to find bargains, poke in the garbage. Just in case something good was thrown out, they will take it. At home a fire burns in the fireplace. Supper is being cooked. The men are in the synagogue at evening prayers. Night falls – hush, peace and quiet!

.....

Next page is from "Those Days" by Mendele Mocher Seforim http://www.jewishgen.org/yizkor/slutsk/slu246.html

The Decree of the Schools

The town of Kopyl was perplexed, and the Jews there were in deep mourning: they were disturbed by one of the maskilim, named Valilnatel, who along with his friends was the cause of this evil. This person would go around, at the behest of the king and his ministers, to all the cities with a Jewish population. He would gather crowds together and preach to them about the benefits of the school [a modern school]. The Jews of Kopyl would curse him, as did their brethren in all other places. They took council together to decide what to do. They decided to decree a public fast upon the community, to recite Psalms, and to implore the dead in their graves to request mercy on their behalf. The faces of the melamdim [teachers] were blackened like the bottom of a pot, for they were worried to the depths of their souls. These schools would destroy their livelihood, and if there were no salvation and respite coming to them from the Blessed G-d, they would become bloated with hunger, and would go to their graves before their time. From here you can learn why the melamdim were so concerned, and why they complained so vociferously against that decree. The townsfolk were standing in prayer, fasting, and reciting chapters of Psalms in the synagogues. The women were prostrating themselves upon graves, and were shedding rivers of tears in the synagogues. Even the schoolchildren were fasting. Shlomole fasted for the first time in his life during this fast of the schools.

The entire summer was a time of mourning and lamentation, and even the few gentiles in town looked like mourners. The gentile and Jewish residents of the town earned their livelihoods together and lived in peace. Everyone participated in the grief and joys of each other. If there was a wedding feast in a Jewish home, the gentile acquaintances would send gifts: this one a fattened chick, and that one a few dozen eggs, this one a loaf of bread, and that one a container of honey, fruit and vegetables, each according to his means. The Jews did the same to them. Therefore, the weeping of the Jews at that time affected the hearts of their gentile neighbors. They wondered, why and to what end is this weeping?

The Jews, even though they were fasting and tearing open the heavens in prayer and supplication, did not rely on a miracle. Until such time as the merit of their forbears would have effect and G-d would have mercy upon them, they did what they could and married off their young children – and the time was a time of great "confusion!" The shadchans (marriage brokers), emissaries of G-d, labored on behalf of the Children of Israel with love, and made haste to bring the young boys and girls to the marriage canopy. Why all this? So that, if Heaven forbid, the decree of the schools should be fulfilled, there would not be found even one child among all of the Jews, for everyone would be married, all of the "young Jews!" To insure that the dowry of the young girls would not be inflated, a rumor was spread in the city that the young girls would be taken away for work in far off colonies.

The Kopyl Fair ... A different version of the same story as above.

Here is the fair! The marketplace, which was quiet on all the days of the year, took on a different appearance and nature during the time of the summer fairs. At such times, the marketplace was teaming with people. New people, and various characters and faces came from villages and towns, all types of noses could be seen – elongated, out of place, sharp, witty, crooked, and peaked. Wild heads of hair were seen, as were various locks of hair, thick beards, thin beards, and people wearing headdresses, caps and frightening hats. There were people wearing linen cloaks, skin coats, wide cloth pants and pantaloons. There were people with shoes, and nailed sandals. There were people covered with tar and smelling of kerosene. These were the villagers. They came with their wives. The "ugly" wives, with outstretched arms and bare chests, with necklaces of glass and coral around their necks, wearing embroidered and woven linen dresses. They would be sitting on wagons filled with bunches of onions and baskets of eggs. At their feet would be a young two-week-old calf, with all four legs tied up, fainting from thirst for its mother's milk. The spotted cow would be tied to the back of the wagon by its horns, waiting to be sold along with its child – she for milk and the child for slaughter, woe unto both of them.

From the valley, from below the mountain, a camp of horses with rolled back tails and straight manes, approach with a noisy, angry gallop, as they bump into each other in the crowd. Their drivers goad them on with a whip and foot, as they urge them on with a roaring call and a scream towards the horse marketplace, and line them up there! Immediately, the merchants come one after another, testing and examining the teeth of each horse, evaluating their beauty, debating the price, slapping the horse on the back, and passing their hand over the hindquarter.

And could it be possible to have a fair without a gypsy? – He too, Grishka, the gypsy, was there! His face was flushed and sweaty from overwork, his hat was tilted to the back of his head. His quiver and his utensils, a knife, pins and iron hooks were attached to his belt. Grishka would walk along, and a tall horse, led by a halter, would go along with him, its skin smooth, with torch-like eyes – it appeared literally like a lion! Leizer Hirsch, the town water drawer, saw the horse in all its beauty and was astonished. He sighed and said to himself: "Oh miser, do not covet what you cannot afford." But his desires got the better of him, and he opened up his mouth and said: "Oh Grishka, what is the price?" They would converse, and the gypsy would continue with the conversation as he rode easily on the horse, running to and fro. The buyer and seller would haggle, one zuz 2, two zuzim. Both would plead with each other, literally in a weeping voice, take oaths, shake hands, and each one would take hold of the corner of his cloak and bring it to the nose of the other to consummate the deal. Finally, the deal would be established, and they would congratulate each other and share a drink, as was customary! Leizer Hirsch got a bargain. He took hold of the horse and led it home, joyous and glad of heart!

Large crowds of people, young men and women, mothers and children together, would gather together and come. There would be the sound of laughter and the sound of conversation as the eyes were raised upwards. The circus tent was there in the market, with amazing pictures posted on the outside. There were pictures of man-eating beings, frightening pictures of animals, flying dragons and various winged beings, photographs of magicians and sorceresses, as well as images of demons, and wild haired, naked spirits. On top of them, on the roof of the tent stood the clown, like one of the nonsensical 4 clowns of the world, a renowned clown, with large multi-colored curls on his hair, dressed in colored clothes with sparkling glaze. He would toot a trumpet, play around, and take a bow before the mothers and girls, daughters of the uncircumcised, whose mouths would be filled with laughter. He would continue to clown around, as he enticed them to come into the tent to see the performance.

Music could be heard from all corners of the land. One man, who considered himself to be a musician, would turn the organ wheel with his hand, as it played a song to the audience by itself. A young girl, wearing boys cloths and pants, would dance and leap with all her might through the round opening of a barrel. Next to her, a sickly young boy would do gymnastics, spreading himself out completely, and standing on his head with his feet in the air. The loud noise of the crowd could be heard on the opposite side of the marketplace, as people were gathering in confusion and with the sounds of strife. Leizer Hirsch and Grishka were fighting in the middle of the crowd and arguing as a horse stood in front of the gypsy, annoying him. The horse was old and weak, without stature and without splendor. The gypsy cheated me!" shouted Leizer Hirsch, as he turned over his case to the crowd – this cheater, may his spirit be crushed, inflated his horse under its skin in order that it should look like an inflated ball, and he even fixed up its teeth with a mouth file. He had given it a wine and spirit spiked potion to drink, so it became drunk, and was able to display the strength of an eagle and run like a deer! The crowd accused the evil gypsy, knocked him down, and beat him profusely in accordance with his evil.

Sources of Livelihood in Kopyl ... also a different version of the story you read a few pages back.

The largest source of livelihood of the Kopyl community, which gave it fame in all of the towns of Lithuania, was a form of textile for women's headdresses. Astrakhan was a thick cloth, colored dark green, rolled up and folded into many pleats and served as clothing for the poor. The cloth of the headdresses was thin and ironed, with the dimensions of a napkin. The weavers of the town made both types of cloth. The women would put this white headdress on the hairnets atop their heads and position it so that its two ends flow down their back like two heart shaped droplets. Each one had a small, short heart on its side. A kerchief would surround the hatted head, round like the opening of a jar. The ends of the kerchief would be tied up in one knot, and each loose end would go over the side towards the ear, and be hidden there. The older, more modest women would have this knot in the front between their eyes, while the younger women would place it more towards the back. The wives of the rich people would wear a silk, Arab or Turkish style kerchief on Sabbaths and festivals. Each kerchief had an embossed, colored design on it.

The parents on the groom's side would send as gifts to the bride a Turkish kerchief and an embossed kerchief. The bride's family would send a streimel for the Sabbath to the groom. The mothers would be very careful to ensure that the headdress was always clean, ironed and smooth. Two women, homeowners, who were partners in this enterprise and supported themselves, did the smoothing of the headdress. The smoothing was done as follows: these two women would stand opposite each other at the distance equivalent to the length of the headdress. Each one would stand in her place, holding the widthwise edges of the headdress in her two hands. In this manner, the headdress would be stretched out between them in the shape of a gutter. They would place a large stone, glass or iron ball into the trough. One would raise her arms slightly, and the ball would roll from her towards her partner. Immediately, the partner would raise her arms, and the ball would roll back. Thus did the ball roll back and forth in the headdress until it was very smooth.

The gentile weavers in the town would weave these headdresses in their homes, and local Jewish traveling merchants would purchase them with money and with balls of thread that were needed by the weavers. The merchants of Kopyl were for the most part young married men being supported by their fathers-in-law, who were not yet penniless. Even the married sons of Reb Chaim engaged in this business. The headdresses would be passed over to large-scale merchants, who would distribute them throughout the cities of Lithuania. The headdresses of Kopyl were well known in the world, and many purchasers jumped upon them. Livelihood was found in the town, and many people were supported by the headdress business. This business was passed down from father to child.

Kopyl, memories ... by Abraham Jacob Papirna

I do not know if any of my readers have seen my dear hometown Kopyl or if anyone has heard of its existence. But those who have seen it found it impossible to believe that this small, poor shtetl possessed a very special past. In the seventeenth century it was the capitol of Lithuanian princes – the house of Lelevitch-Algerdov.

It is historical fact. You can still see in a cone shape on the mountain, surrounded below by rampart – "the castle" ruins which are still visible, silent witnesses to its past richness and glory.

It is a sad fact that the princely residence in Kopyl became the jail for Slutsk District, Minsk Province. The castle mountain that had once been so lively, full of passion and richness has now become a playground for schoolboys on Saturdays.

It was in this condition that I found Kopyl in 1840, where I was lucky to enter the world.

I met this shtetl of wooden buildings covered with straw or shingles and overgrown with moss. The first time I really looked at it, I was left with an oppressive feeling, but with time I became used to it and also came to love the beautiful area, the mountain, fruitful fields, meadows and hilly forests.

Kopylites in general were great optimists; even fires rarely broke out there. During my childhood, around 1845, I was a witness to a fire that destroyed half the shtetl, and in 1865 there was another fire that burned down almost the entire shtetl.

What the Kopylites were most proud of was their struggle and defense against Hasidism that spread a "shulkhan arukh" way of life.

In this struggle they were the victors. When the Hasidim gathered in their "shtibl" to pray or talk together and tell about the great wonders of their sage, the Kopylites immediately took out their drums and beat them loudly with venom so the Hasidim could not pray or talk. That is how the Kopylites stopped them and the shtibl remained closed forever.

At that time there were about 3,000 people in Kopyl from three different populations, beliefs and groups: Jews, White Russians and Tatars. The three groups were different from each other in language, customs and beliefs. Even their history represented three different worlds, and still they lived a peaceful, quiet life together.

They were inevitably united as neighbors and in their economic interests. There was no enmity between them because they had no reason to be jealous of one another. It was difficult for all them to make a living, and because their businesses were different, there was no competition between them. The groups communicated by fulfilling the needs of each other and paying for these services.

The Jews, who made up the majority of the population, were storekeepers, selling bread, wood, flax, and various other products that they would buy in the fall from the peasants at the market.

During the winter they traveled by sled to Stoybts on the Nieman to sell their products to the rich merchants who would then send them on to Konigsberg and Memel. All the storekeepers and bread sellers dealt in small sums of money because there was not a large source of money in Kopyl. Thus, there were a lot of traders, and the competition between them was fierce.

Others were busy selling beverages and tavern fare. Some were wagon drivers, teachers, and artisans. There were a large number of artisans. Many of them could not find work in the shtetl so they traveled to the villages and worked there.

There were about fifteen Tatar families in the shtetl. They were gardeners. They peacefully did their work, were by nature clean, and stuck close to the Jews. The White Russians worked in the fields and as weavers. (If you reached this deep into these essays you will notice a difference of opinion as to who the Kopyl weavers were, White Russians, who would have been the Orthodox or the Tatar Muslims. Although, it could have been both and the Jews bought their products and sold them elsewhere.)

The shtetl and surrounding area then belonged to Count Wittgenstein, Prince Radziwill's heir, and all the houses stood on royal land. So, as the income from working the fields was not sufficient to live on, the Christians took jobs during the winter weaving white linen that was needed and used by Jewish women. Jewish merchants ordered the goods, furnished the raw material, paid the workers weekly, and sold it at the fair in Zelva. Kopyl linen and especially "Kopyl veil" were famous and renown in the Lithuanian market places.

The above-mentioned groups settled separately from each other: Christians and Muslims were on the side streets on and behind the mountain. The Jews took the best part of the shtetl on the highest part of the mountain where the marketplace was located. This included the street where the synagogue courtyard was located. All the special Jewish religious and community institutions were there. Occupying such a respected place with its large Jewish population who carried on such lively commerce, Kopyl gave the impression of a clean Jewish community.

Religious and Community Institutions

The marketplace and the synagogue courtyard-the two Kopyl main centers-were complete opposites in their activities. In the synagogue courtyard a Kopylite felt a heavy sense of religious obligation.

Their spirits were calmed. At the marketplace that same Kopylite looked for work and food for the family. Many Jewish institutions were located in the Synagogue courtyard, too many for such a small, poor community. The Christians had one church, but the Jews had four synagogues in the courtyard: the groyse shul [the Great Synagogue], a besmedresh [house of study, synagogue, meeting hall], the Kloyz [prayer house] and a Tailor's shul. (Tailoring is a transferable skill. My grandfather Sam Kroloff from Kopyl-Kapulia, after arriving in the USA, allegedly spent some time as a button-hole maker in New York City. GK)

The Synagogue courtyard was in the old style. The walls were fantastically painted with symbolic figures taken from the chapters of the Tanakh [Old Testament, Five Books of Moses]. The cemetery was located right at the shul. In the shul one would find the highly esteemed Ber'ke Chazan [Cantor], tall, handsome, with a black beard, black eyes, and a sweet, sonorous voice. As his salary did not provide a living wage, he worked as a shochet [ritual slaughterer].

He also had a distinctive calligrapher's handwriting and was knowledgeable in Jewish religious and State law. Thus he also served as a "writer." People would turn to him to have written various proshenyes [petitions], contracts and wills. He was responsible for writing about people and events in Kopyl's Pinkus [Jewish community record book of important events, probably destroyed by wars and Holocaust].

The besmedresh was used for prayer, mainly by the middle class. The besmedresh was also used as a general meeting hall, as the Talmud Torah [a school, free of charge, for orphans] and "kootoozke" [jail], with iron doors and iron bars on the windows. In this building "recruits" were held under guard until they were sent to provincial capitals as soldiers.

Not far from the besmedresh, in the shul courtyard was the rabbi's house, always open to everybody. Men and women would come here to have questions about rituals clarified. Others came for advice or with accusations. As Kopyl did not have a courthouse, the Christians took care of their own differences with fistfights or made peace in the tavern over a drink. But all Jewish money and family conflicts, as well as other business, was taken care of through the rabbi's court of justice. Everyone had full confidence in the rabbi's court, even Christians in their conflicts with Jews. The rabbi heard the accuser and sent his beadle to call the accused. This person would come immediately (nobody refused to come). Both sides sat down at the table and gave their accounts. A short time later the decision was given, and it was carried out without the help of the police. The rabbi's authority was that strong.

The kloyz was the only stone building in the shtetl and served also as a prayer house for Kopyl's scholars, Orthodox Jews, and philanthropists. These were honest Jews, with strong principles who kept their word and were respected by the townspeople. Dressed in black satin kapotes [long, black coats worn by Orthodox Jews in Poland] with collars and shtreimels [round fur hats worn by Orthodox Jews] on their heads, they made a great impression on everyone. They were known as the "handsome, silk men."

The kloyz was used as a sort of reading room, or a school for grown young men, where they, leaving all business and worries to their wives, were busy after morning prayers or after evening services. Each one was busy either with a page of gemore [the part of the Talmud that comments on the Mishnah] with a chapter of mishnayes [six volume set of the Mishnah which is post biblical laws and rabbinic discussions of the 2nd century B.C. and forms part of the Talmud], or with an Ein Yankev [well-known collection of stories from the Talmud]. The kloyz also served as a sort of club: The men would gather around the oven to discuss everything: religion, world affairs, politics and personal questions.

The Men of the Kloyz

I can still see them. Reb Chaim'ke is standing right there and with him are his four brothers – men of property, bosses in the marketplace and aristocrats, relatives of the Iventsiskes – rich men. First among them is Reb Chaim'ke, a man whose appearance does not make much of an impression. But he is a G-d-fearing man, a man of prayer. He prayed quietly, but cried, moaned and shed tears. He was called "the Great Weeper." Thanks to his qualities and crying he was selected as one of the community leaders.

At first the Kopylites were afraid that, because of his good-heartedness, Reb Chaim'ke would not be able to lead a government that demanded strength and, in certain cases, ruthlessness. But their fears were unfounded. Reb Chaim'ke took the government in hand, and, when necessary he set aside his politeness and became stronger and more heartless.

Also standing there at the eastern wall is a tall man with a lined face and silver hair. He is my uncle, Reb Layzer'ke the son of my late grandfather, Rabbi Ziskind who had been a rabbi in Kopyl. My uncle inherited his father's shtreimel, fox coat, orthodoxy, and his great knowledge of Talmud. At earning a living, he was good for nothing. He served as a judge in the rabbinic court, was a teacher, and in certain circumstances also a marriage broker. But from all these professions, he did not see many blessings. He appeared skinny and pale, but held his head high, and his eyes shone with pride with the knowledge that he fulfilled his religious duties honestly. But he grieved and his voice was full of tension, so tormented was he by "Jewish pain" – in a word his troubles poured out while he prayed.

He prayed, screamed, and clapped his hands making the bitter sound of protest. In his prayers I always heard: "Truthfully, My G-d, what do you do in your world? You offered your Torah to the seventy peoples of the world and none of them wanted to take on such a burden; but we willingly agreed and carry out the sacred six hundred thirteen laws and thousands of other oral commandments – where is the reward for all this? Like sheep we are led to the slaughter – where is justice?"

My poor uncle! He never made peace with the Diaspora.

Reb Leyb'ke ha-Kodesh [the holy man], a man of medium height, with a blond beard, a yellow complexion and a high forehead, at the top of which was a knob. He specialty was Kabbalah [a Jewish mystical philosophy] and his favorite book was the Zokhar [holiest, mystical book of Kabbalah] in which he was always searching to learn the hidden secrets of the Torah and raise the level of his wonderful riches.

About anxiety, Reb Leyb'ke knew nothing. He owned his own house on the market place and his wife was a wonderful, capable woman: she discovered a drink of an indefinite color and the taste-not quite beer, not quite kvass [a fermented drink]. The Kopylites called it "unter beer" [under beer]. The Kopylites knew him as a generous man. On Shabes, after a salty, satisfying lunch, long lines of men, women and children went to Leybke's house to refresh themselves with this famous drink.

Leybke's wife did not work on Shabes, but allowed everyone to ladle from the barrel without measuring how much each one had taken. The price was well known: a groschen [penny] for each portion-no money changed hands. Everyone was known and was given credit. Everybody paid. This is why Leybke was able to give his time to Kabbalah. Kopylites did not think his undertaking was important and many laughed at him.

The keen minded Nach Hasles gave him the name "ha-Kodesh" and Leybke waited for an event when everyone would be convinced of his wonderful, sacred, secret craft. It came about in 1853 during the war with Turkey and the Crimea, a difficult, bitter time. Taxes were demanded with merciless strictness. Military divisions passing through the shtetl would throw people out of their houses and take it over. Men were often drafted into the army. In truth, they were captured. Then Leybke put his heart into searching for the "ketz" [the end of time, messiah's coming]. And he found it in Psalms 4th verse chapter 126, "Like streams [returning] to the Negev desert"-according to the first letters: after the death of Alexander Pavlowitz, Constantine will reign several days. During the days of Nicholas redemption will come.

Leybke's discovery spread throughout Lithuania and people waited with joy for redemption. But the joy did not last long. That year Nicholas I died and Leybke's "ketz" came to naught. Beaten, embittered and disappointed with himself, he died shortly thereafter.

Close by is Reb Leyzor Yankel, a tall man with long hands, whom nature insulted by not giving him a beard. He would nibble, tear and pinch his chin, in vain. Despite his efforts there was no sign of a beard. Therefore he had long, thick ear-locks that he would put in his mouth and chew especially when he was thinking or studying. A sagacious man, he knew how to move mountains, turn white into black and black into white. His brain worked well. He knew that his accomplishments had no real significance. It was art for the sake of art. Reb Leyzor Yankel was an artist, a painter who lived in the Talmudic sea and built castles in the sky.

The "Kloyz" Youngsters

The Kloyz also served as the high school where the best students from the shtetl's grade schools received a thorough education in Talmud and Rabbinic literature. At the start of the 50th year, two young boys, Sholem and Shlomo, drew attention. They gave themselves full time to studying Tanach [Five Books of Moses] with commentaries. Studying a book such as the Tanach turned out to be a waste of time. One of the "lovers" of Tanach, Sholem, a tall young boy, was fated to become one of the best representatives of modern Hebrew and Yiddish literature, known by the pseudonym "Mendele Mocher Sforim".

Unmarried young men and those living away from their wives in order to study also studied in the Kloyz. When a young man appeared with a bundle on his shoulder, he would be surrounded, made welcome and provided with "days." [Students from other towns would eat in private homes, one day here, one day there, but generally only a few days a week.] When a young man had a place to eat, enough candles and books, a place to sleep in the kloyz on a hard bench, what else could he want?

They studied aloud and diligently, with great success.

The young men lived peaceably together and helped each other.

When a dispute broke out, a sort of fight about the meaning of something, or a course of debate in Talmud and in commentaries; it would start quietly and then became a tumult. Every debater had to show his brilliance, quickness, dialectic, logic, even sophism. Others joined the dispute, taking one side or the other. In one word: it was transformed into a war between two sides. It became noisy and tumultuous; seeing the chance of victory, people quickly changed from one side to the other, until one of the debaters gave in and were beaten by his opponent's arguments.

The yeshiva young men who were not Kopyl residents sooner or later married Kopyl daughters, and became sons-in-law for Kopylites. They served as the nucleus of the scholars. These young men, furnished with "kest" [room and board provided by the father-in-law so that the son-in-law could continue studying] at their father in-law's home, would often have to search for a position as a rabbi, a Hebrew teacher, or other religious profession in distant regions (in Podolia, Volyn, Novorosaysk region) where the knowledge of Talmud was not wide spread.

Community and Private Libraries

In order to meet the needs of so many keen minds and various tastes, there was a large, rich library in the Kopyl kloyz. Along with the Talmud, with the codex and rabbinic books, there were also books on Kabbala, philosophy (Moyra Nevuhim [Guidebook for the Perplexed] by Maimonides (Rambam), "Kuzani" [an important philosophical book by Reb Yehuda HaLevi], "Ikorim" ["Principles"], "Shalsheles Ha-kobolla" ["Chain of the Received Wisdom"], and "Paths of the Upright." Books concerning History were also there, such as: "Seyder Hadoros" [The Order of Generations], "Josephus," "Shalsheles Hakabballah" and others.

But the library did not have modern literature such as the "Berliner" which originated in the 18th century in Berlin, and continued after in Galicia and in Russia. This was considered a forbidden book, but it soon arrived in Kopyl secretly smuggled in.

In Kopyl there were a lot of small, private libraries. Everyone had procured books according to their tastes. A bookcase with a full set of Shas [six books that make up a set of Talmud], bound in red leather beautified every Jewish house like diamonds and earrings for a wife. In case of need, it could be sold, or pawned. If worse came to worst, it could be used as a daughter's dowry.

The women had their own libraries for spiritual development and their particular needs. These were mainly Yiddish books, as women were not taught Hebrew. Mostly, these were books of a religious nature such as the "Tzenerene ", the Five Books of Moses with legends [translated into Yiddish], "Menoyres Hamoer" [Bright Candlesticks], instructive stories from Agadah [ethical part of the Talmud] and Midrash [body of post-Talmudic literature of Biblical exegesis]. There were also books of a historical nature such as "Gdules Yosef."

There were also secular books, translated from other languages, such as "Bobe Mayse" (Bava Karalevitz), "Thousand and One Nights" etc. In forty years there were from time to time various biographies and humorous stories by talented writers such as the father of the new Jewish literature A. A. Dick, a strong supporter of Hebrew literature. Thanks to Dick, this literature was available to a lot of readers. At the beginning the readers were simple Jews and women, earnest Jews, with a smile they would think of their wives and daughters who pursued "funny stories", but the youngsters soon understood that the writer did not mean to be only funny and read them with interest.

Erudite Kopylites were not friendly with the poor-the artisans, coachmen, etc. A learned Kopylite would not arrange a marriage with an artisan for such a thing would have brought shame to the family.

I would often hear my mother say, "Thank God there aren't any rogues or artisans in our family."

The aristocrats had all the respected positions and places in the synagogue, leaving the back bench near the door for the common folk. The artisans left and built a separate building and felt exactly like the aristocrats: they bought Torah scrolls, had their own trustees and their own "rabbi" who explained and taught them. Unfortunately the richer aristocratic tailors took over the management of the shul and insulted their fellow tradesmen and gave them lesser seats. This brought about quarrels and even fights. So the latter had to search for another place to pray.

The Shul-Klapper, the Bathhouse, and Finke the Bath Attendant

Yudel the "Shul-klapper" called everyone to shul for prayers in the morning. He would go around with hammer in hand and knock twice at every Jewish house. This was the sign that it was time to pray. Whenever, God forbid, somebody died, he would let everyone know by knocking three times. On Shabes he would go around the shtetl and call out with a ringing voice: "Jews, go to shul!" Friday at noon he would call out with the same voice "Jews, to the bath!" For penitential prayers (conscience-stricken) it was his custom to knock and pull the shutters until he was convinced that somebody was up.

Yudel was a shoemaker and lived from his labor; he did not receive a salary from the community. Even the hammer that was usually used to hammer nails into boots belonged to him. The only use and right Yudel had was to take part in weddings, betrothals, circumcisions and to gather donations for tasteful purposes. They made allowances for Yudel because of his sedateness, his strong hands and feet, and his pleasant voice.

Having the same person call the men to pray and bathe gave the bathhouse status. It was located in the same place as the mikvah [ritual bath used by women], which gave the place a religious character. Also for the men it was customary to take a steam bath and wash every Friday in preparation for welcoming the Sabbath Queen.

The Kopyl bathhouse was the property of the community and was rented for ten Polish zlotys (one ruble and 50 kopecks). This money paid the rabbi's salary. It was an old, blackened, bent building, with many posts and supports and always looked as if it was about to collapse. As it wanted to draw importance from its existence, it continued, during my twenty years in Kopyl, aside from Fridays and Shabes, to serve as a candle factory, where Finke the bath attendant made cheap candles. It also served as the "almshouse" for the poor, old, and sick, and also as a place to sleep for poor travelers. The price for a bath was set at two Polish groschen per person, a high price, but Kopylites were not stingy and as soon as they heard the klapper's voice shouting "Jews, to the bathhouse!" they all left their businesses and went to bathe.

On Friday Kopyl wives did not feed their husband until sundown. This was done, first of all, so that the husbands would have a proper appetite at dinner shabes evening. Secondly and mainly, the wives did not have the time. From Thursday on, with the daughters, the women toiled, without sleeping the entire night. Not by choice, but from fear that they would not have finished preparing by sundown. The women were nervous and edgy, so the men thought it would be smarter and better to be somewhere else and not underfoot. And the best place for them to be was the bathhouse. And they stayed there until dusk, steamed, washed, whipped themselves and each other with brooms and at intervals sat on the benches-aristocrats in front and the common people behind, just as in shul. They talked about politics, the news of the day, and tried to be witty and smart. My uncle, Reb Layzer'ke, after washing would go to the barber-surgeon's space where he had his head shaved and had cut, cupping glasses put on his head and back. Although Reb Layzer'ke was white as a sheet, he was convinced that one of the causes of his illness (there were seven in all) was in his blood. In any case he liked to have his blood let. Twice a month he would go through this. According to his custom, not only was water poured at the bathhouse, but also blood.

Finke the bathhouse attendant was a versatile, distinguished man. Besides being the bath attendant he was the manager of the candle factory, the gravedigger and a badkhn [entertainer at a wedding, specializing in humorous and sentimental semi-improvised rhymes]. He was an excellent badkhn. Before a young couple was led to the chuppah [wedding canopy] he told them about ethics and indicated the important significance of their new life. He also told them that they must not devote themselves to joy and comfort because life is a temporary matter. When the young couples were orphans, he did not forget to remind them about their dead parents, indicating that a person is like a flower in the field. Today it grows, blooms and tomorrow-see, it is withered!. He said this with feeling and everyone was in tears.

But when the couple and the guests sat down at the table full of food and drink, Finke changed and became a joker and a juggler. He sought to bring joy, to amuse everyone, and drinking one glass after another, he was in ecstasy, sang folk songs, told happy stories, anecdotes, jokes, epigrams, and puns. He cracked jokes about the "silk men," the rich, and the rabbis, and all this was expressed in verse. With his hands he divided his face in two. One side laughed, the other cried; showing his two professions as badkhn and gravedigger.

The Administration

All management functions were in the hands of the Police Commissioner, Sheriff Zdroyevsky, who ruled over Kopyl and surrounding area for more than ten years.

There was no other authority in Kopyl, which was far from the beaten path, other than the Police Commissioner. The higher authorities did not look into anything there. The character of the ruler was independent. Under this kind of authority it was not possible to differentiate "the saddened population," especially for the Jews. Expressed by the noted A.M. Dik: "Every Jew can go the hospital, put on a gown, lie in bed-and the doctor will examine him and certainly find something wrong with him. In the same way a policeman can collar him and drag him to the District, and they will find out that the Jew had committed some offense." In Russia there were many laws and for Jews many more.

These were not good times-the era of Nicholai's evil decrees, one after the other, terrifying and unbearable.

Zdroyevsky, the Police Commissioner, was tall, and had broad shoulders. He spoke Polish and bad Russian, and he would scold mainly in Russian and only in a correct manner. The Kopylites were convinced that the devil was not as terrible as men made him out to be. One morning a drum was heard at the market place, which meant a new evil decree. The Police Commissioner arrived and announced that Jews must dress in ordinary clothing. They must not wear beards and ear-locks. The women are not allowed to shave their head and wear wigs.

The Jews claimed that these were conversion decrees. They prayed, decreed a fast, but, alas, without success. The rural police would catch prominent Jews, drag them to the district police and without ceremony would cut up their kapotes, shave their beards, and cut their ear-locks to the root. Bonnets and wigs were torn off respectable women in the street.

A delegation presented itself to the Police Commissioner and he put a stop to this business.

The rural police ceased to rage. For those who had their kapotes cut up, they had new ones made and the beards, ear-locks grew with time, and everything was as it was before. The Police Commissioner lived in harmony with the Jews. On Shabes he would go to someone's house to drink a couple of glasses of wine or schnapps, snack on fish, and never said no to a Jewish cholent [casserole of meat, potatoes and vegetables served on the Sabbath, kept warm overnight in the baker's oven].

He did not pay particular attention to the business of hygiene and building plans. People built as they wished and where they desired. The slaughterhouse was located in the center of the market place. Terrible bellowing was heard from the animals being slaughtered. Blood flowed and terrible odors spread and remained in the air until it rained and the smells were carried away with the storm water.

The road from Kopyl to Slutsk was a difficult one when coming down the mountain. On rainy days there were terrible obstacles. The drivers had to keep their heads when going to the city with wagons. In order to descend, men had to be very careful and courageous. The peasants would often break their wagons and injure the horses. This hazard was accepted as a natural thing, just like thunder and lightening or an earthquake. There was nothing they could do-they were helpless.

The investigator is coming to the shtetl. His visit brings fear to everyone. Only the Police Commissioner is advised of his arrival. A storekeeper says: "Why are you terrified, what are you afraid of? We do not deal in contraband. A big deal-an investigator!" Reb Chaim'ke looks at him, grabs him by the beard and yells: "And this is not contraband?"

In the meantime Zdroyevsky tries to restore calm. The investigator is a good friend, even a distant relative. He will go easy and it will not be expensive. He advises them not to look him in the eyes.

On the day the investigator arrived, there were only young women in the stores and streets. The older Jews were sitting at home, and the young children were not allowed out from school. The investigator, accompanied by the Police Commissioner, visited the stores. He ate a good lunch at the Police Commissioner's in the company of the priest and clergy. The Jewish representative was Reb Chaim'ke. On the second day the investigator left and the storm was over.

Kahal, Tributes, Monopoly, Excommunication

The duty of the Kahal [Jewish Community Council] was to take care of religious affairs and be the go-between for the community and the government. During my time, the affairs of the first part were carried out without any help from the community, according to long standing customs. They were in charge of registration and especially the books of the population, collecting taxes, giving them to the government, and furnishing recruits.

The Jewish population in Kopyl was very poor. Artisans and peddlers worked with a capitol of 50 to 100 rubles and barely made a living. Many residents left for other places to search for work and left behind their families at the mercy of God and help from goodhearted people. Forty or fifty lucky people (those who were counted among Kopyl's bosses and storekeepers, who worked with 500 to 1000 rubles) had to carry not only the expenses for all the community institutions but also had to help the poor. In all the Lithuanian Jewish communities, around 20% of the population was poverty stricken. They had to pay all the taxes for the religious and community institutions. There were many more taxes than just those for the general government. Provincial and state taxes were levied, especially for Jews, on items like candles and boilers. The military recruits ate up a lot of money. It was necessary to support the secret agents and guards and feed the recruits until they were turned over to the military. The Kahal was always in need of money. Community and religious expenses were covered by the meat tax on kosher meat, but it was never sufficient, so the Kahal had a monopoly on various products such as candles or yeast, and this brought in a certain yearly income.

In order to enforce local buying, if people got their products from other villages, it meant excommunication.

The text of the excommunication was terrifying. The offender was cursed in this world and in every world, separated from the community and the synagogue. The excommunication was strong and terrible. It was forbidden to have any contact with an excommunicated person, and he could not receive help. The ban on a certain person was announced in the synagogue with extraordinary ardor. The rabbi, surrounded by his helpers, would make the announcement near the Holy Ark from which the Torah scrolls had been brought out. Black wax candles were burned, and the shofar [ram's horn] was blown.

The Rabbis of Kopyl

Kopyl's rabbis were respected in Lithuania and renowned throughout the region, thanks to the great rabbi Yom-Tov Lipman (the last quarter of the 18th century), the grandson of the famous commentator Yom Tov.

A grandson printed Rabbi Lipman's remarks on the Talmud with the title "Holy Commentaries" or "Holy Yom Tov." It was very popular in the rabbinic world.

During his life, Reb Yom Tov did not publish his interpretations and did not care to compete for a rabbinate in one of the better, first class communities in Lithuania. He spent his entire life serving the poor community of Kopyl.

He gave his entire being over to the study of the Torah, far from worldly pleasures. He would be home only on Shabes and holidays. The rest of the time, he spent in the kloyz in a corner behind the oven (that remained "holy and historic" from that time on). He ate, slept, studied, took care of religious and community affairs and wrote his interpretations there.

According to his grandson and the Kapulier Pinkus:

After the death of "the last" Vilna Rabbi, Rabbi Shmuel, the Vilna Kehilla [Jewish Community Council] selected Reb Yom Tov as the next Vilna rabbi. A group of well-known Vilners came to Kopyl with the news that he had been chosen as the Vilna rabbi. Arriving in Kopyl, the delegation did not meet him in the rabbi's house. The rabbi's wife did not want to call him in order not to disturb his studies. The messengers had to wait until Shabes when Reb Yom Tov would be at home.

Having found out what the Vilners wanted, Rabbi Yom Tov called a meeting after Shabes with the Kopylites and let them know that his salary of 35 groschen a week was not enough.

In order to stay, he would need a small raise, or he would have to go to Vilna. This information grieved the Kopylites. On the one hand, it would hurt them to be separated from their great rabbi, and on the other hand, where would they find the money to give the rabbi a raise?

As both sides were dear to each other, they found a solution. The rabbi was given an increase of one and a half groschen, and he stayed in Kopyl.

Not long after his death, as written in the Pinkas-Reb, Yosele Peimer was invited to be a Rabbi in Slutsk. He was known as Rabbi Yosele Slutsker.

On the way to Slutsk, he spent a Shabes in Kopyl, where he heard about one of Rabbi Yom Tov Lipman's pronouncements. He was astonished by Rabbi Yom Tov's profound knowledge and wisdom. Rabbi Yosele said that if in Kopyl, almost a suburb of Slutsk, there was such a prominent learned man, he would not dare be a rabbi in Slutsk. When he was told that Rabbi Yom Tov was already dead, Reb Yosele remarked: "In that case, I will go to Slutsk. I am not afraid of the dead."

Yom Kippur, when Kopyl Jews sat in the synagogue and prayed, Reb Elia left the kloyz and did not return. The young men went looking for him. They searched for a long time and finally found him at the "poor house" (where the sick lived).

There stood Reb Elienke. He chopped wood and put it in the oven and cooked soup for the sick. One can imagine how surprised these people were. They called him an apostate, left quickly to go back to the kloyz and told him what they had seen. The last person to hear about it said: "It is a shame that the young people know better than their elders about how to spend a holy day!" Rabbi Ziskind's authority worked and calmed everybody down. They did not talk about and discuss this for long.

(Translated from Russian to Yiddish by Nach)

From Kapulie to Slutsk by Joseph Morgenshtern, Cleveland Translated by Judie Ostroff Goldstein

For a young Jewish boy who had to eat at strangers' tables in his own hometown because his hard stepfather did not want to feed his wife's children, going to the nearby city Slutsk with its yeshivas was very attractive.

There would be "essen teg" [eating days, free board by days in several houses] at strangers' tables, only they would not be in Kopyl where everyone knew me, but in Slutsk where all the young boys who came to study from far off towns were doing the same.

Besides, Slutsk was famous for its yeshivas. I hoped that in Slutsk, my studies would open possibilities for me.

I traveled the forty versts [former Russian measure of distance, about .66 of a mile] from Kopyl to Slutsk with my friend Noach, a boy my age. We traveled by wagon, crushed in with other passengers who were traveling to Slutsk on business. The scenery over the forty versts was beautiful, but it is not necessary for me to describe it because our great "zayde" [grandfather], Mendele, has already described it so masterfully in his book. I will immediately continue with the Slutsk situation and my personal survival there.

My friend Nach and I reached the kloyz [study house] together.

The kloyz was renown It was not only a yeshiva where young men rocked over an open gemore [Hebrew gemore, part of the Talmud that comments on the Mishnah (post-biblical laws and rabbinical discussions of the 2nd century B.C.E.)] night and day. It was also a sort of reserve station for all those who needed a place to lay their heads.

In order to be provided with "days," people had to come to Reb Israel, who was in charge of the accounts for all the householders who had given certain days to the yeshiva boys from other towns. The yeshiva boys did not get "days" from Reb Israel just like that – without any reason.

For every "day" that Reb Israel granted for the "semester," the yeshiva boy had to pay him fifty kopecks in cash. In order for a student to be given all seven days of the week for the semester, he had to pay Reb Israel a ruble and five kopecks. And when a boy did not possess such a sum, nothing good came of it.

Therefore, a boy who had a little cash was able to buy more than seven days.

So, the story was that not every day was an eating day. There were also some that we, the young boys, called "mezumene" [cash, money].

The latter were at women's stores who did not have the time to prepare a meal at home for the yeshiva boys, so they received the boys in the store and gave them several kopecks with which to buy their food.

With these "days," Reb Israel had a good business. I was able to get nine "days". Seven "eating" and two cash. The latter two, which cost thirty kopecks, gave us better value for the money.

Once in a while, there was a little trouble. This would happen when a storekeeper decided to go home and cook a meal for the family and for the yeshiva boy. In such a case, the student ate two meals and consoled himself by praying twice that day, for which he would obtain double merit in the world to come.

Sleeping in the kloyz was not bad when there were no nuisances with the crazies.

There were a lot of crazies in Slutsk who would get together there from the entire area. They could be seen in the streets, heard in the marketplace cursing the bosses, and at night at least one of them found a resting place in the kloyz.

It was a difficult semester for me in Slutsk. I was drowning in the dark, so before the term finished, I returned to Kopyl.

At that time, I became a Bar Mitzvah boy and suddenly felt a sense of shame towards eating "days." Is this what one is supposed to do with one's time? So I put an end to it. I went to my Uncle Shimon, who had an iron store at the marketplace and who could use my help. The main thing was that I began to earn my daily bread by working every day in my uncle's iron store, but I hadn't counted on my Aunt Brayna:

During the week, you work for your food, but on Shabes, you do not work, so why should I feed you? So, Aunt Brayna was right, and I celebrated the Sabbath in hunger.

In the evening hours, I studied in the besmedresh [house of study, synagogue, meeting hall] under the supervision of Reb Shlomo Shvitzitzer.

Reb Shlomo Shvitzitzer was a modern Jew. When he studied a page of gemore with us poor boys, his voice was loud, but as soon as he finished the lesson, nobody was there.

People called him Shvitzitzer because he came to Kopyl from the nearby village of Shvizitz, where he had lived for a long time with his wife, four sons and an only daughter. He was a tenant farmer in the villages.

Being a Jewish scholar, he taught his children Yiddishkeit [Judaism] and was happy when a Jew strayed to him, and he was able to perform a good deed by giving him a place to stay. On holidays, he came to the shtetl just like all the tenant farmers in the area. He hoped, God willing, to arrange marriages for his children as God commanded. But suddenly, a great misfortune struck, and it broke him entirely.

His only daughter, who was the apple of his eye, fell in love with a neighboring peasant's son, and there was no saving her. He left Shvizitz with the family and settled in the Kopyl besmedresh when a priest married his daughter to the man she loved in church. To this day, I cannot forget Reb Shlomo Shvitzitzer.

Kopyl Gets Other Faces

One began to see young men wearing Russian shirts and hats in the streets of Kopyl. Their language was a juicy Yiddish – also entirely different.

These young men had been brought from other places, mostly from Bialystok, for Fayvel Riplis's tannery, which at that time grew to be a large enterprise.

The air in Kopyl was full of words like "Socialism", "strike", "bourgeois" and others. There were songs like "Shvester un Brider" ["Sisters and Brothers"], " Az es falt, falt der Bester " [It so happens, the best fall] and " Baruch Shulman Der Groyser Held " [Baruch Shulman the Great Hero]. In short, Kopyl had suddenly and unnoticed been given a good shake.

I felt a strong pull towards Zionist ideals.

At the same time, with the new speeches and songs from the young men who were brought to Kopyl, one also heard speeches and songs about Israel.

The main speaker was the Jewish apothecary in Kopyl, who wrote for the daily Hebrew newspaper from Vilna "HaZman." Every day, I ran to him to see if leaving for Israel was possible.

The subject of Israel for Jews who would return there from Kopyl, Slutsk, and other towns and villages captured my young heart. So, I joined a youth group that collected money for Zionism.

We said that they should know that we, poor Jews, also stood with them.

At that time, we heard the news that there would be a Zionist meeting in Minsk. The city of Minsk grew in my eyes greatly and mightily, and it was my dream to go there.

A small matter, Minsk! Minsk began to seem like the greatest center in the world.

All the ideals of Zionism and Socialism were bubbling up there.

It was said that in Minsk, Jewish sons and daughters refused riches that their rich parents possessed. They went off to fight for the people and for a better and freer world in the form of glory and purity that, for me, was embodied in the form of the famous revolutionary Gershony.

I was drawn to the large Minsk library, where books were free for everybody. It was what had drawn me to Minsk, and I began to make plans to reach Minsk.

This material is made available by JewishGen, Inc. and the Yizkor Book Project for the purpose of fulfilling our mission of disseminating information about the Holocaust and destroyed Jewish communities.

THE GREAT TRANS-ATLANTIC MIGRATIONS...

The mostly untold story

Many Quotes below are from "The Great Transatlantic Migrations, 1870–1914" by Walter Nugent and "On the trail of the immigrant" by Edward Alfred Steiner(1906). Others are from Peter Roberts book, "The New Immigration." (1912) These are among the sources for many of my references regarding immigration.

Permission to leave: In many areas, it was not possible to just pack up and leave without permission of the authorities. In the late 1880s, the Italian government passed laws to make emigration easier. Although Nugent states that many emigrants did leave their homelands illegally. See my essay on Uncle Jake's great escape.

"In Russia, before one may emigrate, many painful and costly formalities must be observed, a passport obtained through the governor and speeded on its way by sundry tips (bribes). It is in itself an expensive document without which no Russian subject may leave his community, much less his country. Many persons, therefore, forego the pleasure of securing official permission to leave the Czar's domain, and go, trusting to good luck or to a few rubles with which they may close the ever open eyes of the gendarmes of the Russian boundary. Austrian and Italian authorities also require passports for their subjects, but they are less costly and are granted to all who have satisfied the demands of the law." pp. 31-32 of Steiner.

Booking Passage: "These formalities over, the travelers move on to the market square... There also, the agent of the steamship company receives (with just as much feeling) their hard earned money in exchange for the long coveted 'Ticket,' which is to bear them to their land of hope." p. 32 of Steiner.

"The Hamburg-America Line (HAPAG) developed a network of agents in various spots in Russia and East Europe from the early 1870s onward. Through them it served Russian Jews escaping from pogroms as early as 1871, and also German-Russian Mennonites and Bohemian farm families. The terrible cholera epidemic that killed thousands in Hamburg in August 1892 nearly shut down HAPAG for almost two years, but in the fall of 1894, together with the government of the city-state of Hamburg, it built another 25,000 square meters of port facilities, including baths, disinfection facilities, restaurants, sleeping quarters, churches and synagogues, and a music pavilion. Quarantines were enforced in accord with new rules, both German and American." p. 32 of Nugent. (Photo Liverpool, England, Jews waiting for the ship.)

To the Port: Emigrants, who increasingly heard from relatives and former neighbors living in the New World of opportunities there, accordingly availed themselves ever more often of the expanding railway networks to reach the seaports. Those from the Austro-Hungarian Empire nearly always departed from Hamburg or Bremen; those from Russia went through Hamburg; and Germans themselves left from either of those ports or from a Dutch or French port. Swedes and Danes appear frequently on the Hamburg passenger lists. People leaving Italy embarked from Naples, Genoa, Trieste, or Marseilles; those from the Balkans, Trieste usually; and many from the Ukraine and the Russian Pale after 1900 used Odessa." p. 33 Nugent.

From the small windows of fourth-class railway carriages, they get glimpses of a new world, larger than they ever dreamed it to be...

Guided by an official of the steamship company whose wards they have become, they alight from the train, but not without having here and there to pay tribute to that organized brigandage (gangs) by which every port of embarkation is infested. The beer they drink and the food they buy, the necessary and unnecessary things that they are urged to purchase, are excessively dear by virtue of the fact that a double profit is made for the benefit of the officials or the company that they represent.

The first lodging places before they are taken to the harbors are dear, poor and often unsafe...

Yet, admirable as is the machinery which has been set up at Hamburg for the reception of the emigrant, these minor abuses have not all passed away ... The Italian government safeguards its emigrants admirably at Naples and Genoa, but other governments are seemingly unconcerned. When the official is done with the emigrants, they are taken to the emigrant depot of the company (which in many cases is inadequate for a large number of passengers), their papers are examined, and they are separated according to sex and religion. At Hamburg, they are required to take baths, and their clothing is disinfected, after which they constantly emit the delicious odors of hot steam and carbolic acid. The sleeping arrangements in Hamburg are excellent. Usually, twenty persons are in one ward, but private rooms which have beds for four people can be rented. (*The fumigation arose after an epidemic.*)

The food is abundant and good, plenty of bread and meat are to be had, and luxuries can be bought at reasonable prices. At Hamburg, music is provided, and the emigrants may make merry at a dance until dawn on the day of sailing.

The medical examination is now very strict, yet seemingly not strict enough; for quite a large percentage of those who pass the German physicians are deported on account of physical unfitness." pp. 32-35 of Steiner. (Sent back from America because American doctors at the port thought they were sick.)

The Voyage: "The day of embarkation finds an excited crowd with heavy packs and heavier hearts climbing the gangplank. An uncivil crew directs the bewildered travelers to their quarters, which in the older ships are far too inadequate and in the newer ships are, if anything, worse.

Clean they are, but there is neither breathing space below nor deck room above, and the 900 steerage passengers crowded into the hold of so elegant and roomy a steamer as the Kaiser Wilhelm II of the North German Lloyd line are positively packed like cattle taking a walk on deck  when the weather is good, absolutely impossible, while to breathe clean air below in rough weather, when the hatches are down is an equal impossibility. The stenches become unbearable, and many of the emigrants have to be driven down, for they prefer the bitterness and danger of the storm to the pestilential air below. The division between the sexes is not carefully looked after, and the young women who are quartered among the married passengers have neither the privacy to which they are entitled nor are they much more protected than if they were living promiscuously. Photo boarding ship. https://www.thoughtco.com/germans-to-america-1421984

The food, which is miserable, is dealt out of huge kettles into the dinner pails provided by the steamship company. When it is distributed, the stronger push and crowd, so that meals are anything but orderly procedures.

On the whole, the steerage of the modern ship ought to be condemned as unfit for the transportation of human beings, and I do not hesitate to say that the German companies, and they provide the best for their cabin passengers, are unjust, if not dishonest, towards the steerage.

Take, for example, the second cabin, which costs about twice as much as the steerage and sometimes not twice so much; yet the second cabin passenger on the Kaiser Wilhelm II has six times as much deck room, much better located and well protected against inclement weather. Two to four sleep in one cabin, which is well and comfortably furnished, while in the steerage, from 200 to 400, sleep in one compartment on bunks, one above the other, with little light and no comforts. In the second cabin, the food is excellent, is partaken of in a luxuriantly appointed dining room, and is well cooked and well served, while in the steerage, the unsavory rations are not served but doled out with less courtesy than one would find in a charity soup kitchen.

On the steamer Noordam, sailing from Rotterdam three years ago, a Russian boy in the last stages of consumption was brought upon the sunny deck out of the pestilential air of the steerage. I admit that to the first cabin passengers, it must have been a repulsive sight--this emaciated, dirty, dying child; but to order a sailor to drive him downstairs was a cruel act, which I resented. Not until after repeated complaints was the child taken to the hospital and properly nursed. On many ships, even drinking water is grudgingly given, and on the steamer

Staatendam, four years ago, we literally had to steal water for the steerage from the second cabin, and that, of course, at night. On many journeys, particularly on the Furst Bismark of the Hamburg American line, five years ago, the bread was absolutely uneatable and was thrown into the water by the irate emigrants.

In providing better accommodations, the English steamship companies have always led; and while the discipline on board of ship is always stricter than on other lines, the care bestowed upon the emigrants is correspondingly greater." (from On the Trail of the Immigrant, by Edward A. Steiner, published in 1906.)

"In the early eighties, every steamship had compartments for steerage passengers, in which hundreds of men were huddled together in berths which afforded bare room to lie down. The berths were two deep, and each passenger paid a small sum for a mattress of straw made to fit the berth; he also provided himself with a platter and cup, knife and fork, and spoon, which he had to keep clean and stow away for safekeeping. There was no room provided to place hand baggage, or small trunks save in the berth. When the man got in, the baggage got out so that during sleeping hours, the small baggage occupied the pathway leading to the berths; if the vessel rocked hard during the night, the rattle of tins and crockery was great, and, in the morning, it was no easy task to locate the grip or small trunk that had slid away.

Towels and soap, comb and brush, were nowhere in sight, and the washroom and toilet accommodations were far from decent. The air in the compartment was foul at all times, and every passenger spent as little time there as possible. None of the immigrants thought of undressing when they went to rest – they took off their shoes, removed their coats, and turned in, and with the dawn they were again on deck. No dining room was provided, but the space between the two rows of berths served as one. Some smooth boards, resting on wooden horses, served as a table. In front of the tables were benches. When the meal bell rang, a rush was made for these; then the stewards brought bread, meat, vegetables, etc., each passenger in turn being served as the waiters passed from one end of the table to the other. The bread was good; the meat, tough; the coffee, poor; and the tea – slop....: p. 2-3 of Roberts

Roberts goes on to describe the "Improved Conditions" of the ships of today [1920]. "In this are found inclosed berths to accommodate from four to eight persons. Room is provided for small trunks or hand baggage, and there are hooks upon which to hang clothes. A stationary washstand with towels is furnished, and the button of an electric alarm is near each berth, so that the occupant may, in case of need, summon a steward. The occupants of these quarters secure a degree of privacy that enables them to remove their clothes before they retire. The lavatories are decent, and the conveniences provided are ample and always usable. Regular dining rooms are provided, and the utensils used are furnished by the company and kept clean by the stewards. The food is ample and of good quality, providing care has been exercised in its preparation. These improvements are not common as yet – they are only found on some ships carrying steerage passengers from the northwestern countries of Europe,..." pp. 3-4 of Roberts

The New World: Steiner describes the fear of the emigrants as they prepare themselves for entry to the new country. The fear of the immigration agents, the medical, and of the unknown. "Yes, those are heavy hours and long, on that day when the ship is circled by the welcoming gulls, and the fire-ship is passed, while the chains rattle and the baggage is piled on the deck..." pp. 54-55 of Steiner

"At last, the great heart of the ship has ceased its mighty throbbing, and but a gentle tremor tells that its life has not all been spent in the battle with wind and waves. The waters are of a quieter color, and over them hovers the morning mist. The silence of the early dawn is broken only by the sound of deep-chested ferryboats that pass into and out of the mist like giant monsters stalking on their cross beams over the deep. The steerage is awake after its restless night and mutely awaits the disclosures of its own and the new world's secrets. The sound of a booming gun is carried across the hidden space, and faint touches of flame struggling through the gray are the sun's answer to the salute from Governor's Island.

The steerage is still mute; it looks to the left at the populous shore, to the right at the green stretches of Long Island, and again straight ahead at the mighty city. Slowly the ship glides into the harbor, and when it passes under the shadow of the Statue of Liberty, the silence is broken, and a thousand hands are outstretched in greeting to this new divinity into whose keeping they now entrust themselves." pp. 59-60 of Steiner

The Officials: Cabin and steerage passengers alike soon find the poetry of the moment disturbed, for the quarantine and custom-house officials are on board,...

The steerage passengers have before them more rigid examinations which may have vast consequences; so in spite of the joyous notes of the band, and the glad greetings shouted to and fro, they sink again into awe-struck and confused silence. When the last cabin passenger has disappeared from the dock, the immigrants with their baggage are loaded into barges and taken to Ellis Island for their final examination." pp. 62-63 of Steiner

"Before they leave the boat, they put on their best clothes, for they are anxious to look their best and make as favorable an impression as possible upon the representatives of the government;..." p. 34 of Roberts

"The barges on which the immigrants are towed towards the island are of a somewhat antiquated pattern and, if I remember rightly, have done service in the Castle Garden days, and before that, some of them at least had done full service for excursion parties up and down Long Island Sound...

With tickets fastened to our caps and to the dresses of the women and with our own bills of lading in our trembling hands, we pass between rows of uniformed attendants and under the huge portal of the vast hall where the final judgment awaits us. We are cheered somewhat by the fact that assistance is promised to most of us by the agents of various National Immigrant

Societies who seem both watchful and efficient. Mechanically and with quick movements, we are examined for general physical defects...

From here, we pass into passageways made by iron railings, in which only lately, through the intervention of a humane official, benches have been placed, upon which, closely crowded, we await our passing before the inspectors.

Already, a sifting process has taken place, and children who clung to their mother's skirts have disappeared, families have been divided, and those remaining intact cling to each other in a really tragic fear that they may share the fate of those previously examined.

One by one, we passed the inspectors; we showed our money and answered the questions, which were numerous and pertinent.

The examination can be superficial at best, but the eye has been trained, and discoveries that seem rather remarkable are made here.

Four ways open to the immigrant after he passes the inspector. If he is destined for New York he goes straightway down the stairs, and there his friends await him if he has any; and most of them have. If his journey takes him westward, and there the largest percentage goes, he enters a large, commodious hall to the right, where the money-changers sit and the transportation companies have their offices. If he goes to the New England states he turns to the left into a room which can scarcely hold those who go to the land of the pilgrims and puritans. The fourth way is the hardest one and is taken by those who have received a ticket marked P.C. (Public Charge), which sends the immigrant to the extreme left where an official sits, in front of a barred gate behind which is the dreaded detention-room." pp. 67-68 of Steiner

"Each railroad on the Jersey shore has an immigrant room to which the newcomers are taken by ferryboats from Ellis Island. In these rooms the immigrants are kept under strict guard until the immigrant train is made up – invariably at night...." p. 38 of Roberts

"Steerage immigrants must take the immigrant train or secure a first-class ticket on a regular train. Those destined to points within fifty miles or so of New York City are put on the first local train leaving after they are brought to the depot; but if they go eighty or more miles, they must take the immigrant train, which may be made up of a full complement of cars or of one coach which is attached to a regular train. The train starts at night, -- about nine o'clock, -- transporting to their destination the people examined that day at Ellis Island...." p. 39 of Roberts

The People. Steiner, Roberts and Nugent agree that the major reason for the emigration of most of the people was one of economics, especially of those from the southeastern European countries. There were, however, some cases, such as the Jews and the Russian Mennonites, who left due to persecution or on religious grounds. Many of those from the northeastern parts of Europe came as families but Roberts claims that a great many from the southeastern parts came to earn money and then return home. He goes on, "The new immigration, as before stated, differs much from the old. The people of south and eastern Europe are poor, illiterate, and unskilled as compared with those of the Baltic nations; they have lived under forms of government which that are oppressive and autocratic, their religious concepts differ widely from those of nations to the northwest; and yet these men of the new immigration have aspirations and hopes much like the immigrants of previous generations." p. 9 of Roberts.

"No one doubts that the flow of migrants out of Europe accelerated in the nineteenth century, beginning in the 1840s and 1850s, then leaped forward after 1870 when steamships almost completely replaced sailing ships. Early in the century, the voyage from the British Isles to North America took four to six weeks, plenty of time for contagious diseases to ravage passengers and crew. Up to and including the Irish Famine emigration of the 1840s, deaths from typhus, cholera, or other contagions frequently swept away 10 percent, and occasionally 25 percent, of the passengers during a crossing. In the 1850s mortality fell sharply, thanks to voluntary and government-imposed health and sanitary regulations and faster ships, which began to combine steam power with sails.

Nugent (P 32) reported the Hamburg-American Line "HAPAG" served parts of Russia and East Europe as early at the 1870s serving Russian Jews, German-Russian Mennonites and Bohemians. Cholera killed thousands in Hamburg, "nearly" closing the port in 1892 but in 1894 the shipping line and Hamburg government "built another 25,000 square meters of port facilities, including baths, disinfection facilities, restaurants, sleeping quarters, churches and synagogues, and a music pavilion."

(P 33) Nugent reported that many emigrants, responding to messages from friends and relatives transplanted into the New World ever more often used expanding railway networks to reach seaports. "Those from the Austro-Hungarian Empire nearly always departed from Hamburg or Bremen; those from Russia went through Hamburg; and Germans," from their countries' ports or Dutch or French. Meanwhile Swedes and Danes were on Hamburg passenger lists ... Italians leaving from Naples, Genoa, Trieste, or Marseilles. Balkans usually used Trieste and after 1900 many from Ukraine and Russia's Pale left from Odessa.

(P 32)"Technical improvements in the stroke and bore of propellers and the efficiency of engines brought migrants westward ever faster" he wrote.

Jews: "Somber Jews come, on whose faces fear and care have plowed deep furrows, whose backs are bent beneath the burden of law and lawlessness. They come, thousands at a time, at least 5,000,000 more may be expected; and he does not know what misery is, who has not seen them on that march which has lasted nearly 2,000 years beneath the burden heaped by hate and prejudice. Both peasant and Jew come from Russian, Austrian or Magyar (Hungarian) rule, under which they have had few of the privileges of citizenship but many of its burdens. From valleys in the crescent shaped Carpathians, from the sunny but barren slopes of the Alps and from the Russian-Polish plains they are coming as once they went forth from earlier homes; peaceful toilers, who seek a field for their surplus labour or as traders to use their wits, and it is a longer journey than any of their timid forbears ever undertook." pp. 22-23 of Steiner

Poles: "The Poles were the next of the Western Slavs to be drawn out of the seclusion of their villages; those from Eastern Prussia being the earliest, and those from Russian Poland the latest who have swelled the stream of emigration.

"The largest number of the Polish immigrants is composed of unskilled laborers, most of them coming from villages where they worked in the fields during the summertime, and in winter went to the cities where they did the cruder work in the factories. The Poles from Germany's part of the divided kingdom have furnished nearly their quota of immigrants, and those remaining upon their native acres will continue to remain there if only to spite the Germans.

"The Austrian Poles who have retained many of their liberties and have also gained new privileges, have had a national and intellectual revival, under the impulse of which the peasantry has been lifted to a higher level which has reacted upon their economic condition; and although that condition is rather low in Galicia, (where the Gordick's came from) as that portion of Poland is called, immigration from there has reached its high water mark. The largest increase in immigration among the Poles is to be looked for from Russian Poland where industrial and political conditions are growing worse, and where it will take a long time to establish any kind of equilibrium which will pacify the people and hold them to the soil." pp. 24-25 Steiner.

Read more: Polish Americans - History, The first Poles in America, Significant immigration waves, Acculturation and assimilation, (http://www.everyculture.com/multi/Pa-Sp/Polish-Americans.html#ixzz1AU8inwAb).

Whereas the essay about Uncle Jake's trip from Ukraine to Liverpool only mentions Hull in a few sentences, this reveals the importance of that port city and what the England part of the trip to Liverpool was like. Probably nothing about it ever appeared in your family's memoirs.
http://www.bbc.co.uk/legacies/immig_emig/england/humber/article_1.shtml

Then, there was train travel in the USA during the 19th Century.

TRAIN TRAVEL IN THE 19TH CENTURY

Recently, on a popular website, the question was asked, "How would you prefer to travel?" Many chose the steam train. I loved steam engines and the cars they pulled. Except for two points,… no air conditioning and tunnels.

In 1948, my grandfather, Sam Kroloff, and I took the choo-choo from Chicago to Atlanta and back to visit Uncle Max, Aunt Mary, and their kids Chuck and Carol. The red soil of Kentucky was sparkling. The clickety-clack from where one rail was jammed against another and the wheels hitting the joint was mesmerizing.

That year, Harry Truman continued an old presidential election campaign trick to draw crowds by taking a train tour and addressing people from the back car on a platform. Viola. Sam and George's train had a back parlor car with a platform. Georgie, wanting the Truman experience, went onto the platform. It was fun for about three minutes.

Then, the train went through a tunnel.

Steam engines burn wood or coal and spew out dark smoke, embers and soot … lots of soot, lots of smells and (at least for me) lots of snot. I was coughing and "emberized" from head to foot.

Earlier, for immigrants, the discomfort of rail travel began at the station house or depot, often misdescribed as a sort of charming social center. The truth is that these depots were a favorite lounging spot for loafers and the homeless. Spittoons sat everywhere, lying in wait for some unsuspecting traveler to accidentally kick over. As in saloons, "spitters" often missed so that almost as much spittle covered the floors as filled the spittoon. The lack of "no smoking" areas meant the air was thick and gray with smoke from cigarettes and cigars. My grandad Sam had a spittoon in his bedroom in Aunt Ina's Sioux City house to avoid midnight toilet runs. He often missed.

There was no such thing as a "check system" for luggage, which had to be identified and retrieved by the passengers themselves. This resulted in frequent arguments and the occasional smashing of trunks and bags, not to mention theft. Not only did baggage handlers not care who owned which bag, but they also gave no thought to how they treated the luggage in their care. No wonder their nickname was baggage smashers.

Train schedules of the great immigration period left much to be desired. Connections were more missed than hit. A traveler from Woodstock, Vt. in 1888 took two days to get to New York City. The response to his inquiry about when a certain train would leave was "sometime." A journey of twenty-five miles could take two and a half hours.

The bulk of passenger traffic came from the middle class, but the conditions they endured came closer to matching emigrant carriages than private rail cars. The wood-burning locomotives belched cinders that pattered on the roofs overhead like hail. Smoke and steam engulfed the train until, at the journey's end, the traveler appeared as though he had labored in a blacksmith's shop all day.

Travelers could close the windows and instead suffer the stink of whiskey, tobacco, and closely packed bodies. That was if they could open and close the poorly designed windows. Noise added to the discomfort, often drowning out all but the loudest of voices.

European trains often offered small compartments to reduce noise and bodily discomfort, but American railroads herded sixty to seventy passengers into each long car. The backs of the seats were too low to act as headrests, and if a passenger managed to nap in spite of the noise, he was soon awakened by the "trainboy," a peddler of books, candy and sundry goods whose visitations were constant and disruptive, according to one observer.

Mark Twain, on his way West, was badgered by what he called their "malignant outrages." He also noted that passengers looked "fearfully unhappy...doubled up in uncomfortable attitudes, on short seats in the dim funereal light ... like so many corpses who had died of care and weariness."

George Pullman's self-contained sleeping cars, introduced in the late 1860s, were considered a milestone in transportation luxury. Getting dressed in one, it was said, could only be accomplished if the person were expert at dressing under a sofa. Bad air trapped behind heavy curtains, the jolting of the train, and the overall cacophony of snores and crying babies made sleep nearly impossible. (As a kid, I took a Pullman from Chicago to Sioux City, Iowa. I thought it was great, but that was about a hundred years later.)

Food on board was up to the passengers, who brought with them baskets and containers loaded with whatever suited their fancy. One prominent odor in rail cars came from cabbage cooked over the stoves provided for heat. The Pullman dining car, when it came along, sounded like heaven but received few rave reviews from visitors of the times. Anyway, most travelers could not afford to eat in such cars. If possible, they gobbled down quick, greasy meals at lunchrooms along the line.

Add to this were train wrecks due to broken trestles (bridges), poor track, exploding boilers, faulty signals, and careless engineers and switchmen, producing an accident rate in the US five times that of England. According to one report, in 1890 alone, railroad-connected accidents caused 10,000 deaths and 80,000 serious injuries.

All in all, it doesn't sound like the most pleasant method of travel, but at least it was over much sooner than wagon trains or ocean travel.

MANIFEST DESTINY

Manifest Destiny is a "divine sanction" for capturing new territories. That's one reason an "alpha" nation like the USA uses as an excuse to force its own values upon others. It was the growing understanding of two different versions of Manifest Destiny that helped push the Krulevitskys out of The Pale.

Manifest Destiny in the US created jobs for immigrants even as Native Americans were being crushed and herded into their own small Pale of Settlements called Reservations. The "destiny" of the United States to occupy "The West" was propelled in large part by the Industrial Revolution. The picture is a once-popular depiction of American manifest destiny. For a discussion of the picture and manifest destiny see https://arthistory327.wordpress.com/2012/08/25/bombastic-art-manifest-destiny-and-john-gasts-american-progress/

Those tired, poor, huddled masses yearning to breathe free from around the world saw

North America as a land of opportunity. Our Russian cousins also were attracted by the USA's relatively humane values.

In their Tsar-dominated homeland, Manifest Destiny was quite different. The name "Tsar" is a Russian synonym for the ultimate European ruler, Caesar. Like him, Tsars were driven to expand their borders. Unlike Julius Caesar, the Tsars also believed that all people in the lands they controlled should convert to their religion, Russian Orthodoxy, an offshoot of Catholicism.

Other European rulers wanted Jews to convert *to* the old-fashioned Roman Catholicism. The Tsars, as titular heads of the Russian Orthodox Church, wanted to be the popes of Eastern Europe. So, they wanted the Poles who came under the spreading cloud of Russian control to convert *from* Roman Catholicism to Orthodox Catholicism (the Russian kind). Tsars and their minions made the lives of Jews and others who didn't submit to their religious and other wishes quite unpleasant.

Religion, power, money, and control are interconnected. Russia's leadership was pressured to protect a large number of businesses, farms, and a variety of jobs from Jewish competition, not unlike what other Europeans had been doing for centuries. The Tsars dearly wanted to be more European than even the French. And the French had perfected antisemitism. Someday, you might want to research "The Dreyfus Affair." And, don't forget, the French started the Inquisition. https://en.wikipedia.org/wiki/Inquisition

The outside world intruded now and again. One author wrote, "In 1853, during the war with Turkey and the Crimea, there was a difficult, bitter time. Taxes were demanded with merciless strictness. Military divisions passing through the shtetl would throw people out of their houses and take them over. Men were often drafted into the army. In truth, they were captured." Generally, 19th-century Jews under Russian supervision were determined to stay different. "The Chosen People" chose not to change their dress and demeanor, even though their "ways" were considered strange and feared.

CHICAGO

MARY AND JOSEPH

The Fire, the Neighborhood, the Mob and the Shabbos Goy.

I am pretty sure all the following is right.

Introduction

This short essay examines a mere sliver of our Chicago connections. Other essays in this series, "WHY DID OUR FAMILIES DO THAT?" contain much more about age-old developments in the New World, Old World Europe, and South Africa, which affected decisions our ancestors made that are relevant to our lives today.

The Fire. In 1875 or 1876, Mary Levy Kauffman's mother and father (Louis and Sarah Mann Levy) emigrated from Poland to Chicago. For the next 25 years Louis and Sarah lived a

few steps from the site on Dekoven Street where Mrs. O'Leary's cow allegedly kicked over a lantern while being milked. The lantern's flame is said to have ignited most of the O'Leary barn, which along with a lot of other factors, led to The Great Chicago Fire of 1871.

Mary Levy was my grandmother.

That catastrophe (the fire, not Mary) was a defining moment for Chicago and the entire Midwest.

Mary was the Levy's second child to be born in Chicago. From 1875 through the year she left, Chicago and its East Coast partner, New York City, were the most important engines driving the development of the US. Mary moved to Sioux City, Iowa, with her new husband, Joseph Kauffman, in 1900.

During her childhood, Chicago was nicknamed *The Windy City* by some New Yorkers. Not because of the brisk breeze that blew in from Lake Michigan but because of Chicago's loudly boasting politicians and other promoters. By 1900, when she arrived, Sioux City's boosters, especially the land speculators, were puffing up their chests and proclaiming their metropolis was "Little Chicago." Proportionally, it probably had a bit less corruption.

In their infancy, both communities had been pretty rough port cities. One is on the Missouri River, and one is on Lake Michigan. Neither of the two was restrained enough to quietly ease into a placid adulthood.

While the Fire and the bustling Dekoven Street neighborhood were relevant to our family, something else defined Chicago and touched our family and all other Chicagoans… Al Capone's Mob, also known as The Gang or The Syndicate. I'll get to that in a few paragraphs.

But first, some of the back story. The 1880 U.S. census listed my great-great grandfather Louis Levy as a "huckster." Officially, that was a very broad census category. He might have gone door-to-door peddling, probably food. Maybe he had a cart on a street from which he sold vegetables or household items … just as did many relatives whom he would never know in South Africa and Iowa.

By the time Mary Levy was in her teens, her dad and mom had moved up the food chain and owned a street-level grocery shop among the tenements along Dekoven Street, a few blocks north of Chicago's famous downtown, known as The Loop. Louis and Sarah Levy and their kids lived above the store.

The Neighborhood. Coincidentally, the Dekoven Street area in the 1890s was the most studied poor urban immigrant community in the United States. Because of that, as seen in another essay, we can know a lot about her daily life.

In time, Ben Behr married Mary Levy's younger sister, Annie. Conversations with him over 50 years ago revealed that he and nearby teenagers lived a life almost identical to those depicted in the movie and play *West Side Story* ... without the music or dancing, of course. There were teen gangs, turf wars, ethnic divides, fights, and knives.

The neighborhood was very loud and smelly. Sometimes, the garbage and human waste were picked up, often not. The picture was taken near Dekoven St. https://commons.wikimedia.org/wiki/File:Chicago_street_vendors_postcard_(Front).png

While the Chicago Fire had attracted huge amounts of New York money to rebuild the smoldering center city, the fire did not burn much of Dekoven Street. Prevailing winds carried the murderous flames and ash north and east. Curiously, the O'Leary barn burnt to a crisp, but their house survived.

The avalanche of East Coast money financed hundreds of thousands of jobs in Chicago, which helped attract a million or more procreative people from across the USA and the world. Some were good, some vile. Almost all who settled on Dekoven had one thing in common. By today's standards, they were poor.

So, in 1900, when Mary Levy married Joseph Kauffman of Sioux City, Iowa, and moved west, her new home in a nice house with a big yard must have seemed absolutely serene.

That serenity would be broken up by the occasional movement of a herd of cattle down the street on which they lived, headed for the large Sioux City stockyards, where the cows and steers would be slaughtered, cut into pieces that often would be packaged in paper wrappings. By the time the bits and pieces of those herds reached most urban customers, the acts of birthing, raising, massacring, and marketing the cows, pigs, and sheep they ate were completely severed from the reality of the moans, bleats and blood.

Random fact: The white building (left), built in the 1880s, sat on the O'Leary lot where it was photographed in the 1940s. It had a plaque commemorating the site. The building on the right looked similar to the Levy's place on the next block. All were razed when the city, appropriately enough, built a training facility for Chicago's firefighters.

The Mob. My parents were raised in Sioux City and moved to Chicago before I was conceived. Like every Chicagoan of a certain age, I could not help but run into the Mob. For just one of many instances: In the mid-1950s, I dropped out of college to work in a disgustingly filthy old warehouse to earn enough cash to finish college. The union I had to join was controlled by The Mob. Each month, two extremely large knuckle-draggers would accost us and collect the union dues. I shudder to think how the money actually was used.

In any event, I'm the kid with the dark sweater. The guy pictured in front of me with the sweaty, very soiled shirt had been a "chauffeur" in the Capone Gang. He often drove Al's brother, whose nickname was "Bottles."

My co-worker was named Vince or Vic. He told me about the time he was at the wheel of a car ferrying a long-forgotten politician with ties to The Mob. While stopping at a light, gunmen from a rival gang dramatically opened the car's back door. One machine-gunned the passenger and, poof, the crooks disappeared. Just like in the movies, but it was real life. (I checked this out by looking at the microfilm of The Chicago Tribune, which reported the incident just as Vince/Vic related it.)

The Shabbos Goy. About the same time that Joseph Kauffman went to Chicago in search of a bride (1900), that scrawny warehouse drunk was a kid. Amazingly, he claimed he was the Shabbos Goy in the Levy apartment above their store on Dekoven Street. (A Shabbos Goy is a non-Jewish helper who does the forbidden Sabbath activities in an Orthodox household, such as lighting cooking fires.)

And you may ask, "Why is it necessary for a non-Jew to light the cooking and heating fires during the Sabbath?" There is an answer, and it is contained in some of the words of a song in the highly acclaimed Broadway musical and Hollywood movie titled "Fiddler on the Roof." The milkman Tevye and the chorus explain …

(Chorus) Tradition, tradition... tradition

(Tevye) "Because of our traditions, we've kept our balance for many, many years.

Here in Anatevka we have traditions for everything...

how to eat, how to sleep, even, how to wear clothes.

For instance, we always keep our heads covered and always wear a little prayer shawl...

This shows our constant devotion to God. You may ask, how did this tradition start?

I'll tell you - I don't know. But it's a tradition...

Because of our traditions, everyone knows who he is and what God expects him to do."

WHAT MARY LEFT

This essay is relevant to every nation's continuing discussions about immigration, jobs, and healthcare, and it is a part of the American story. It is about a neighborhood in Chicago during the late 1800s that today has been pretty much dug up, paved over, or rebuilt. Some call it gentrification. Others call it erasing history. Nevertheless, we are what we are and who we are because of our history. And some of our history began there.

Cousin Hal Mendelsohn asked if I had heard stories about our grandmother Mary's early life. The answer is no, although my mother, Florence Blossom Kauffman, said Mary had been taken to see the great Chicago World's Fair in 1893 by her father, Louis. Yet The Levy's neighborhood and its lifestyle are well documented, some of which are summarized below.

Mary was born in 1877, the second of Louis and Sarah's kids. There appear to have been ten children, six of whom survived. According to the 1880 census, the eldest, Moses, was born two or three years earlier. It is probable that Louis's father, Reuben Levinsky, and possibly his mother, Ida, were in Chicago before the Great Fire of 1871. Others of our families followed. They went into several businesses, including taverns, craftsmanship, and groceries.

They were among the earliest Jewish/Polish residents of Chicago. The family emigrated from Warsaw in what today is Poland.

After the Fire, which fried all of Chicago's downtown area, the city was in the midst of a frantic rebuilding spree financed, in large part, by New York money that likely would have been put to other uses in other places.

The investment in Chicago was a hot topic among people in St. Louis, Sioux City, Savannah, and Seattle who thought they deserved a larger "part of the pie."

That capital (money) quickly built an already robust infrastructure, like railroads, that survived the fire and a business culture that made Chicago the non-political capital of most of the USA. Its domain was a huge area bordered by the Appalachian mountains to the east and the Rockies to the west. There were jobs in The Windy City, and jobs attract the jobless like bears to honey.

The Levy/Levinsky's history in Poland is impenetrable. In different USA census reports, they were listed as coming from Poland, Russia, and Poland/Germany. That's probably because, Poland had been split into several parts, partitioned into areas under the control of Prussia (Germany), Austria, and Russia. And the borders shifted over the years.

Chicago historians contend that most of the Russian and Polish emigrants in the 1870s and later were from poor rural communities with Jewish populations. The towns were called shtetls.

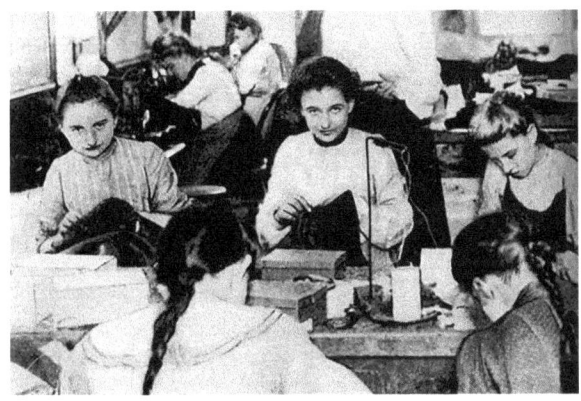

Chicago and Warsaw had some similarities, covered in another essay. But the place the Levys lived, on Chicago's near South Side, around Dekoven and Maxwell Streets, was a bit like a Shtetl with an old-fashioned European lifestyle. It also was a bit like Warsaw and Liverpool and a lot like what some people think of as the American Melting Pot or the American Stew or what the country was like in its "salad days." Within a few square blocks was an amazing mixture of cultures. Much more varied than around the biblical Tower of Babel.

While the Levys' neighbors were from all over Europe, not far away were neighborhoods that pretty much recreated the communities they left. Among them were Pilsner (Slavic), Chinatown, Little Italy, Little Warsaw, Andersonville (Swedish), Bridgeport (Irish), Polonia (Polish), Greektown, Jewtown (Maxwell Street), and The Black Belt. Maxwell Street was an American version of the markets in East European communities … such as towns where many of my other ancestors lived … Slutsk and Kapulia in what now is the country of Belarus, along with a town named Mena and one called Chernush in Ukraine.

I remember my folks taking me to Maxwell Street as a kid to buy clothes. It was loud, lined with pushcarts on the streets, crowds on the sidewalks, and a few blocks of stores. People were yelling from every side about how good their goods were and, sometimes literally, shoving their merchandise at us. For a kid, it was scary. I also remember the music. The Jewish merchants often had electricity and long extension cords for the loudspeakers used by musicians. The merchants liked the crowd-appealing music.

I had no idea I was experiencing the birth of urban blues played by previously rural black men who had come north to survive. Maybe you remember the song "The Rock Island Line," which was "a mighty fine line." It was one of the railroads that helped bring the black diaspora from the American South to the urban north.

The Blues Brothers movie with John Belushi and Dan Aykroyd vividly depicted the Maxwell Street scene as I remember it. Something similar occurred in the Lower East Side in New York, where newcomers were taking their first bites out of The Big Apple.

IN 1878, MARY WAS A TODDLER, AND CHICAGO WAS A "TODDLIN" TOWN

Compared to European cities, Chicago was, like Mary in 1878, a toddler, still maturing and with unrestrained optimism. The lyrics of a hit song recorded by the popular 20th Century singer Frank Sinatra, appropriately titled "Chicago," said it was a "toddlin" town.

Toddlin had at least two meanings. First, it referred to a boisterous dance craze (The Toddle) of the 1920s when the song was first recorded. Second, it referred to a maturing city with unrestrained optimism but still a toddler who walks like a person who had too many drinks.

Many of Chicago's boosters, sometimes called blowhards and "windy," certainly exhibited wild optimism. Others, maybe not so much. The city was a huge magnet for the poor, and hungry, yearning to breathe free. Young Mary's neighbors were poor, hungry, and because of extreme air pollution, still yearning to breathe free.

Across the city, there were thriving areas, prosperous people, and progress. Downtown was quickly rebuilt after the fire, and suburbs were popping up like daffodils in spring.

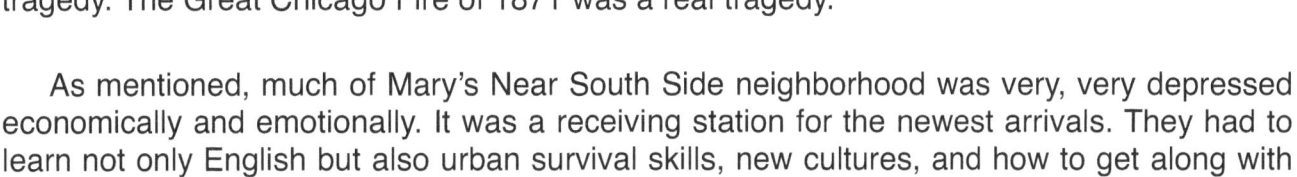

Every material item *anyone* would want was in Chicago. Even if that *anyone* was not there, like in Omaha or Oregon, it was available. By the 1890s, Chicago's bulky Sears or Montgomery Ward's mail-order catalogs were stuffed with over 25,000 items each. Some items were small like a button, others were as big as kits for houses, ready to be shipped directly to a site upon which they would be built. Shipments to and from Sears, Wards, and the huge meat-packing business in Chicago helped pay for the spreading network of railroads that tied the United States together.

Like after wars, there is money to be made in rebuilding from tragedy. The Great Chicago Fire of 1871 was a real tragedy.

As mentioned, much of Mary's Near South Side neighborhood was very, very depressed economically and emotionally. It was a receiving station for the newest arrivals. They had to learn not only English but also urban survival skills, new cultures, and how to get along with people next door they never imagined existed in their rural spread-out or tightly-packed slum or ghetto communities.

Louis and Sarah were somewhat successful, I guess because everyone in the neighborhood had to eat. And they sold food.

A hint of their economic status is in the 1900 Census. They rented the building where they lived and had the store. When Louis died in 1899, the newly widowed Sarah (Mary's mother) and Sarah's younger children still lived in the building. Also renting there was Sarah's son Moses, who then called himself Morris, and his young family. The logical assumption is that they were not living in a cramped tenement and renting some of it out to others. After Louis died, Sarah ran the store, and Morris was an iron salesman, whatever that meant.

To better answer cousin Hal's question about Mary's world, I lifted information from several mid-1890 reports published by Jane Addams' Hull House, the most important settlement house in America because it provided so many services to the surrounding area while also instituting social reforms. It was where Benny Goodman took music lessons.

Interspersed are a few of my comments. Unless otherwise noted, words within quotation marks come from the Hull House essays, all written by women.

Dark photo is from museum collections showing area around Maxwell Street when Mary was a pre-teen. Modern photo is from a Chicago architectural river tour 2017 ... both about the same spot.

The approximately one-square-mile area that the nearby Hull House chronicled in the early 1890s consisted of two separate areas. On the east side of the Chicago River's South Branch was a "third-of-a-square-mile that includes…a criminal district which ranks as one of the most openly and flagrantly vicious in the civilized world. West of the river (the top part of the black and white picture) was the poorest and probably the most crowded section of Chicago." That's where Mary lived, a couple of blocks from the river.

On the dark side, or the bad side of the river, were houses of ill repute and a jumble of polluting industries, railroad yards, stacks of lumber, etc. The befouled, bubbling South Branch of the Chicago River was a constant presence. Depending on the wind direction, in addition to the neighborhood smells, there were very strong odors coming from the huge Stockyards and meat packing factories to the Southwest with thousands of cramped, moaning, then bleeding animals … and their awful offal.

Just a few blocks west from Mary's house were several residences that gave "the impression of a well-to-do neighborhood." About a mile further away were mansions of the wealthy.

Even in the rather small, seemingly well-to-do area near Hull House, landlords sought maximum income from available space. Where backyard gardens might have been planted, wooden buildings sprang up. A Hull House report said, "It is customary for the lower floor of the rear houses to be used as a stable and outhouse, while the upper rooms serve entire families as a place for eating, sleeping, being born, and dying."

The colors for each occupied tenement show the predominant languages spoken in each residence. The white in the front of the Levy's building indicates residents spoke English. The red in the back is the symbol for Russian speakers, which in their case must have meant Yiddish, and the parallel lines are the code for Polish speakers.

The map shows the Levy's building at 113 Dekoven. Mrs. O'Leary had lived at 137. The street was re-numbered a few years after Mary left to live in Sioux City, and 113 became 524. In 1880, when Mary first appeared on a census form, her family lived about a mile north on Canal St., a neighborhood that would have been torched by the 1871 fire and rebuilt. https://www.digitalcommonwealth.org/search/commonwealth:3f4636086

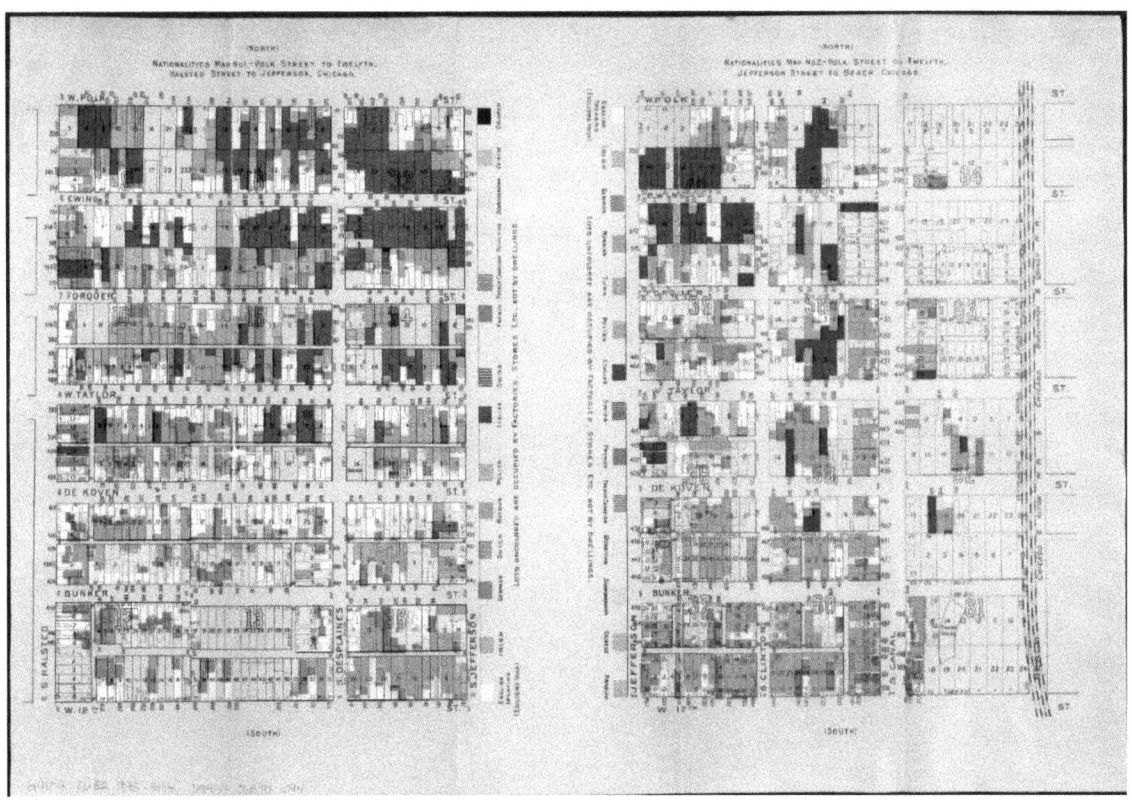

SEVERAL HULL HOUSE MAPS REPORTED THEIR AREA LIKE ABOVE. THIS IS THE REAL WORLD MARY LIVED IN … THE REAL WORLD OF BROAD SHOULDERS … HOG BUTCHERS TO THE WORLD … THE BUILDUP TO THE CAPONE MOB … AND AMAZING ADVANCES, EVEN IF THE MOB GOT A PART OF IT … IN CITY INFRASTRUCTURE (WATER, GAS, SEWER, ELECTRICITY, TRANSPORTATION, WAGES, SCHOOLS, ETC., ALONG WITH A FEW MOB MURDERS, CONTROL OF BOOZE, AND THE FACT THAT THE HOTEL PUBLIC TOILETS HAD MONITORS WHO OFFERED ONE A TOWEL AND EXPECTED A TIP, HALF OF WHICH WENT TO THE CAPONE MOB OR ONE OF THEIR COUNTERPARTS. I FOUND IT CONFUSING AT FIRST BUT JUSTIFIED LATER WHEN I LEARNED THE HOTEL MANAGER MIGHT BE SHOT IF HIS "PROTECTION" CHARGE WASN'T PAID ON TIME. FAR AS I COULD TELL, GRANDMA MARY WAS A PIECE OF WORK. NO WONDER SHE WAS SUCH A STRONG INFLUENCE IN THE SIOUX CITY COMMUNITY WHEN SHE MARRIED JOSEPH AND MOVED THERE.

If you are interested in how Mary lived and how that might have influenced your life, please look up the Hull House on Google. There is a lot there, and it once again may prove that you are what they were. Mary must have been, like many immigrants to America, influenced by a society that expressed Medieval ethics, a very strong person. Your ancestors were, too. They were able to absorb the American ethos (Manifest Destiny and saying all are equal, but not acting as if all are equal.). It was like a high wire circus act. We come from strong stock. Or maybe we don't. People are the same thing but different.

MORE ABOUT MARY'S NEIGHBORHOOD AND INTRO TO THE WHITE CITY

Dekoven and other close-by streets contained a collection of "tobacco-stands, saloons, sordid looking shops, factories and occasional small dwelling-houses," built for one family, but generally "tenanted by several, and occasionally serving as bakery, saloon or restaurant as well as residence." (Illlustrations in this section from Newberry library, Pinterest and Wikipedia.)

Liquor and just about any other "vice" was available everywhere around young Mary. There were "eighty-one saloons west of the river (in her neighborhood), besides several delicatessens, restaurants, and cigar-stands where liquor was sold." Keep in mind a nearby neighborhood a few blocks east and across the South Branch of the Chicago River was considered much worse.

From 1877 to 1900, plenty of people born in the USA, as well as immigrants, moved to Chicago. According to Hull House maps online, it looks like the tenements in Mary's neighborhood housed people from at least 18 nations. Almost all adults were immigrants from Europe.

Although attitudes about child labor were changing, there remained a strong need among poor families for the youngsters to work. Thus, not all kids went to public school. Pictures: show a typical tenement kitchen in Mary's neighborhood ... above and a nearby sweatshop at left. See the essay, Smart Elek, for more on child labor in the mines and Pennsylvania mills around the Gordicks.

Several smallish areas in the Windy City were considered ghettos ... Italians on a few blocks, Russian and Polish Jews on another few blocks, Bohemians (Czechs and

Slovaks) on a separate few blocks, and Irish, Germans, Scandinavians, Chinese (in basement laundries, we were told), and a few people from the Mideast.

After scouring a dozen or so of the Hull House maps, I only found two African Americans. Many had begun to settle a few blocks away into what became known as The Black Belt. Chicago was a very segregated city by skin color, religion, and homeland. Interestingly, Some of these were ghettos where people wanted to reside.

Hull House maps documented what people claimed were their weekly earnings. They chronicled residents of each building in the Dekoven neighborhood. If I have it right, half of the Levy building residents were, in total, earning $20 or more a week, and the other half between $10 and $15 a week. Not sure what that meant in terms of their wealth vis-a-vis those days or these days. An online calculator shows that $15 in 1900 would be about $450 in 2020. I'm also not sure that is accurate.

The picture shows the O'Leary residence. Its barn burned, but the O'Leary home didn't because the prevailing winds pushed the fire away from it. Dekoven Street, like most of Chicago, was unpaved. Water from homes and businesses emptied into the street and eventually carried almost every imaginable amount of pollution to the Chicago River and Lake Michigan, which were the sources of drinking water. After a huge engineering project, the river was reversed, flowing from Lake Michigan, which provides clean water. Any city sewage now flows down river toward the Mississippi River.

Notice the raised wooden sidewalk at the O'Leary's with flowing street water, maybe after a rainstorm. Two reasons for the quick spread of the Chicago Fire were those elevated wooden walkways and a weeks-long drought. Millions of dry leaves were crammed under the miles of raised walkways. The leaves needed only a spark to ignite. The city's bone-dry wooden buildings were like kindling.

In addition, there had been a communications breakdown hampering the first responders. Most were exhausted from coping with fire-after-fire around the city as a drought deepened.

A much bigger fire occurred about the same time north of Chicago in Wisconsin. It was in an almost uninhabited area and received little notice. Like today, if it wasn't reported widely, it just didn't happen.

Jumping forward twenty years after the fire, the Hull House investigators reported a high turnover in the tenements around Mary and the site of the O'Leary house. Frequently, residents who were unable to pay their rent were evicted. It was not unusual for a packed tenement to morph into a lodging for emigrants from a single country, often relatives. Some landlords rented beds, not rooms … 12 hours for the day shift, 12 for the night.

Nearby Mary were hot, humid sweatshops and their "sweaters." Sweaters as in sweat/perspiration. Most sewed parts of a garment, such as coat sleeves or button holes. Others assembled the parts into dresses and suits.

Some kids sewed, and others rolled cigars in overflowing apartments. Still others toiled in small factories, maybe painting pottery with toxic lead-based colors. They were paid by the "piece" … each sleeve, shirt, skirt, cigar, or piece of crockery earned a few cents or maybe less than a penny. Men, women, boys, and girls worked from dawn to long after dusk. Pictured on the previous page is an 1890 New York family of four rolling cigars at home.

In New York, Chicago, and elsewhere, the profit margins for sweatshops were usually slim. Nonetheless, the cut-throat market for clothes grew in tandem with America's rapidly expanding population. The pictures in the annual Sears and Montgomery Ward catalogs showed the latest fashions to people all over the country. (I saw a report somewhere that, for a while, there were more people in Chicago's "needle trade" than any other trade in the city.)

A Hull House writer who peeked into the back doors of factories said she continually saw "bent figures stitching."

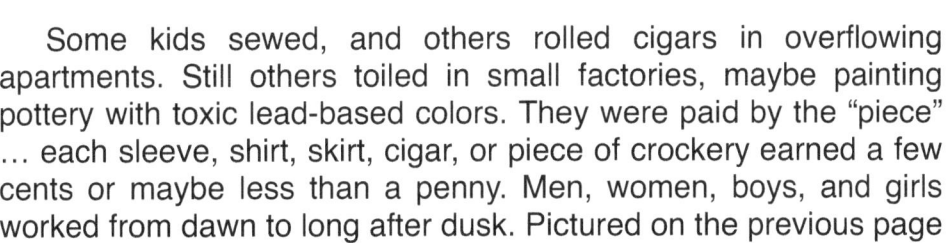

"People are noticeably under-sized and unhealthy," an observer wrote. The many workers in the tailoring trades "look dwarfed and ill-fed; they walk with a peculiar stooping gait, and their narrow chests and cramped hands are unmistakable evidence of their calling." This was hard, tedious work. Especially in summer, they sweat.

"Tuberculosis prevails…and deformity is not unusual. The mortality among children is great, and the many babies look starved and wan."

Germs dripping from the noses of sick sweaters became embedded into the fabrics and cigars they handled. Those germs stealthily moved from sweater shops to clothes shoppers. The malicious microbes helped cause mini-epidemics.

Like today, there were fashion "seasons." The "needle trade" sweaters and their bosses feverishly worked on manufacturing the new clothes-lines and then suffered payless downtime waiting to see if the products sold and if they would be reordered. Being paid a pittance by piece and with growing families to feed did not easily lead to savings accounts or "rainy day funds."

Smaller kids and unemployed older ones ran up and down the fetid stairwells and along sidewalks and alleys unattended unless their parents were out of work. Most of the tightly packed houses on Dekoven had little if any, air circulation in interior rooms. People slept on windowsills or wherever they could, especially in hot weather. Photo from U of Illinois. Much more background and photos, including this one at https://ecrp.illinois.edu/v2n1/bhavnagri.html

In the mid-1890s, Mary's adult neighbors spoke broken English, if they spoke any English at all. (I noticed 50 years later that my immigrant relatives spoke English with a Yiddish accent. Their kids apparently spoke Yiddish with an English accent. The same must have been true for Dekoven St. families speaking German, Italian, etc.)

Hull House and other institutions, including religious and government agencies, provided self-help services like English as a Second Language, discussion groups, entertainment events and inadequate but useful medical services. Native language newspapers were widely circulated, and there were plenty of poster announcements. Churches and synagogues abounded. (The picture above is an alley near where Mary lived. Picture below shows dead horse in street near children playing.)

Not far away were the humongous, odious Chicago Stock Yards and meat packers. Biggest in the world. Wastes (from those animals, some still alive and what was left of them after they were butchered) flowed into the ever more sickly, sticky, stinky Chicago River, which, in turn, flowed into Lake Michigan, which as mentioned before, was the source for the city's drinking water.

A Hull House essayist wrote that "omnipresent midwife" signs were "announced in polyglot" languages on every hand.

In 1900, the year Mary left Chicago, the river was reversed, helping clean up the lake's water and sending the effluent away from the lake all the way to the Mississippi River and, assumedly, the State of Mississippi.

Autos and trucks were the future. Horses and their manure were never far. Some dead. Looking at photos of long dresses on women crossing the streets and what must have stuck to their bottom hems congers up unpleasant thoughts.

People did not regularly wash. Hull House encouraged neighbors to walk over for weekly baths. There also were bath houses that charged a fee.

As I was growing up in a mid-20th Century Chicago middle-class neighborhood, the air remained polluted, and the streets were not pristine. We said the first sign of Spring was not the first robin-redbreast or dandelion struggling between sidewalk cracks, but when black soot-besotted slush would melt to reveal the remains of a winter's harvest of frozen doggie poop.

The dirty slush captured residue from thousands of coal-fueled railroad engines, plus the burning of coal in the Far South Side steel mills and the millions of coal-fired cooking stoves and furnaces. "The Smart Elek?" essays center on coal.

Even after the 1871 Fire, as building codes were strengthened, many wooden structures remained. Some eventually just collapsed and were replaced by brick. Some were jacked up onto moving platforms "and deposited on property in the outer areas of the city. Chicago had been jacking up and shipping out still-usable buildings to suburbs since 1858. (The drawing from 1865 shows one of the brick structures carried away. Sometimes with the tenants still inside.) http://www.connectingthewindycity.com/2019/06/june-11-1923-masonic-temple-building.html

As mentioned, trash, along with human and other wastes, were all around. Their smells were not erased by stiff breezes from Lake Michigan. The good odors from cooking usually lost out to the bad. Alleys, where they existed, were dangerous places for children or anyone. In the alleys, "refuse and manure are sometimes removed," said a Hull House observer.

"In front of each house stand garbage receivers — wooden boxes repulsive to every sense, even when as clean as their office will permit."

On the brighter side, a Hull House report stated that nearby were "fruit stands to help fill up the sordid streets, and ice-cream carts drive a thriving trade."

As bad as things were around Dekoven, hope was tantalizingly near. State Street, known in song as "That Great Street," was a merchandiser's dream. The lakefront and an extraordinarily large number of well-tended parks were open and free. The parks were good places to sleep during oppressively hot summer nights. Unless you were a person of color, "the sky was the limit," even if it might be darkened by raining coal ash.

Nonetheless, racism and hate for the "others" like Jews, Catholics, Poles, Italians, Irish, Asians, and all people of color was rampant. "No Irish Need Apply" signs in store windows and the inability of Jews to buy houses in some areas, get into certain lines of work, or attend many schools and clubs were the norm. But, Chicago overall had an aura of optimism, an attraction, a feeling that the future could be bright.

And then, with great fanfare, there appeared on the South Side, a gossamer view of the best of the present and the even better future.

The Chicago World's Fair of 1893 drew millions into the city … about a quarter of the population of the US attended, it was claimed. By 1891, over 40,000 skilled laborers and workers had been employed in the construction of the fair. The Fair was so successful that novelist Hamlin Garland wrote to his parents, "Sell the cook stove if necessary and come. You must see the Fair."

The exposition area was called The White City because its massive buildings were painted white and brightly lit.

Once inside the gate, visitors saw the marvels of civilization and the Industrial Age. Outside were the fantasy worlds of the Wild West, foreign lands and just plain fun, like the first Ferris Wheel. When possible, Dekoven St. residents slipped away from their corner of the Near South Side and took affordable public transportation to see the fair. It really was the biggest extravaganza anywhere in the world. My mother said her aunts and uncles had gone to the fair.
https://exhibitcitynews.com/the-fair-that-changed-america/

DEATH, MARRIAGE, URBAN TO RURAL

That year, 1893, Mary was a teenager and must have been thinking of marriage and her future. Whatever she hoped was dramatically affected by her father's death a few years later. She must have dreamed. But, her grandkids, like cousins Hal and George, who hardly knew her, never heard what she wanted or about what she did in Chicago and how she lived. All we know is that about a year before the turn of the century, The Maiden Mary's father, Louis, died. Mary's mother, Sarah, was left with a bunch of kids and a store.

By the end of the century, the 20-something Mary apparently knew no Prince Charming from a land far away to sweep her up in his arms so the two could ride away on a gilded carriage.

Then, POOF arrived in the form of Joseph Kauffman, a young and very successful grocer from Sioux City, Iowa.

According to family legend, Joseph had convinced a friend or friends to take a train to the Big City, have some fun, and seek a bride. He and Mary somehow met and clicked. He left and soon came back. They married. It was 1900, a turn of the Century and a turn of fate.

She followed her new husband, Joseph, to his home in semi-rural Sioux City, where residents still talked of the soldiers garrisoned along the Missouri River during the Indian Wars. Sioux City was a gateway to the West.

As reported in another essay, Joseph Kauffman was a very quiet presence, not surprisingly, since his household included his mother-in-law, sister-in-law, wife, and five daughters.

In 1900, there were about 33,000 residents in the whole city. She left about 1.7 million in Chicago. The Iowa air was much cleaner than Chicago. The neighborhoods were quieter. The corruption was not as obvious, and almost every child went to a reasonably good school. Yet, according to a book published about Jews of Iowa around 1900, the Russian Jews of Sioux City were the poorest in the state. (Family photo of Joseph and his store.)

But not Joseph, who had been born in or near the Russian town of Slutsk in what now is Belarus. For their first 20 years of marriage or more, the Kauffman's income was pretty good. His daughters claimed that Joseph never brought Mary a gift for birthdays, anniversaries, or other occasions. He told his wife to get whatever she wanted because they had accounts at all the stores at which she would shop.

One thing not strange to Mary, what with the nearby constantly expanding Sioux City Stock Yards and packing houses, and horses everywhere, was the occasional familiar scent in the air. My mom's sister Leah remembered cattle being driven up their street as a braying herd headed toward the nearby stockyards. That might have been around 1910.

According to first cousin Gloria Ginsberg Marks, "Grandpa bought the house on Virginia Street, and eventually he bought the whole quarter block to house relatives who moved to Sioux City. ... His was the first house to have an indoor toilet and bathtub on the block. Grandma used to make root beer in the basement," she said.

About 50 years later, a few of the Levy family gathered in Sioux City for an event. Back left is Ben Behr. He was the neighborhood kid who once bragged to me about outwitting the ethnic gangs of boys around Dekoven St. They constantly harassed youngsters of other religions or homelands. I thought Ben must have been quite a badass as a kid. He married Annie Levy (seated far left next to Mary). Is there a Levy nose and chin?

Ben and Annie stayed in Chicago, had a family, and owned a couple of picture-framing stores. On the right is Eva, Mary's youngest sister, who followed her to Sioux City along with their widowed mother, Sarah. Eva married and had a family in Sioux City. Who knows what happened to Mary's other siblings, and so far, Who is not telling? Just like there probably is a Who (as in Louis and Costello) in your family, not repeating the good stuff.

Mary must have been quite a dynamo. I knew her in her dotage, and I was a kid. But, big city girl Mary moved to Sioux City after marrying Joseph. Allegedly she was pissed that the Orthodox Jewish synagogue they joined wouldn't let men and women sit together, and she wanted to be next to her husband. So she set in motion the fundraising for the first Conservative synagogue west of the Mississippi River. As luck would have it, her cohort in this caper was Dr. Max Helfgott, a close cousin of my other grandmother, Sarah Helfet Kroloff.

When I was about ten, my cousin Chuck and I spent a few days in Sioux City. We went to something billed as a family picnic in a big park. In my eyes, it seemed we were related to the entire community.

BOSTON AND CHICAGO NOTES

A slew of our relatives have Boston roots. Just a year after the Great Chicago Fire, a massive blaze burned much of Boston's center city. Many fewer lives were lost than in Chicago, and it destroyed a smaller area. According to Wikipedia, "Because over-insurance of buildings was common, many businesses had enough insurance money to begin rebuilding soon after the fire. In less than two years, Boston's financial district was rebuilt." Thus, the reconstruction of the city did not suck up as much investment money as did The Windy City.

In 1870, when the first Levinsky group probably arrived, Boston, Chicago, and Warsaw had populations hovering around 300,000.

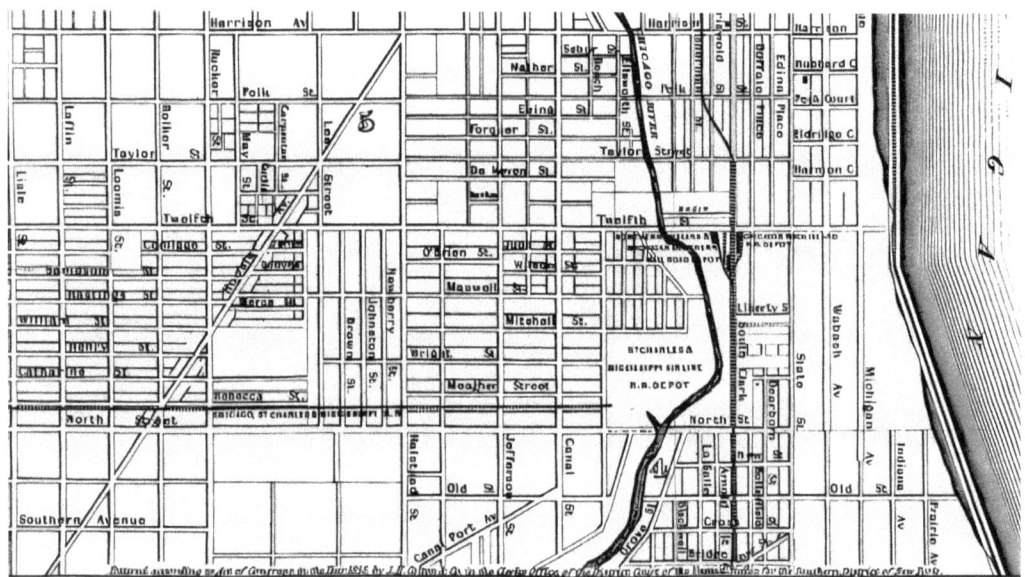

Tracing a family's roots can be way too complicated. For example, in 1909, Chicago renumbered streets outside The Loop, the city's commercial center. So, 473 S. Canal Street, where the Levys lived in 1880, became 1114 S. Canal. The Levys 113 Dekoven residence became 524 Dekoven. The O'Learys lived at 137 Dekoven. That lot became 558 W. Dekoven. It was a few doors away from Canal Street. And, just for the record, Louis Levy's father, Reuben Levinsky, was listed in the 1885 Chicago Directory as a grocer at 151 W. 12th St., which today is known as Roosevelt Road. This was their neighborhood map.

The arrival of the first railroad into Chicago (1855) brought a large influx of Irish, German, and Bohemian immigrants. Many were housed in quickly built wooden structures on Maxwell

Street (see the middle of the map, an east-west avenue) and the surrounding neighborhood, which was just west of a RR station. That was before it became known as "Jew Town."

Hull house maps showing wages, nationalities, etc., in every area building around 1895. You will need a magnifying glass to learn more info than you expect.

When Mary Levy was a teenager, about a 20-minute walk east of the Levy's residence to Clark St. were 50 brothels in 1895.

This 1921 map is an exclamation point on Chicago's importance as a railroad center. The map is from Chicago The Greatest Railway Center in the World By Robert J. McKay, Vice-President for Fort Dearborn National Bank, From Fort Dearborn Magazine, December 1921.

WHY THEY CAME TO AMERICA AND CHICAGO

The good, The bad, The ugly are summarized in two great poems.

The New Colossus (A poem mounted on The Statue of Liberty)

By Emma Lazarus, 1883

Not like the brazen giant of Greek fame,
With conquering limbs astride from land to land;
Here at our sea-washed, sunset gates shall stand
A mighty woman with a torch, whose flame
Is the imprisoned lightning, and her name
Glows world-wide welcome; her mild eyes command
The air-bridged harbor that twin cities frame.
"Keep, ancient lands, your storied pomp!" cries she
With silent lips. "Give me your tired, your poor,
Your huddled masses yearning to breathe free,
The wretched refuse of your teeming shore.
Send these, the homeless, tempest-tost to me,
I lift my lamp beside the golden door!"

The Colossus referred to Castle Garden the entry point at the foot of Manhattan Island. It closed when Ellis Island opened in 1892.

The picture and one girl's story at https://thechroniclesofhistory.com/2021/03/08/u-s-history%E2%95%BDarriving-at-ellis-island-the-diary-of-sadie-frowne-her-experiences-in-the-promise-land/

CHICAGO

By Carl Sandburg

Hog Butcher for the World,
Tool Maker,
Stacker of Wheat,
Player with Railroads and the Nation's Freight Handler;
Stormy, husky, brawling,
City of the Big Shoulders:

They tell me you are wicked and I believe them, for I have seen your painted women under the gas lamps luring the farm boys.

And they tell me you are crooked and I answer: Yes, it is true I have seen the gunman kill and go free to kill again.

And they tell me you are brutal and my reply is: On the faces of women and children I have seen the marks of wanton hunger.

And having answered so I turn once more to those who sneer at this my city, and I give them back the sneer and say to them:

Come and show me another city with lifted head singing so proud to be alive and coarse and strong and cunning. Flinging magnetic curses amid the toil of piling job on job, here is a tall bold slugger set vivid against the little soft cities;

Fierce as a dog with tongue lapping for action, cunning as a savage pitted against the wilderness,

Bareheaded, Shoveling, Wrecking, Planning, Building, breaking, rebuilding, Under the smoke, dust all over his mouth, laughing with white teeth, Under the terrible burden of destiny laughing as a young man laughs,

Laughing even as an ignorant fighter laughs who has never lost a battle,

Bragging and laughing that under his wrist is the pulse, and under his ribs the heart of the people, Laughing!

Laughing the stormy, husky, brawling laughter of Youth, half-naked, sweating, proud to be Hog Butcher, Tool Maker, Stacker of Wheat, Player with Railroads and Freight Handler to the Nation.

Remember, it was named "Windy City" by New Yorkers sick of Chicago boosters who wouldn't shut up.

Carl Sandberg wasn't kidding about those big shoulders. The Levy-Levi-Levinsky family moved to Chicago just as one of the most outlandish projects in America was coming to a close.

The center of the city with offices, stores, and hotels was built on land near the River and Lake at water level. Thus, rains and sewage could not always drain into Lake Michigan or the Chicago River, they just sat in the streets like big, long, muddy, smelly bathtubs. Among the many reasons Chicago was the city of "Big Shoulders" was that the city fathers had the business district buildings lifted up and set on new foundations above water level. A few were put on huge skids and moved to the suburbs. See more about this incredible activity at https://en.wikipedia.org/wiki/Raising_of_Chicago

One amazed British traveler wrote home in 1867 after watching workmen raise a hotel 4½ feet: "The people were in it all the time, coming and going, eating and sleeping — the whole business of the hotel proceeding without interruption!" http://interactive.wttw.com/loop/loop-then-now/lake-street-between-clark-street-and-lasalle-street also see wiki commons.

THE SEMINAL EVENT OCCURRED OCTOBER 8, 1871

A long drought. A city of wooden homes and stores. Miles of raised wooden sidewalks with millions of dried leaves accumulated beneath. The fire men, already exhausted from small blazes around the city, were too tired to service their equipment. There was the very bad luck in the barn of Mrs. O'Leary near the corner of Dekoven and Jefferson Streets. Here is the backstory for The Great Chicago Fire. Pictures from Wikipedia and museum exhibits. Fuller story Wikipedia.

The Fire burned from Sunday, October 8, into early Tuesday, October 10. Possibly 300 humans were killed, some vaporized in the inferno. The polluted Chicago River burst into flames. The few bridges heading east toward Lake Michigan were blocked as panicked citizens on foot and in horse-drawn vehicles jammed them.

The red skies rained superheated, burning bits of wood that once were furniture and lifelong treasures. They were carried aloft by "heat winds" called "Fire Devils" that reached near tornado speeds. The temperature was so intense that supposedly fireproof stone structures burned from the inside out.

Thousands eventually found safety along and in the waters of Lake Michigan, where individuals and horses had fled.

Later tragedies in Chicago claimed more lives, but none of them brought such devastation. By the time a drizzle and calm winds arrived, the equivalent of four square miles in the city's heart lay under damp ash and still-glowing remains of homes, apartments, offices, stores, and other businesses. Picture: after the fire. Rebuilding Chicago, Oct. 1871; Rufus Blanchard and Bulkeley & Kellogg, Lithograph.

Counter-intuitively, the tragic Chicago fire turned out to be the most positive event in the city's history ... and for the family headed by Louis and Sarah Levy, my mother's grandparents.

The two Levys arrived about 1875, following the earlier footsteps of other family members. Chicago already was on its way to becoming America's most important city after New York ... The Second City.

Outside of the devastated area, Chicago remained in good shape. It still was America's most important railroad hub. It still was an important inland port, although parts of the docks along the Chicago River were burnt to a crisp. The black and white picture shows river activity before the fire. From WTTG documentary on Chicago River. View is east of Rush Street Bridge, toward the mouth of the Chicago River, heavily congested with ship traffic. The footing of the Rush Street Bridge is visible in the foreground. At left, the McCormick Reaper Works can be seen, and on the left, one of the Sturges and Buckingham elevators is visible. Note on back reads: "A reproduction of a photograph taken before fire of 1871. Photo courtesy Chicago History Museum

Chicago had huge stores of lumber shipped down Lake Michigan from the north that were untouched by the flames, and it had a population ready to roll up its sleeves and work hard (for money).

Only two weeks after the fire, an eyewitness wrote ... "Suddenly (we) find ourselves in the midst of a hurrying throng of people and vehicles on Canal Street, which, so lately a street of lumber yards, factories, and freight transportation for river and railways, is now one of the chief mercantile thoroughfares, and the adjacent streets are full of people and noisy with the hum of activity."

By 1880, about five years after emigrating from or near Warsaw, Louis and Sarah Levy had four children. Coincidentally, they lived in a building at 473 S. Canal Street, housing three larger Polish immigrant families and a large Bohemian family. The structure may have been just at the edge of the fire zone, so unburned, or was built over the ruins. The census of that year listed Louis as a huckster. Hucksters were people who sold goods door-to-door or had a cart of merchandise on a street or sidewalk. The picture shows State Street, probably in the 1890s. Notice electric street cars well before automobiles arrived on the scene.

In 1900, Chicago already had the second-largest cable car network in the country. There were street cars, commuter railroads, and the fabled "L." The elevated railway circled the city business center, called The Loop, it sat about three stories above the street and extended across the city. No matter how crooked the city management was, it was a pretty easy, straightforward, and cheap town to get around.

Sioux City had its own short-lived elevated railroad. Liverpool's was famous. New York, London, and several other big cities had subways as well. Urban transportation may have had as much influence in creating the urban and industrial transformations of the Northern Hemisphere as did the speedy steamships and choo-choo trains.

Chicago was feisty and wanted to be ahead of New York in every way … even the bad ways. The city and its residents had "an attitude," an abundance of optimism. They spoke loudly and carried a big stick (shtick?) even before Teddy Roosevelt suggested the idea. The Levys' Chicago suffered and lavished in its outlandish crime and sprawling stockyards that smelled to high heavens. According to my Aunt Leah, Harris Levinsky must have been very rich

(maids, chauffeur, etc.). He was in the liquor business. A branch of the Levy/Levinsky family was named Bobinsky. By the end of the 1800s, the Bobinskys, if I read the records correctly, owned at least three saloons near what now is Chicago's Loop, the heart of the city. I assume they were in "the trade" in the old country and wonder what they did during Prohibition. 1900 Loop picture and background opinions about construction   https://chicagology.com/transportation/unionloop/

Earlier, amid America's Civil War, Chicago overtook Cincinnati as America's hog slaughtering capital. By 1870, when the first of the Levy-Lewinsky-Bobinski family was getting settled, the South Side's meat processing center was handling 2 million animals a year. By 1890, it was 9 million. Fortunes were made, and tens of thousands of workers were employed, though not without plenty of rich-vs-poor tensions. Picture is the "L" downtown, before the appearance of autos.

So, in Chicago, there were jobs, lots of them, even when economies elsewhere were sour. For most of white America, there was a sense of optimism about the future (as in Sioux City at that time) and relief that Europe was so far away.

Chicago was a renowned center of architectural innovation. Mary Levy was in Chicago when the first real skyscraper reached toward the high heavens, The Home Insurance Building, built 1885. Picture from old post card.

She saw electricity and phones spread. And watched as the first few autos were scaring the daylights and the not quite fully digested meals out of horses on the streets.

The Levys were there when the gritty steel mills employed thousands to produce the railroad tracks that carried people and raw materials into the city and manufactured goods out. They were there when the Pullman Works built the glossy sleeper and dining cars to move to and fro across America over those same railroad tracks.

The Levys were there when public transportation made getting around relatively easy, starting in the 1880s. Streetcars, horse-pulled vehicles that looked like railroad cars, the horse pulled cabs, the "L" and the commuter trains pulled by smallish steam engines chugging above ground and in tunnels and below bridges carrying the bums, bailiffs, businessmen, and barristers to their daily jobs of gulling or gilding customers. Pictured are early cable cars.

Mary was there when the Chicago mail-order business blossomed with Sears and Montgomery Ward. They, in turn, helped finance Rural Free Delivery and Railway Express, important predecessors of the modern Postal Service, UPS and FedEx. The mail order giants were an early Amazon, bringing by mail anything an aspiring debutante in Dubuque, Iowa, might want, or a ready-to-build kit for a suburban family-sized house delivered to the address where it would be built by a family in Decatur, Georgia… or any of the 15 other places in the USA named Decatur. Picture of inside/outside Montgomery Ward downtown building https://chicagology.com/goldenage/goldenage015/

Mary was there during some of the biggest and most bloody labor strikes and when the major crime syndicates of the Prohibition Era were beginning to mature. The Mob, in one form or another, had long controlled the local government as well as businesses far beyond what the law allowed. As noted elsewhere, one of the Capone Mob's chauffeurs, the young son of Italian immigrants with whom I worked, allegedly was the Shobbos Goy in the Levy's household. (Later, I had clients who turned out to be part of the "Syndicate.")

The Levys were there in 1893 when the great Chicago World's Fair, with its 200 specially-built buildings, arose on the South Side. Some were huge, displaying advances in science, sanitation, arts, and household articles, and provided prestige for the city as well as a spectacular show of America's industrial optimism.

One fine fair feature was the first Ferris Wheel, It was 25 stories high and could hold 2,160 people at a time.

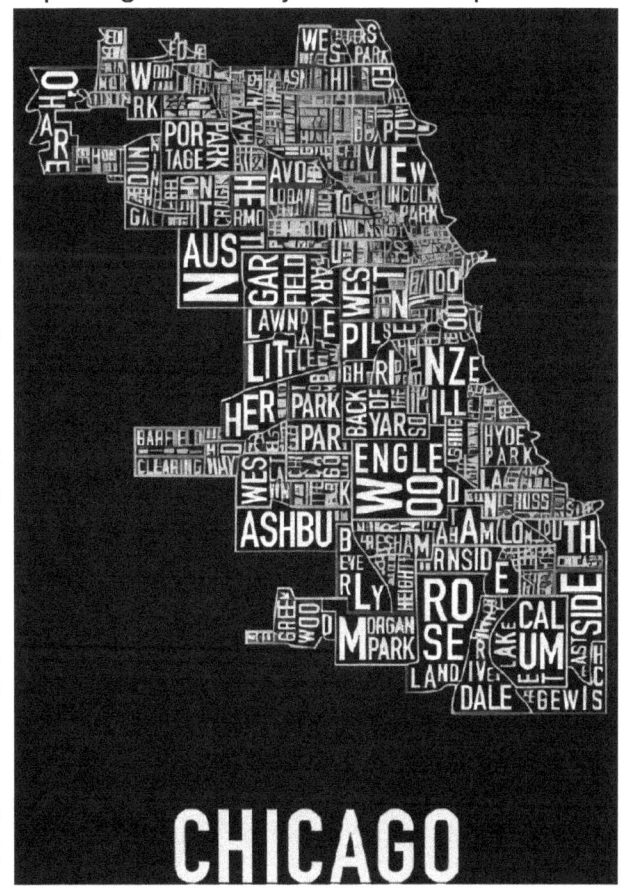

The wildly successful Fair, The "White City," was a mile-long exposition. Its "firsts" included Aunt Jemima Syrup, Cracker Jacks, Cream of Wheat, Diet carbonated soda, Juicy Fruit gum, Pabst Beer, Shredded Wheat, Hamburgers, electric innovations, and so much more that long books have documented its awe-inspiring vastness, creativity and world cultures.

The Fair was easy to reach by land and boat. Today's University of Chicago sits on the area that was the fair's "Midway." See more about the fair in the following essays.

Just for the record, Chicagoans live on the North, South, or West sides. Not in them. But

Chicagoans do live in one of the city's 77 neighborhoods, like Rogers Park or Hyde Park. There is no East Side because that is Lake Michigan. But the lakefront does curve to the east, so there is a Southeast side. The map shows neighborhoods. Levys lived in what today is called the South Loop, near the Lake in the middle above the large NZ (Bronzeville). Get your magnifier glass.

In the Levy neighborhood, there were public schools, access to a few hospitals, and a growing number of community services unknown in the Old Country. It appears to me that there also were family support systems that reminded them of Poland.

Pictured below are homes built around 1880 several doors west on Dekoven Street from the Levys. The white building is where the O'Leary house and barn stood. The pink building on the right has a street level store, probably like the Levy's. http://forgottenchicago.com/articles/the-little-house-on-polk-street/

There must have been tension within the family as women were wage earners and much more independent than in the Europe they had left behind. Picture: Men and women in a garment sweatshop around 1900, a couple of blocks from the Levy store.

Chicago dominated commercial life in most of the country, from the Appalachian mountains to the Rockies.

It was an irrepressible magnet for people and investment. The resources that poured into the city sucked the life out of other infrastructure projects around the U.S. (As people in Sioux City would lament.)

A cynical view of the city around the time Mary left for Sioux City comes from the book, "CLARENCE DARROW, Attorney for THE DAMNED," by John A. Farrell. Page 137. "The anything-goes attitude reached beyond the streets of the Levee" (The Levee District was home to many brothels, saloons, dance halls, and similar places, says Wikipedia.) "Factories were dangerous. The air was thick and black, and the waters were polluted. The alleys were strewn with garbage, and the street cars were crowded, filthy, and freezing in winter ... the Municipal Voters League announced that 'Of sixty-eight aldermen ... fifty-seven were thieves.' "

To summarize: In The Second City, there were opportunities (some foul, some fair) on nearly every corner.

Mary's move to relatively bucolic Sioux City was a very large lifestyle change.

A confession. I was a very biased Chicago booster even before I became the manager of press relations for the Metropolitan Area Chamber of Commerce. That was my last Chicago job before moving to Washington, DC, in the early 1960s. There was another serious fire south of Chicago's Loop in 1874 that displaced hundreds of prostitutes, East Europeans and African Americans. It burned over 40 acres.

THE LEVYS' CHICAGO WAS THE SAME THING AS THE LEVY'S WARSAW, POLAND ... BUT TOTALLY DIFFERENT

The Levys lived near Maxwell Street, which eventually morphed into a thriving bazaar that replicated a shtetl or small town European market. The market first appeared after the Great Chicago Fire of 1871 with few Jews. Several years later, Yiddish became Maxwell Street's Lingua Franca. The Levy kids, like most immigrant children, also spoke English. Maxwell Street, in what sometimes was referred to as "Jew Town," was like the Lower East Side markets in New York, which, in turn, were like the weekly or monthly shtetl markets. (Maxwell Street, right, shtetl market, left.)

In 1880, my great grandparents' oldest child, Moses, was five years of age. The Census Taker was told he had been born in Illinois. Was Sarah pregnant on the trip across the Atlantic? Was he born in Poland and she told the Census Taker he was born in Chicago to make him a citizen?

That year, Louis was 30, and Sarah claimed to be 24. Neighbors were from Hungary, Prussia, Bohemia and Poland. Nearby were Germans, Swiss, Scandinavians, Irish, Italians, French, French Canadians and a few Chinese.

In 1900, nearly 80% of Chicago's population was either foreign-born or the children of foreign-born immigrants. As this is being drafted in 2019/2024, the same arguments by white Protestant European immigrants against people of other religions and colors were being shouted again in the USA.

The city's German Jews looked down upon the Russian Jews. Like they did in Sioux City and New York City. Chicago's wealthy Reformed German Jews tended to live near Lake Michigan in Victorian style homes with many amenities. The European Orthodox greenhorns were shoehorned into squalid tenements. The Conservative movement in Judaism had yet to gain a toehold.

Orthodox Christians, plus Polish and Irish Catholic churches, like new dogs in the neighborhoods, soon marked their own territories. Gangs often were kids from the same religion. There were numerous small synagogues in the heavily Jewish areas, close enough that the Jewish Orthodox could walk to services. Unlike in Europe, there was no government-organized warfare between the religious fiefdoms. No progroms.

At least among adults.

According to Uncle Ben Behr, who lived in the Levys neighborhood, teenage gangs sometimes made it difficult for other teens to wander across streets because gangs would be protecting their territory for their own kind, just as in the movie and the play "West Side Story."

One block might be controlled by Italian kids, another by Irish. Since the Irish, Italian and Polish Catholic parishes had little to do with each other, it wasn't unusual for gangs associated with one parish to harm or rob people from another Catholic parish. Or any other intruder. (Photo by Jacob Riss is from NYC. Just like Chicago … don't mess with a tough guy holding a stick!)

Chicago sizzled, steamed and sweated in the summer and offered frozen-solid eyelashes in the winter. Yet the city's melting pot simmered with a cultural and ethnic stew that outsiders found particularly scrumptious.

The stew in Mary's neighborhood was centered on Maxwell Street. In a controversial move, it was eaten up by a combination of developers of the University of Illinois campus in Chicago and developers of high-end apartments and stores. In the mid-1900s, gentrification paved it over. I remember the crowds, smells, and raucous salesmen grabbing my dad or me. They tried to force us into their clothing store or look at the goods displayed in their push-carts. That's where my parents took me to get a bar mitzvah suit in 1948.

Returning to a previous theme, the Levys were early adapters but not pioneers. Chicago was incorporated as a town of 350 people in 1833. In 1847, German Jews, mostly from Bavaria, formed a synagogue. Over the ensuing years, many were merchants, craftsmen and members of the Reform movement. They thought of themselves to be of higher "status" than the hordes of poor Eastern European Jews in the second wave who came from the East of what now is Germany.

The many synagogues within walking distance of Mary Levy were much smaller and not as elaborate as the more affluent Reform temples. The Los Angeles Breed Street Shul pictured on the previous page was modeled on Chicago houses of worship near Mary. (I'm not sure where the women sat. I think the pews shown were for men only.)

Even though the support systems for greenhorns were in their formative stage, the Levys probably were OK with their surroundings. Almost every adult in the neighborhood was an immigrant who did not speak The Queen's English. They were not in a ghetto, in the European sense, but Yiddish, their language, would often have been heard on the streets around them, as would Polish, Italian, Swedish, etc.

Some of the social "help" groups were religion-based, some run by the city or a local alderman, and others like Chicago's pioneering and non-sectarian Hull House were supporting a wide spectrum of the residents around the Levys. Hull House, a short walk away from Mary, was the nation's most influential "settlement" house, offering just about everything an immigrant needed to be an American. But that was not until about 20 years after the Levy family had arrived in the U.S. from Poland.

Another aside: Chicago's education, police, health, garbage collection, and other struggling support systems for greenhorns that evolved around the Levys during the last quarter of the 1800s were mirrored across the globe. It wasn't just a Chicago phenomenon.

Remember Leon Helfet, my great uncle in South Africa? He was born in the part of Russia, now the independent country of Ukraine. After a few years in Liverpool, he morphed into a British-raised greenhorn and benefitted from Jews who arrived before him in Cape Town.

In the early 1900s, when Mary Levy had moved to Sioux City, she helped welcome greenhorns into their new world. It is not recorded that Mary helped Sarah Helfet when she first came to Sioux City. But Mary and husband Joseph Kauffman, would have known Sam Kroloff, a rival grocer. The Kauffmans were good friends of Dr. Max Helfgott (a Helfet cousin). Mary and Max were leaders in conceiving and building the first Conservative synagogue in Sioux City. I was told it was the first one west of the Mississippi.

The picture shows Chicago's downtown around 1900, the time Mary Levy left for Sioux City. Still no automobiles. Picture from Newberry Library collection.

THEY CAME FROM A LAND THAT CONSIDERED ITSELF POLISH, BUT ...

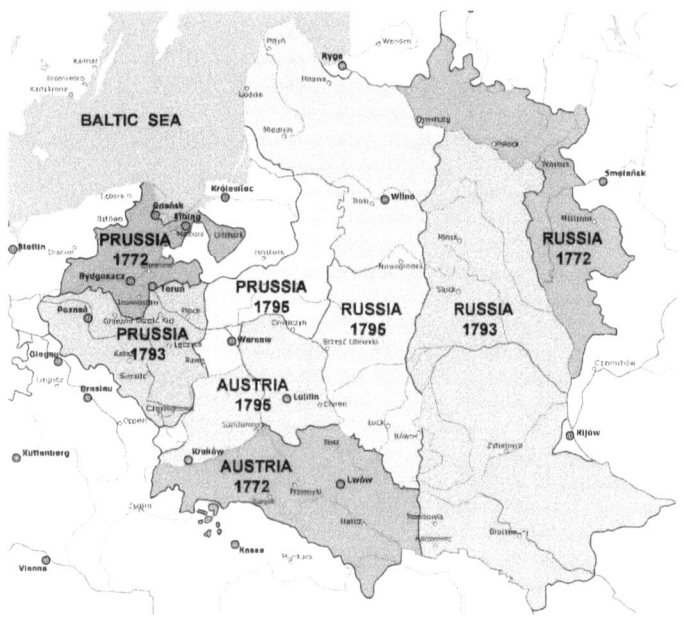

Actually, there wasn't a Poland in the 1800s. While most residents may have considered themselves to be Polish, they were ruled from afar. From the late 1700s until after the First World War, what we now think of as Poland had been conquered, lost, reconquered, and finally sliced and diced into three areas or zones of influence, controlled by the Austrians, the Prussians, and the Russians.

Poland was a coveted territory after the vast and powerful Polish–Lithuanian Commonwealth died. Russia was gaining strength. Prussia and Austria wanted Poland as a buffer. As with other items lightly brushed upon in these essays, it really is way, way more complicated.

Needless to say, Poland was a land to die for, and Napoleon, Tsars, Kings and Queens were willing to force tens of thousands to do just that.

The idea of Manifest Destiny in America is discussed in other essays. But, a Russian version of the "deity-driven" need to expand was similar. The Tsars wanted to control more land and people, expand and protect their borders, and not necessarily make nicey-nicey on the rulers of other European countries... even though some rulers were the Tsars' cousins.

The Tsars were more successful in Europe than in Asia. In 1924, Joseph Stalin became the modern and even more brutal Tsar. By the end of World War II and deep into the Cold War, he had control, or primary influence, over more land than the Tsars could have imagined in their longest drug-induced dreams. That influence included Maoist China and the "Stans"... like Pakistan, Afghanistan, Kazakstan and the others. Historical pendulums swing, and some of that influence has waned.

Nonetheless, as this is written in 2019-2024, the Russian leader Vladimir Putin is doing what Stalin and the Tsars did … extending Russia's borders as far as possible. For instance, Crimea, which once again is Russian, has historical and religious significance to Russia.

It was because the Polish borders changed every few years that the Levy-Levinskys sometimes identified themselves as being born in Russia, sometimes Poland, and in at least one document, they were listed as "Polish/German." Obviously, they lived in an area where borders moved over the years. Or maybe family members moved on their own or were forced by a decree from a government to move.

In the Russian zone of influence, there were serious uprisings in which Jews played a part. Two major ones were the Polish-Russian War of 1830–31 and the unsuccessful 1863–64 rebellion against Russian rule. That one resulted in the imposition of tighter Russian control over the region. The rebellion began in Warsaw, and its results likely were major considerations as the Levys began to plan their emigration or escape nearly ten years later. The picture above is of a Polish insurrectionist coming home in 1831. https://polishcitizenship.blog/?p=35

Polish Jews and Catholics saw increased pressure from their Russian overlords to convert to the Russian Orthodox religion. By the mid-1840s, some Catholic and Jewish youth were being conscripted into the Russian army for 25 or more years.

And pogroms began springing up again in The Pale of Russia. Word spread. Fanaticism festered on all sides. It is alive today.

The 1899 painting, left, by Mykola Pymonenko, illustrates a victim of fanaticism.

The picture documents an event in Ukraine that the artist read about. A Jewish woman was attacked by members of her community for falling in love with a Christian convert. The townspeople are raising sticks and fists. Her parents are shown to the right, denouncing her. From the Wikipedia article "History of the Jews in Russia."

BACKTRACKING ON THE LEVY EXODUS

Harris Levinsky was my great-great uncle. He's the one who told the 1900 Chicago census taker that his birthplace was "Poland/Germany." His version of the family heritage appears to be different than my grandmother Mary's version. Over the years, Mary told Census Takers that her family was from Poland, except for when she said Russia.

Anyway, Mary's parents and grandparents crossed the Atlantic for a complex set of reasons.

Overpopulation tends to be a very important motivator that is masked in most family histories. Although they were rudimentary, new medical treatments and ideas on sanitation were spreading into rural areas and city slums. More babies were surviving. Fewer mothers were dying during childbirth. "Bubbehs" and "Zaydehs" (grandmas and grandpas) were living longer. The high number of births per family didn't fall until well into the 20th Century. In the late 1800s, it was not unusual for a man to sire ten or more children. Often, wives died young, the men remarried, and more kids popped out. https://www.ebay.co.uk/itm/IMPERIAL-RUSSIA-VILLAGE-SCENE-PEASANTS-ORIGINAL-KEYSTONE-STEREOVIEW-PHOTO-/291807974176?hash=item43f11c5320:g:AZYAAOSwbYZXdlKi

In a place like America, unlike much of Europe, more people usually meant more business opportunities. In that new optimistic world, there was a need for more farmers and factories, more clothes, cookies, crockpots, and the occasional crackpot to fulfill the needs, including entertainment, of the expanding population.

Context: I found this throughout the history of my wife Susan's birth family, the Simmons' of Blue Mountain, Mississippi. The essays that begin on P261 trace her birth father, Bob Simmons' ancestors, settling in eastern Virginia 12 years before the Puritans and Pilgrims landed at Plymouth Rock. Bob died when Susan was seven years old.

For about 400 years, the Simmons tribe slowly spread West, through the Cumberland Gap of the Appalachian Mountains into Kentucky and Tennessee, and later South into the newly formed state of Mississippi. There, they would be caught between waves of the North and South armies flowing back and forth during the early Civil War.

After their men went to war, the women and children were at the mercy not only of pillaging soldiers but also of ravaging gangs picking over what the military hadn't already taken. In one reported case, it was just a string of popcorn off a Xmas tree.

TRAINS, TAVERNS, TENEMENTS, AND TIDBITS ABOUT EVEN MORE STUFF

Like in Chicago, by the 1850s, a web of iron railroad tracks was spreading outward from Warsaw. Some headed toward seaports where metal bottom steamships were replacing wooden vessels. Cross-Atlantic trips went from taking a couple of months to a couple of weeks and then half that time. The first oceanic steamships combined sails with paddle wheels on their sides. https://www.norwayheritage.com/gallery/gallery.asp?action=viewimage&categoryid=4&text=&imageid=1411&box=&shownew=

The ships of choice eventually became lighter, stronger steel-hulled, without sails and propelled by screw propellers. Ships, like trains, were becoming bigger, faster and safer.

There were thousands of seats, beds, and spaces for cargo to be sold.

I could not find records of the Levys' trip to the USA, so it is unclear how much European rail travel was used by the family in the 1870s. Even if they made their way from the middle of Poland to an Atlantic Ocean port by horse-pulled cart they would have taken a train to Chicago from wherever they landed in the USA or Canada. Trains from New York, for example, were already heading out of New York for Chicago by 1852.

An aside about those railroads: In the 1880s, it was claimed that a Roosevelt Road (12th Street) bridge in Chicago was the greatest railroad-watching site in the world. It was within walking distance of the Levys. Just imagine a youngster like young Mary Levy or her brother coming home after an hour or two of standing above the smoke belching choo-choo trains covered head-to-toe with soot from dozens of coal and wood burning engines passing underneath them. That bridge is in the background of a picture.

Trains were more efficient movers of families, businessmen, merchandise, food and drink. Investors funded large distilleries and breweries in cities from which high volumes of spirits flowed at low costs. The one-two punches, trains, and technology had killed a lot of Jewish and other small businesses in the Pale of Settlements and throughout central Europe. Emigrants, of course, tried to find American jobs using their European skills.

Even though there were all kinds of official and on-the-ground practical restrictions regarding travel in The Pale, the stirrings of the Industrial Revolution, along with some government decrees and changes in the economy, were pushing families from rural areas all around Poland, the Austro-Hungarian Empire and elsewhere into large towns. Wars, weather, epidemics, and decrees from on high were forcing populations back and forth. Jews were among the most unsettled because, unlike most other European "tribes," they were expelled from cities and sent to the rural areas, and sometimes vice-versa. The artwork left shows a rural roadside inn, probably similar to the Krulevitsky inn in Kapulia. https://gatchina.bezformata.com/listnews/hudozhnik-gatchinskoy-ohoti/111329120/

The explanation of the Chaos Theory, also known as the Butterfly Effect, mentioned in the introduction of these essays is relevant. The wings of a butterfly in the Tsar's garden were flapping as his regents walked the palace's well trimmed pathways, talking about drafting more young men to fight in ever expanding border wars. Their talk helped set off chaotic actions in The Pale and Poland, which caused sometimes small and sometimes mass emigrations.

The Chaos Theory provides three important scientific and historic truths. 1. Small actions can cause large calamities. 2. Everything that looks and feels chaotic is part of a larger pattern. 3. Everything in the world, the solar system, the galaxy and our universe is interconnected. That is why real science is much more interesting to me than science fiction or even politics. There are other real-life examples in other essays in this series.

The Levys of Poland must have been adventurous, very scared, or both. They were able to gather enough money to get whatever documents they needed (maybe with bribes), obtain ship passage to North America, and rail tickets to Chicago. Who met them and who, if anyone, helped is a mystery. The family of Reuben and Ida Levinsky (Mary Levy Kauffman's grandparents) planted roots in Chicago on or before 1870. They apparently made some money and sent for their sons Harris and Louis and maybe more relatives.

For the most part, the Polish Jews and Polish Roman Catholics did not have much to do with each other in their homeland, except if business relationships evolved. At home and usually in public, they spoke different languages, Yiddish and Polish. They tended to live in different parts of their neighborhoods. When they came to Chicago, not only were there separations between the Polish Catholics and Jews, but the Polish Catholics generally belonged to their own parishes, and they had little, if anything, to do with the Roman Catholic Italians or Irish. They all used oils for various parts of their worship ceremonies, but the oils didn't mix, just as oil and water don't mix. Picture, Warsaw, 1867, around the time first Levys left for Chicago, USA.

Nonetheless, the city's magnets were powerful. Chicago became the second largest Polish city after Warsaw as millions of poor Polish Roman Catholics and Polish Jews emigrated to the US. For a while, it was the third largest German city. By some estimates, as late as 2019, Chicago also was the third largest Greek city.

Like large American cities in the 1800s, Warsaw had four-to-six-story tenement houses that lacked elevators, running water and privacy. They consisted of small, crowded rooms, smelly garbage, and horse dumping outside. Ventilation inside was non-existent. The noise of neighbors and outside events was constant. Warsaw, like Chicago, had trams and trains by the 1860s. Pictures, Warszawa - Marszałkowska-1867 from wikimedia, and Warsaw peddler carts at a market.

By 1870, each city had a population of about 300,000. There were other similarities because the spread of education, technology, information and hate was moving at a pretty constant rate through Europe, Canada and the US. They both had busy railroad stations.

Unlike Europe, in North America, after the Civil War, there were fewer worries of being caught between opposing armies.

In the early 1800s, life in Warsaw's "Jewish Quarter" was restricted, but it improved somewhat in the 1860s. Jews participated in Polish uprisings against the Russians. The Russians won. Not great for Jews.

For a while, Warsaw's Jews, according to a few reports, made up more than half the workers in commerce and were involved in the crafts. Some lived in dumps, others lived very, very well.

Also, during this period, Jews reportedly had monopolies in the sale of salt and, as mentioned before, alcoholic beverages. That would change.

Russia took unforgiving control of Warsaw after Napoleon was defeated in 1814. Russia's nationally-sponsored antisemitism rose much higher than simply being tolerable. During the first half of the 1800s, when Louis and Sara Levy's parents were born, it appears that Polish Jews who emigrated tended to go to nearby countries, relatively few to the US. That also changed.

Like Chicago, Warsaw was a city on the make in the 1870s. Both municipalities had freshwater pipelines, for instance. Both cities were manufacturing centers. Both were filled with immigrants who tended to smell and talk differently than other residents. The cities teemed with people and vermin, arts, crafts and ideas.

These two pictures might be the same place in Warsaw, over 150 years apart.

Both pictures from Wikimedia Commons.

The personality of a city actually will affect the personality of the citizenry. Warsaw's might have seemed to be pretty much downbeat, and, if you were a Jew, for many, it was beat-up. Yet, it was a manufacturing, banking, business and intellectual center.

Whether they liked it or not, Judaism set them apart. It shaped who and what they were. It gave them a framework to follow for what to wear, when, what and how to eat, and a feeling that eventually things maybe, possibly, hopefully, with a little luck and with a lot of help, might be better. Of course, that tenuous hope too often referred to what would happen after dying. Like a long list of Western religions, parts of Judaism are fixated on living a regimented life that will make whatever comes after death better.

Thus, the Levy/Levinsky transit to the US in the 1870s and 80s followed many years of severe persecution, interspersed with fewer years of lower, but still oppressive, persecution. Like a yo-yo, the daily limits on the lives of Jews in the former Polish/Lithuanian empire spun up and down. Picture is from wikimedia.org, showing Warsaw Jewish merchants and a kid, maybe examining jewelry.

Warsaw's Jewish population estimates show growth from about 41,000 and 26 percent of the residents in 1856 to about 150,500 or an estimated third of the city population in 1887. That probably wouldn't be natural growth, it must have included quite a bit of immigration, mostly, I guess, into ghettos. In Poland, however, there were Jewish industrialists, bankers and philanthropists, intellectuals, authors, rabbis and entertainers of note.

By the late 1770s, what we now call Poland had approximately 14 million people. It was a multicultural and multiethnic. In total, it was estimated that there were more Lithuanians, Latvians, Germans, Russians, Byelorussians, Ukrainians, Gypsies and Jews than ethnic Polish Catholics. There were Protestants, Eastern Orthodox, and Unitarians in the mix. Of course, there was some grit between each other when they met.

Red shows areas of Russian dominance in the Pale. https://fromshepherdsandshoemakers.com/2017/01/15/those-infamous-border-changes-a-crash-course-in-polish-history/

The transition to Chicago from one urban area to another urban area must have been at least a bit easier than the shocks suffered by poor rural peasants coming to Chicago. Thus, unlike the Jews from small towns like Kapulia in Belarus, Sarah and Louis Levy probably spent at least some of their youth in a crowded, boisterous urban environment or had visited the city ghettos. Chicago had a very different vibe. A very different history.

Another aside regarding booze and trains. In Chicago, Harris Levinsky was a saloon keeper. The Chicago Bobinsky family also had saloons. My mother once told me she thought her grandfather (her dad's father), after he arrived in Sioux City, owned a bar.

For many years, Jews in Poland, Belarus and other Eastern European rural countries brewed beer and distilled booze. They were rural innkeepers and the men who ran urban bars.

The following is from "A Short History of Polish Jewish tavern-keeping" By Glenn Dynner.

"The Jewish-run tavern became the center of local Christians' leisure, hospitality, business, and even religious festivities. Luckily for Jews, the nobles who owned the taverns believed that only Jews were sober enough to run taverns profitably. At the same time, reformers and government officials blamed Jewish tavern keepers for epidemic peasant drunkenness, as the image illustrates, and sought to drive Jews out of the liquor trade." Artwork above: W. Grabowski, After a Quart of Vodka (1883). Courtesy Professor Hillel Levine. Below is from https://commons.wikimedia.org/wiki/File:Gustaw_Pillati,_Fryz_wilanowski.jpg

Booze in Eastern Europe, however, provided a torrent of taxes and evasions. In the USA, too. Before Prohibition banned the legal sale of alcoholic beverages in 1920, some tales of Jewish taverns in the Russian and Polish-ruled lands of the 1700s and 1800s made them look like establishments in America's Wild West … watered down drinks, attempts to steal and bilk the drunks, brothels, other entertainment, food and kowtowing to those in authority. The taverns/roadhouse families often "fronted" for nobles or rich Christians who demanded a portion of all sales.

By the mid-1880s, times were changing. The introduction of railroads led to the demise of thousands of roadside inns with taverns where travelers, teamsters and their horses would recharge at night. As mentioned elsewhere, Aaron Krulevitsky, who rests on top of every Kroloff family tree, was murdered along with two of his children in his Kapulia-area roadside inn.

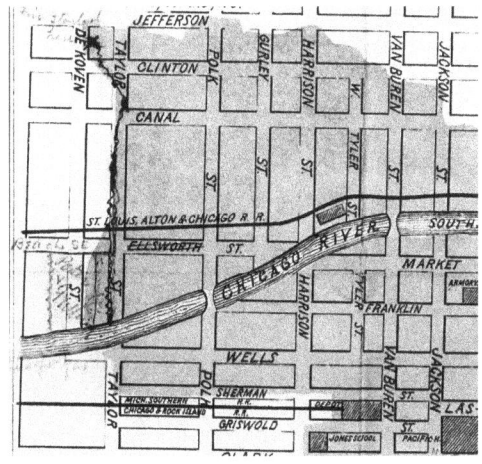

The Levys neighborhood in the 1880s wasn't the center of the American Warsaw. Yet, it did house a fairly large population of poor Roman Catholic Poles.

The places they lived on Dekoven and Canal Streets probably were on the very edge of the fire and not torched. This map shows the fire area in red. The X in the upper left corner identifies the O'Leary residence. Notice most of Dekoven St. was not burned.

As you can see from the Hull House maps of the neighborhood, by the 1890s, each block around Mary was tightly packed with buildings.

As mentioned before, Jane Adam's Hull House, founded in 1889, was America's first "settlement house." It became a rather large complex of about a dozen buildings serving residents in the slum area that included the Levy's. Hull House provided social services. Among them were medical aid, education, concerts and other arts at no cost to the nearby poor working class.

Large studies of the neighborhood conducted by Hull House are online. They offer minute details of working and living conditions in Chicago's Near Southwest Side. They also offer comparisons to conditions in other urban areas and are important in understanding why so many Americans were later able to suffer yet make it through the economic Depression of the 1930s and the severe restrictions and hardships brought on by World War II. In many ways, they lived an easier life than in Europe.

HULL HOUSE MAPS OF NEIGHBORHOOD WHERE LEVY FAMILIES LIVED ON 113 DEKOVEN STREET CAN BE FOUND AT http://encyclopedia.chicagohistory.org/pages/410008.html

The maps show ethnicity, incomes of residents per building, languages and more.

By the 1910 Census, Sarah, Mary and Eva were in Sioux City, and Morris lived at 1605 W. 12th St. He was a wholesale peddler, which might have been anything from a traveling salesman to someone selling goods to others who then retailed them from door-to-door.

I grew up in Chicago during The Great Depression of the 1930s and World War II. Hundreds of thousands of African Americans (then labeled as Negroes) were moving north from the American "South" to the city's South Side. Chicago was well on its way to becoming the most segregated large black-white city in America. When I worked as the press relations manager for Chicago's Chamber of Commerce in the early 1960s, the African Americans of the city, for the most part, were in the shadows except for their jazz, taxes, and low paying jobs. (See Maxwell Street, the Blues, Beatles/Elvis and Merchants.)

Chicago was a melting pot where cultures were blended, a symphony orchestra where each instrument kept its identity in harmony (or was it in dissonance?)

SHORT HISTORY OF CHICAGO JEWS BEFORE 1900

When Civil War hostilities began, the Jewish community in Chicago had increased to the extent that it was able to recruit a complete company of a hundred Jewish volunteers to join the 82nd Regiment of Illinois Volunteers. The Jewish community of Chicago quickly recovered from the Great Fire of 1871, which affected the neighborhood of the German Jews, and from the fire of 1874, which affected mostly East European Jews. The 1871 fire destroyed the new Jewish hospital, five of the city's seven synagogues, many Jewish institutional buildings, and most of the downtown Jewish-owned businesses and homes. Newberry Library. https://archive.org/details/nby_205875-10

The neighborhood of the Russian and Polish Jews received the cognomen "the ghetto" and that of the German Jews, the "golden ghetto." The so-called ghetto was described by a contemporary in 1891 as follows:

On the West Side, in a district bounded by Sixteenth Street on the South and Polk Street on the north and the Chicago river and Halsted street on the east ... one can walk the streets for blocks and see none but Semitic features and hear nothing but the Hebrew patois of Russian Poland. In this restricted boundary, in narrow streets, ill-ventilated tenements and rickety cottages, there is a population of from 15,000 to 16,000 Russian Jews. Every Jew in this quarter who can speak a word of English is engaged in business of some sort. The favorite occupation, probably on account of the small capital required, is fruit and vegetable peddling. Here, also is the home of the Jewish street merchant, the rag and junk peddler, and the "glass pudding" man. (Note: Not sure of the definition of glass pudding. GK)

The principal streets in the quarter are lined with stores of every description. Trades, with which Jews are not usually associated, such as saloon-keeping, shaving and hair cutting, and blacksmithing, have their representatives and Hebrew signs. In a narrow street a private school is in full blast. In the front basement room of a small cottage forty small boys all with hats on, sit crowded into a space 10 × 10 feet in size, presided over by a stout middle-aged man with a long, curling, matted beard, who also retains his hat, a battered rusty derby of ancient style. All the old or middle-aged men in the quarter affect this peculiar headgear.... The younger generation of men are more progressive and having been born in this country are patriotic and want to be known as Americans and not Russians…. The commercial life of this district seems to be uncommonly keen. Everyone is looking for a bargain and everyone has something to sell. The home life seems to be full of content and easygoing unconcern for what the outside world thinks…. (Chicago Tribune, July 19, 1891).

This area contained the famous Maxwell Street Market, which flourished from the 1870s until it was closed by the city in 1994. For many years it was the third largest retail area in the city. Jews lived in the Maxwell Street area in large numbers until the 1920s. Among the prominent people who lived there were band leader Benny Goodman, U.S. Supreme Court Justice Arthur Goldberg, the father of the atomic-powered submarine, Admiral Hyman Rickover, CBS founder William Paley, novelist Meyer Levin, Academy-Award-winning actor Paul Muni, social activist Saul Alinsky, movie mogul Barney Balaban, world champion boxers Jackie Fields and Barney Ross, and a number of well-known local politicians and businessmen.

Economic Activity: Of the large migration from Germany, Prussia, Hungary, Bohemia, and Poland in the 1840s and 1850s, most became peddlers, and later many opened small businesses. In the 1860s Jews began to enter the medical and legal professions; some also went into banking, even founding Jewish banking houses. The new Russian immigrants of the 1880s preferred factory work and small business. The greatest number of them, 4,000 by 1900, were employed in the clothing industry, mainly its ready-made branches. The second largest number, 2,400 by 1900, entered the tobacco industry, primarily the cigar trade, many of them in business for themselves.

The Russian immigrants had been preceded in these trades by the earlier Jewish immigrants, but now far outnumbered them. Among the Russian Jews at the turn of the century were also about 2,000 rag peddlers, 1,000 fruit and vegetable peddlers, and a good number of iron peddlers; others found work ranging from common laborers to highly skilled mechanics and technicians. The growth of sweat-shops in the needle trade in the 1880s with their unsanitary conditions and excessive hours was the determining factor in the development of the Jewish socialist movement and the Jewish trade-union movement.

The Chicago Cloakmakers Union, predominantly Jewish, was the first to protest against child labor, which persisted despite compulsory education, and conditions in the sweatshops. They succeeded only in establishing a 14-year-old age limit and limiting any one sweatshop to the members of one family. In that period there were many short-lived unions and several strikes in the clothing industry in Chicago, mainly by East European workers against German-Jewish shop owners, but the first successful strike did not take place until 1910; it included workers from the latest influx of Russian immigrants, who fled the Russian revolution of 1905 and among whom were many revolutionary idealists. The strike was conducted in the face of the hostile leadership of the United Garment Workers, their union, which sent in strike-breakers. Nevertheless, it was this strike that in 1911 established collective bargaining in the clothing industry. It spurred the New York Tailors locals to organize nationally, and ultimately, laid the foundations for a new and lasting union, the Amalgamated Clothing Workers of America, under the leadership of Chicagoan Sidney Hillman. (More about unions especially in the coal mines, in the Gordick/Elek sections.)

"Each garment center had its own character, greatly influenced by the groups that toiled within it. In New York, the Irish dominated from 1850 into the 1880s. After 1865, Swedes and Germans entered the industry, followed in the 1890s by Italians and Russian and Polish Jews. In Chicago, Germans, German Jews, Bohemians, and a few Americans and Poles established that city's garment center. They were joined in the 1890s by Scandinavians, Eastern European Jews, Italians, and Lithuanians."

Although they began as peddlers and small store owners, German Jews came to Chicago early and with a relatively good secular education. They soon prospered and went into the professions and large business. They ran such well-known national companies as Florsheim, Spiegel, Aldens, Kuppenheimer, Hart Shaffner and Marx, A.G. Becker, Albert Pick, Brunswick and Inland Steel. Julius Rosenwald oversaw the growth of Sears Roebuck. He was a major philanthropist for Jewish and non-Jewish causes and for the establishment of the Museum of Science and Industry. His brother-in law Max Adler, also of Sears Roebuck and a philanthropist, founded the Adler Planetarium. For a number of generations there was some friction between the German Jews and the Eastern European Jews, mainly due to differences in religious beliefs, tradition, language, and economic status. The two groups lived apart and each had their own institutions. Today in Chicago – as elsewhere – the former divisions of the two groups are virtually nonexistent.

Population Growth & Changes: From the 1880s to the 1920s the Jewish population grew from 10,000 to 225,000, or from 2 percent to 8 percent of the general population. In 1900 about 65 percent of Chicago's Jews were of East European origin; in 1920 about 80 percent were.

BORN IN RURAL RUSSIA, NOT ALL HAD ROOTS IN THEIR COMMUNITIES

Pale is an old English word meaning border. Thus, the expression "beyond the Pale" means beyond a real or imaginary boundary.

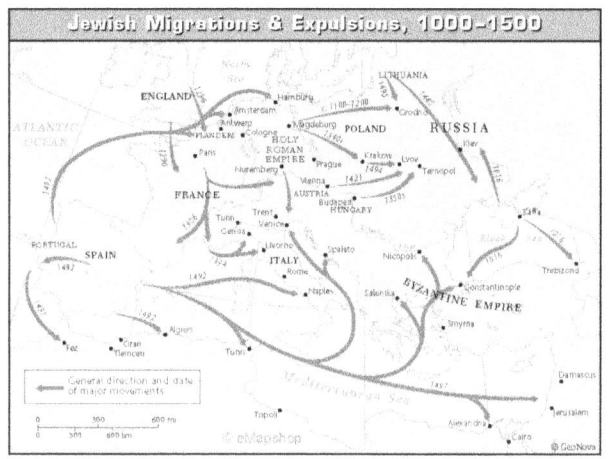

Many of the small villages and towns in The Pale had long histories. Kapulia was already a walled community in the 1200s and was often attacked by Tatars from the south or west, among others. Until the 1790 establishment of Russia's ever-expanding Pale, like most shtetls, there were few Jews in Kapulia. Map and further background https://www.jewishwikipedia.info/diagrams.html

European Jews had been periodically expelled from wherever they lived. Sometimes, they were uprooted, shoved out of a town and forced to walk in the wilds to find a place that would accept them. As kings and other rulers wanted to extend their borders, sometimes Jews wishing to get out of uncomfortable situations were encouraged to settle in uninhabited locations under the protection of the expansionist ruler. The king then claimed his citizens lived there.

Thus, our ancestors may not have had deep roots in their communities. They certainly were not nomads because most travel was forbidden. (Map is before the year 1500. Picture is of an expelled couple.) http://www.jewishsphere.com/JewishCustoms/RussiaDrivenOutAfterPogrom.jpg

So hundreds of thousands from bigger cities were forced to live in small rural settlements where the patterns of daily life were not much different than the year 1000. No electricity, for instance. At times, the reverse, rural residents were forced to live in cities.

Picture on the prrevious page is a prettified reconstruction of a traditional Jewish shtetl built in the South African Jewish Museum in Cape Town as it would have appeared in Lithuania. Why Lithuania? Probably because that was the Old Country for many of Cape Town's Jews.

SHORT REVIEW OF ITEMS THAT MIGHT BE USEFUL FOR STUDENTS SEEKING HELP WITH THE DREADED SCHOOL PAPER DUE TOMORROW ABOUT THEIR FAMILY HISTORY

All of my relatives who first settled in Siouxland along the Missouri River were from The Pale of Russia. Most came from the province of Minsk (or Minsk Gubernia) in what now is the country of Belarus. Others came from a couple of small Ukrainian shtetls in Chernigov and Poltava provinces east of Kiev (Kyiv). All of Susan's birth father Robert's relatives and her birth mother Edith's family came from in or around England. After her father died when she was about seven, Susan and her brother Bob were adopted by Edith's new husband, John Gordick. His family was from Galicia (Austro-Hungarian Empire). Now Slovakia and Ukraine.

- My maternal grandmother, Mary Levy, was born in Chicago as it was rapidly rising from the ashes of the Great Chicago Fire of 1871. Her parents were from Warsaw, Poland. In 1900, she married Joseph Kauffman and moved to Sioux City, where he was a successful young grocer.

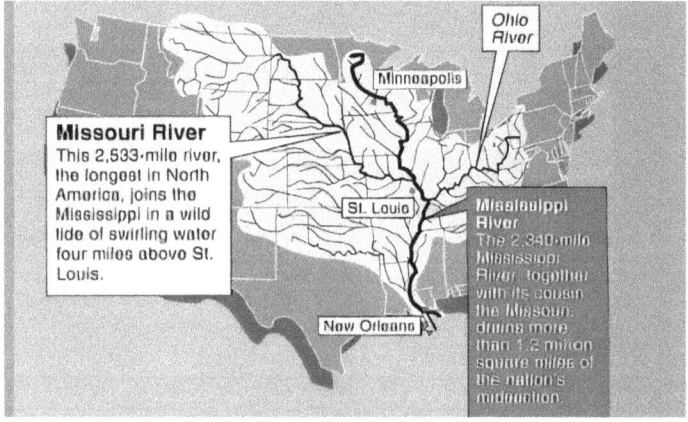

- The Chicago in which Mary was raised … "The Second City" … was the *de facto* Capital and heart of America between the Appalachian Mountains of the East and the Rocky Mountains of the West. That's about 70 percent of the country. Map from PBS.

- America's Midwest is called the Heartland. The Mississippi River *Valley* is its spine. The Mississippi *River* is the aorta. Its tributaries are the cardiovascular system. Its left arm is the Missouri River Valley (Sioux City is at the elbow where the yellow Missouri River box is pointing), and the right arm is the Ohio River Valley. Chicago is near where the human heart would be located on a map of your blood system. Map at https://en.wikipedia.org/wiki/Mississippi_River_System

For many years, the Levys lived "above their store" on Dekoven St. It was a few "doors" from where Mrs. O'Leary's cow allegedly kicked over a lantern in the family's Dekoven Street barn and started the quick-spreading blaze that leveled the center of Chicago.

- With its railroads and stockyards, an abundance of building wood, and many other businesses and services (like street cars) that were untouched by the fire, Chicago became a boom town like no other. It was a magnet for just about everything, good and bad, in the "civilized" world. Around the country, bankers complained because so much East Coast money was invested in rebuilding Chicago that their areas were being short-changed.

- Over the years, as borders changed, Mary Levy told U.S. census takers that her parents were from Poland or Russia. Her uncle Harris once told the census person he was from Poland/Germany. All in the same spot, but borders moved.

- *Mary*'s husband, *Joseph* Kauffman, was a Sioux City resident originally from Slutsk, a town south of Minsk. My cousin Shelly and I like to say, **"for many of us it all started with Mary and Joseph."** That may be overly cute.

- An online list of people being sought by the Russian police reports about a dozen Krulevitski (Kroloff) young men were wanted for evading the draft. All of them were my relatives. If the Tsar's minions had floated a raft downriver from Sioux Falls to Omaha, they could have nabbed all of them. It is unclear why the name sounded like Krolovetski. But there were few Jews in what today is Kapyl, Belarus, before 1790. Maybe when families suddenly were required by governments to have a "last name" and many used where they lived. It may be the family was living in Krolovets, Russia and moved. In Slavic languages like Russian, ski, or sky, the end of a name often meant something like "from."

- Food was a big problem for deeply religious Jewish travelers. Not all ships had Kosher kitchens. Certainly, the railroads didn't. This forced many religious emigrants to break with tradition or starve. It must have been a factor in the changing of religious habits and contributed to the rise of Conservatism and Reform movements in Judaism in the US. Mary Kauffman, my mom's mother, and Dr. Max Helfgott of Sioux City, a close relative of my dad, were two of the leaders who created Shaare Zion, the first Conservative Jewish congregation west of the Mississippi River.

- A retelling of the immigration story from Finland to the USA relates how unhappy the Finns (who often were seasick anyway) were appalled by steerage class food. Their complaint, even when not seasick, was it just tasted awful.

- Uncle Jake Dobrofsky came from a very rich family in Mena, Ukraine, The family suddenly fell upon hard times and fled to Liverpool. The story of Jake's harrowing adventures is the basis for another essay in this series, "Uncle Jake's Dramatic Escape." See (Page 85.)

- Above is a gathering of Kauffmans in Sioux City, circa 1950, in the Ginsberg's living room.

Top row: (left to right)

Dave Ginsberg, Eva Levy Skalovsky, Annie Levy Behr, Ben Behr, Archie Kroloff, Florence Kauffman Kroloff, Bud (Skalovsky) Sanford, Harriet Kauffman Metcalf, Harvey Metcalf, Louise Metcalf

Second row: (l-r)

Leah Kauffman Ginsberg, Joseph Kauffman, Mary Levy Kauffman

Bottom: (l-r)

Mazie Kauffman Mendelsohn, Harold Mendelsohn (with 7up bottle), Larry Mendelsohn, Susan Kroloff, George Kroloff, Gloria Ginsberg Marks, Norton Marks.

A gathering in Sioux City, probably late 1930s

The Levys came from Poland, the Kroloffs came from what now is Belarus, and the Helfets came from Ukraine.

Back: (l to r) Sam Kroloff (my grandfather), Irving Levich (uncle by marriage), Harry Helfet (my grandmother's brother, thus he was my great uncle)

Front: Sarah Helfet Kroloff (paternal grandmother), Ina Kroloff Levich (my aunt), Harry's wife, Anna.

SIOUX CITY, IOWA... THE CHICAGO WANNA-BE

By the time the shtetl folks converged in Sioux City, it was already the ultimate Chicago wanna-be. It had an ego as big as The Windy City, which was Chicago's nickname. The epithet was derived not from the gales that swept in from Lake Michigan but from the loud boasting of its politicians and boosters. Picture is sign from former Sioux City deli.

Like Chicago, Sioux City was a railroad junction (albeit a lot smaller), and it had sprawling, smelly stockyards and several equally odorous and prosperous meat packers that created a lot of jobs. Photo right from Sioux City Journal retrospective story. https://siouxcityjournal.com/news/local/history/photos-sioux-city-stockyards-through-the-years/collection_62c1b4e4-2c30-51cb-9a9b-9e5a45121ac4.html

The city's white population was almost as diverse as Chicago's. There was an effort to segregate the approximately 300 people of color. From historical reports, the city seems to have had plenty of crime and corruption. There was some antisemitism in the community, and it occasionally was bothersome. KKK clans, for instance. Overall, the level of acceptance of the emigrants appeared to far outweigh the slights.

From 1870 to 1920, Chicago's population steadily grew from nearly 300,000 to nearly 3 million people. Sioux City's population figures went up and down. From a mere 3,500 in 1870 to 7,366 in 1880, it dramatically rose to 37,806 in 1890, dipping to 33,111 in 1900, and up to a stratospheric 71,227 in 1920.

The Kroloffs and Kauffmans in Sioux City had seen the rise of an elevated railway (picture left) in 1890 and its bankruptcy in 1893. Notice the small steam engine. Its boosters later claimed the Chicago "L" used the Sioux City design. Unlikely! https://www.facebook.com/SiouxCityMuseum/posts/on-this-day-in-sioux-city-history-the-sioux-city-elevated-railway-opened-for-bus/3752616641446085/

Our relatives saw the introduction of electricity and rampant land speculation that helped buoy and then bust the local economy more than once. They reveled in the spread of newly paved streets, cable cars, manufacturing and stores. Even during the bust years, the town survived as a regional commercial hub servicing people from smaller towns and farms fairly far away.

Until the market for agricultural products crashed after the end of WWI, the city was full of optimism based on what the citizens had seen in the past.

That experience, the continual bouncing back from adversity, is what pushed out our relatives when times went bad and then pulled them back because they knew there was a support system of their kin along the Missouri River. It must have been comforting that some of those supporters were the very same ones who had been part of the support systems in the shtetls in and around Kapulia 20 or 30 years earlier. Their own relatives.

WHO CAME FIRST?

The first person in Sioux City from Kapulia might have been Morris Levich (Yankelovich), who, his grandson Barton told me, had some rare experience with growing potatoes in or around the Kapulia shtetl. Morris tried farming potatoes in the Dakotas. Bart remembers hearing the first year was OK, but the next crop was a failure, and the family moved south a few miles. Morris might have been attracted first to South Dakota by advertising like that pictured below. Similar posters in the local languages were popping up all across Europe. Poster and background on land grants https://en.wikipedia.org/wiki/File:Iowa_and_Nebraska_lands10.jpg

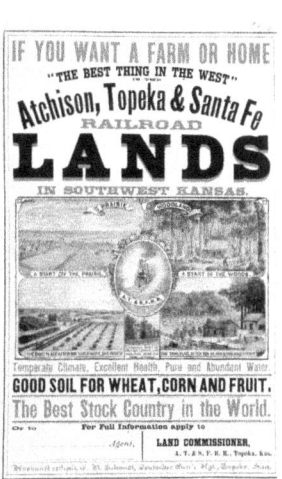

Maybe the first Kapulian to visit Siouxland wasn't Morris but another relative or friend who heard about the newly opened West and wrote a glowing letter home. Or maybe the first from Russia was enticed by an agent seeking pioneers to settle the area and fill jobs being created.

Among the first from Slutsk, the largest community near Kapulia, were the Davidson brothers, who eventually built a large Midwest department store empire. They were not related to us, but their sister had been married to my great grandfather. And they were responsible for him coming to Sioux City. His transportation was part of a deal for him to divorce the Davidson's sister. Like so much in life, it was complicated.

While the rivers were the first circulatory system for the Midwest, the railroads and the telegraph lines that ran parallel to the tracks were the Midwest's nerve system. The railroads provided the nutrients for America's growth. Millions of acres were "granted" by the government to be sold to help finance the laying of rails and to pay for new colleges and universities, at least one in every state. They were and are known as Land Grant Colleges. In Iowa, it is Iowa State.

Farms near the tracks grew the unprocessed crops, cattle and pigs that would fill the freight cars headed to stockyards and meat processing plants. The railroads constructed huge water towers to fill up the boilers of locomotives every few miles. Near the water towers were stacks of wood or piles of coal to turn the water into steam within the locomotive engines and move the rods that turned the wheels. Towns grew up around the water towers.

Freight cars filled with raw food and other materials going to Chicago, for example, returned to the towns along the same tracks with the wonders of the Industrial Age, much of it from Sears Roebuck and Montgomery Ward's catalogues.

HOW THEY WERE DOING

By 1900, the Jewish population of Sioux City was 1,000 and growing. About that time, a book, "The Jews of Iowa" by Rabbi Simon Glazer, proclaimed that Sioux City's Orthodox Jews were the poorest in the state. Of course, not all my relatives were Orthodox, and a few were far from poor.

My grandparents, Mary and Joseph Kauffman, according to the five surviving daughters, were very "social."

Joseph's grocery store was thriving. It was the first in Sioux City to buy a gasoline powered delivery truck. This family photo of him in front of the store must have been taken before the truck was acquired.

While his competitors were delivering to their customers via horse and wagons, his driver was leaving them in his smoke, as their horses, frightened by the vehicle, literally littered the streets.

Among her other activities, Mary, the Polish-American from Chicago, whose English and Yiddish were pretty well honed, donated time to help the "greenhorns," which is slang for new arrivals.

Globalization, which goes back even further than biblical days, was evident in our family. About the time Mary was helping greenhorns in Sioux City, half a world away in Cape Town, South Africa, Jewish merchants were helping new arrivals like my other Sioux City grandmother, Sarah Helfet Krololoff's brother Leon. He became acclimated to the new culture and started several profitable South African businesses.

Our Sioux City relatives, just like the old country, first lived within walking distance of a synagogue or two. That was before they could afford a horse and buggy and, later, a car. Because of its membership, one Sioux City synagogue was nicknamed "the Kapulia Shul."

Antisemitism tended to be difficult both in Calvinia, South Africa and Sioux City, Iowa in the 1920s and Thirties. In and around Sioux City there were robust rallies of the Ku Klux Klan.

One was across the street from the Robinows grocery store. I was told our cousins kept the store open before during and after the rally, because they said these people are our customers and they deserve to be served. Probably wasn't bad for business either.

Less than a generation later, people with the same messages, supporters of the Nazi philosophy, were filtering into Calvinia, South Africa and made it terribly difficult for Jewish residents to stay, so they left for more comfortable surroundings.

When I was in Calvinia a long-time resident said the town began to fall upon hard times when the Jews left. I couldn't determine if he was trying to tell me what he thought I wanted to hear or the truth. If I had stayed a couple days longer maybe I could've found out.

SIX SIDEBARS

1. This convoluted family story might actually be true. It is about the Davidson Brothers' sister.

Actually, there were two Davidson families. One family was from Slutsk, about 30 miles from Kapulia. Brothers Ben, Abe and Dave created a large regional chain of department stores. Logically enough, it was called Davidson Brothers. The headquarters was in Sioux City.

The second Davidson family was made up of Kroloffs from Kapulia and its environs. I don't know the logic of changing their names to Davidson or several other names, nor why they first settled downriver in the Council Bluffs, Iowa area, across from Omaha, Nebraska. But that's what they did. My Davidson cousin Debbie recalls being told the name came when one of the family bought a "bootleg" passport from a man who might have been Scotch. A nice family story. It might even be true.

The wildly successful Davidson brothers, who began emigrating to Siouxland in 1880, had a married sister in Slutsk. Her name was Sippe. The "boys," or maybe their mother, supposedly despised the husband and wanted Sippe to come to Sioux City. My mother, Florence Kauffman Kroloff, claimed a deal was cooked up under which Sippe would get a divorce in Slutsk and come to Iowa. The man she divorced was my great grandfather, Joseph's dad. Like any Orthodox Jewish woman, she had to have the consent of her husband (the one whose name became Kauffman) to obtain the divorce. Thus, there was to be long-term negotiation on the husband's part. Sippe did get her 'Get', which is Hebrew/Yiddish for the divorce paper. By 1883, she was in Sioux City.

Part of the Get, my mother said, was to provide my great grandfather a way to emigrate to the USA. In 1885, Sippe's ex-husband, Gabriel Kauffman, arrived in Sioux City with his new wife and family, including his son Joseph (my grandfather).

My mother also claimed that Sippie became famous when the syndicated Sunday comics feature "Ripley's Believe It Or Not" said that she later married a man named Miner. Therefore, she was a Mississippi Miner. I looked it up, and it's true.

2. First cousin Chuck Kroloff and I were born in 1935 and lived in Chicago. At least a couple of summers in the late 1940s, we jointly invaded Sioux City and stayed with relatives. By then,

most of the area's Jewish families from "the early days" had moved on to Chicago, California, Phoenix, or wherever.

Nonetheless, many dozens remained close to the Missouri River shores from the Dakotas, through Iowa and into Nebraska. On one of those trips, Chuck and I attended a Jewish Community picnic. To our young eyes, it seemed we were related to the whole town. More importantly, it was a celebration of a continuing support system.

3. The Kauffmans' five surviving daughters had an adored brother, Charles. He died at age 13 during the worldwide Flu pandemic of 1918-20. According to a couple of my aunts, their parents no longer were "social" after his death.

4. Regarding the truck that Joseph bought to deliver groceries from his store. Soon after it was acquired, he took it out for a ride and almost immediately crashed into a tree. The family lore is that he swore off driving. Never got "behind the wheel" again. His wife, Mary and five daughters were not taught to drive.

5. One aunt, Harriett, eventually learned a bit more than the basics of driving but not enough to make a left turn. She could go forward and park. So, usually, the only way to proceed was to make right turns. I vaguely remember her telling me that she never would make a left turn. Her trips were longer than most but must have been more scenic.

6. Another of my mom's sisters was Leah, who was short and could not touch the brake and clutch pedals. She was an inch or three shorter than five feet and, of course, did not drive. After a trip to Omaha and back to Sioux City, she was asked about the scenery. Her response was something like this; "Scenery, what scenery? I sat in the back seat, and all I saw were the tops of trees." Or, maybe she was kidding or had just taken a senior safe driving lesson.

WHAT WAS IT ABOUT BOTH CHICAGO AND SIOUX CITY FROM 1880 TO 1900?

It wasn't the odor or the beauty of each.

To those in Europe yearning to emigrate, Uncle Sam might have seemed like the "Carnival Barker," creating colorful and exciting images of what was behind the sideshow curtain. For others, "Uncle Sam" was seen as a lifesaver, or lifepreserver thrown to a drowning person.

Actually, behind Uncle Sam's carnival curtains was an exhibit sponsored by a food company, a ship or rail line, or a state seeking immigrants, a company needing workers, like miners, to work in Pennsylvania or Midwest mines.

The Canadians joined others in the game. The poster (right) is written in Norwegian. Issued in the 1890s, it reads, "Canada: 160 acres of free land for every settler." To learn more about Ukranian emigration to Canada, as in Susan's family try https://www.atastefortravel.ca/31249-grosse-ile-quebec/

Professional promoters, agents, barkers, or other boosters were taking advantage of better printing presses and cheaper paper. They preyed upon the prayers, hopes, and especially the fears of poor Europeans. Traveling salesmen representing companies and governments to the far south, north and central Europe utilized improved mail service, the telegraph, and mostly, word-of-mouth. People who understood English were as scarce as one of those carnival barkers mentioned above working a baptism. But they understood the word "jobs." With improving communications technology, many were hearing from their friends and relatives who already emigrated. Some of the sales stories, or "pitches" were realistic. Illustration and more history https://fr.m.wikipedia.org/wiki/Fichier:Jewish_immigration_Russia_United_States_1901.jpg

There was a joke about streets being paved with gold. "The poor immigrant learns three things upon arrival.

He was expected to pave them. Each Irish tenant farmer of County Cork, Jew of the Pale, Italian from the Foot, Finn from the Fjord, Slav and Slovene from central Europe, and the beleaguered Pole who seemed to be the butt of every practical joke any European ruler or army ever thought up … each had a unique reason to emigrate to America. At least, they thought their story was unique. Below is an Alfred Stieglitz photo, "The Steerage."

As a group, the larger outside influences (caused by a butterfly's wings far away, as explained in The Chaos Theory.) were more or less the same. There was the push of over-population, plagues, discrimination, corruption, bad times for agriculture, wars, and business depressions that, in turn, caused personal depression.

While Europe was depressed, overall, America was on a high, and no two cities during much of the 1880s were more upbeat than Sioux City, Iowa and Chicago, Illinois.

And no better examples of that optimism were the five Sioux City Corn Palaces (1887-91) and Chicago's World's Columbian Exposition of 1893.

The horrendous "Great Chicago Fire of 1871" had burned the center of the city to its foundations. But, its railroads reaching to the east coast, south, north and west, its port on Lake Michigan, and much of its massive granaries, lumber yards and all stockyards survived virtually intact. The Great Chicago Fire I Chicago Stories I WTTW Chicago Visit: https://images.app.goo.gl/DVzqzK4UABZuE1Tz5

In 1875, when Louis and Sarah Levy showed up, money for reconstruction after The Fire was pouring into the city as fast or faster than jobs were being created. It was a tumultuous, glorious, crime ridden cultural oasis … the natural market center for at least half the USA. To most Americans, it must have appeared to be a carnival of epic proportions.

Chicago was every immigrant's optimistic dream and dreadful nightmare. It had a life of its own, day and night, even before electric lights. It already had neighborhoods populated by citizens from the "home country" who, for the most part, welcomed the greenhorns from Europe.

The Europeans who came to Sioux City might have first spent time, maybe only a few hours, in an East Coast port (NY or Philadelphia, or one in Canada), then hopped a train west to Chicago. They would have spent at least the hour or two required to get from the train station at the end of the eastern rail line, across Chicago's newly rebuilt center city, to the station for a different rail line headed west.

Chicago, as previously chronicled, was The City of Broad Shoulders, Hog Butcher for the World. Sioux City, by 1880, wanted to be "The" Little Chicago. The future of both cities was intertwined. Both grew up as frontier towns with a taste for alcohol and a rural connection to farmers and markets.

Chicago dominated. Sioux City wanted a piece of the action. Chicago business liked that Sioux City wanted some skin in the game. Chicago money helped build Sioux City's meat packing houses ... Cudahy, Armour, Swift ... because it was more efficient to build plants next to stockyards to kill, cut up, and package cows, pigs and sheep close to where the animals were raised. It was cheaper to ship stackable, marketable packages than the live or dead bodies of steers and bulls. Then, the rails would bring them to local grocers and butchers far away or close by. Disassociating the blood, gore, and groans by using neat meat packing in the process helps market the packages.

The economy, of course, was the driving force of job creation. And, despite what family myths may linger in your mind, hope of attaining a job usually was the top or among the highest reasons emigrants chose the USA over other nations. This was especially true for the first-to-come, who overwhelmingly were young men.

I strongly believe that the reason so many headed to Sioux City (and the nearby Missouri River towns) in the 1880s and 90s and, more importantly, stayed, even when the economy occasionally went sour, was their early experience of finding jobs relatively quickly and the support systems built-in for them there as family and neighbors from the old-country followed them.

Because of the boosterism surrounding the city's future, no matter how bad the economy tanked, the transplanted Europeans were sure the good times would roll again.

By 1888, Sioux City had a grand opera house (left), and electric wires were being "strung" in residential neighborhoods (above).

As the East Europeans were beginning to arrive, Sioux City boosters hoped the city would grow to 250,000 and were looking for something unique to set it apart from the hundreds of other Midwest cities. To no one's surprise, they found…

CORN

This essay includes further context for my theory about the safety net in Sioux City and optimism about the future. It began in 1887 as our family was establishing itself along the Missouri River. That was the beginning of the good years. It also shows a difference between small-town big-thinking and big-city concepts. (Remember, I was PR manager for the Chicago Chamber of Commerce, then the biggest in the country, and I spent about half my time working on behalf of the chamber's International Trade Fair, then the biggest in the hemisphere.) Below, I have scandalously stolen facts from Iowa historical and other websites.

Picture has appeared in scores of reports worldwide, for instance https://www.dw.com/en/gmos-threaten-production-of-organic-maize-in-spain/a-35990288

PRAIRIE PALACES AND KING CORN

Often, Midwest summers were hot and dry.

In the 1870s, swarms of locusts gobbled up entire grain fields in much of the Midwest. Even in the best of times, farmers had trouble making a profit. Prices for their produce often were low when they had products to sell. They complained that it was expensive to ship crops to market on trains and to borrow money from banks.

Across much of the plains, locusts and dry weather forced many to leave their land and go elsewhere. Typically, those who remained took years to recover.
Picture and background on locust hordes at many sites for example https://todayinhistory.blog/tag/westward-expansion/

The Sioux City area was luckier. There was enough rain, and crops flourished.

The town had grown from about 7,000 in 1880 to over 30,000 people (mostly immigrants and first generation Americans) by 1887. (Again, I apologize that there seems to be some flexibility in varying population estimates.) It was the third largest meatpacking center in America and a busy gateway to the Northwest. As mentioned before, Sioux City residents, many of them in their bravado, believed the city might become nearly as important as Chicago. The city's bankers, business leaders, real estate developers (speculators) and even "common citizens" were promoters.

It was decided that building a corn palace would help meet their expectations.

People already knew how to build barns and houses, but a palace would be harder. For six days, 46 men sawed and hammered.

HELP FROM NATIVE AMERICANS

The nearby Winnebago tribe sold 5,000 bushels of Indian corn to the palace-builders for decorations. Indian corn is blue, purple, red and white. Another 15,000 bushels of yellow corn were used. Corn poster. https://bucksfoodshed.org/meet-corn/

For 15 days, teams of horses hauled additional loads of straw, sorghum, wild grasses and vines. Steam saws sliced and chopped the materials to size. Carpenters thatched the roof with green cornstalks and nailed tons of corn to the walls and around the windows.

Inside the palace, local artists twisted and arranged nature's products into works of art featuring autumn colors and unusual textures. A huge spider made of carrots hung on a web made of cornsilk. For the walls, artists wove scenes of Indians in canoes and buffalo in meadows.

Local women wore corn necklaces to parties, and the men wore cornhusk neckties. Just about everyone learned the myths of Monomania, the Indian god of corn, and Ceres, the Greek goddess of harvests. They wrote songs and poems about "King Corn."

Storekeepers filled their windows with pumpkins and harvest scenes. Brightly colored globes covered the gas lights that arched over the streets. It was a big deal.

SIOUX CITY WAS WHAT THEY CONSIDERED TO BE WORLD FAMOUS

One crisp fall day in October 1887, the palace and festival opened. Businesses placed their newest products on floats for the industrial parade. Another day covered wagons, and groups of Winnebago, Sioux, and Omaha tribes from their tribal reservations paraded down the streets. At night, fireworks boomed overhead. Passenger trains to Sioux City added extra cars to carry the crowds into town.

Chicago, New York and London newspapers and magazines published stories about the Corn Palace in Iowa. From Boston came curious vacationers. Wealthy businessmen from the East Coast were impressed with Sioux City and the enthusiasm of its citizens, and they invested there. More than 130,000 people saw the Corn Palace before the festival ended a week later.

The palace was torn down, as planned. Right away, the citizens of Sioux City started thinking about building another palace the next year.

Every year for the next four years, a new palace was built—always more magnificent than the one before.

In 1888, the carpenters used so much corn and grain to decorate the outside walls that not a single square inch of wood was left uncovered—except for the flagpoles.

In 1889, the palace towers were higher than nearby church steeples. More industrial and agricultural displays were added. Products trending in the big cities appeared, like phonograph records for the new-fangled "talking machines."

In 1890, a giant globe of the world topped the palace. Countries were outlined with kernels of corn. Inside, the ceiling was an imitation of the sky at night. Electric lights shone like stars. A bevy of towns in Iowa had some electric lights by then, but most Iowa farm families would wait at least 40 years before electricity could light their evenings.

    The festival that year was as grand as ever until the last day. Heavy rains ruined the parade, poured through the palace roof, and drenched the displays. More information about the palaces and photos at https://www.siouxcitymuseum.org/history-website/sioux-city-corn-palaces

SIOUX CITY IN FULL FORCE DURING 1889-90

An appropriately decorated train went to Chicago's Republican Convention, with stops along the way to promote the Corn Palace. Later, another train went to Washington, DC, for the inauguration of President Harrison. It also was a Corn Palace promotion.

In 1890, Sioux City's boisterous boosters unveiled the town's own short-lived elevated railway system, like the ones already built or soon to be opened in Liverpool, New York, and Chicago. Some over-the-top locals even claimed the Chicago "El" or "L" was based on the failing Sioux City design. The version was a casualty of the 1893 economic crash and the realization that its business model was not sustainable. A town of 30,000 just didn't need a two-mile-long aerial railroad. Photo from https://commons.wikimedia.org/wiki/File:The_street_railway_review_(1891)_(14574599678).jpg

Meanwhile, the 1891 palace was more than a block long. Visitors hopped on streetcars and rode right through the building. Several states and "South America" sent exhibits. Mexico provided a band. Louisiana shipped live alligators. The updated electricity exhibit was popular.

When the palace was torn down, a man paid $1,211 to salvage some of the corn, lumber, cloth and nails. See Sioux City Corn Palace history.

And then the palaces were no more

In the spring of 1892, the nearby Big Floyd River flooded much of Sioux City. Money was short after the clean up. The Panic of 1893 brought on a three-year economic depression in the US and Europe that crushed any hope of another palace. Flooded Sioux City's economy was in shambles. More about flooding, buildings and Sioux City History at Wikipedia and Google.

WHY PALACE?

The name, Corn Palace, is revealing. As if a city had eyes and could see, Sioux City saw itself first as a rural agricultural dynamo and second as a business and manufacturing center. "Palace" is a European word signaling superiority that would have been familiar to Sioux City's European immigrant population.

Probably no other small city had come up with, and successfully executed, such an audacious example of American optimism and boosterism. Its attempt to build an elevated railway about the same time as the Corn Palaces must have been a strong argument for our relatives to stay there.

The once fearful Belarus Kroloff, Herzoff, Robinow and Levich young men, and later their families, were infected with the optimism of their neighbors in Siouxland. That was communicated back to the "old country." More kept coming.

Those five years were among Sioux City's most confident. The streets were not paved with gold, but they were adorned with the golden corn mined from the fields that stretched as far as the eye could see and silver from the tassels on each ear of corn.

That's the Sioux City my relatives knew, even if they came later. The Corn Palace years seemed to cement a semblance of sensible optimism for the future.

There was an important difference between the boosterism in Sioux City and Chicago.

The city fathers and mothers of Sioux City thought as big as they could. One corn palace a year for a quick publicity and tourism hit, and maybe sell some corn, cows, pigs, produce, or some real estate.

It was meant to amaze and amuse but not to inspire and change the world.

ON THE OTHER HAND, IN CHICAGO

**"Sell the cookstove if necessary and come
You must see the fair."**

--Author Hamlin Garland, in a letter to his parents, 1893

(Sorry, It is too good a quote for me not to repeat it.)

Chicago was a different story than Sioux City. It amazed, amused, inspired and changed the world. It was rhapsodized in songs. For instance, above is the sheet music for a tune about the world's first Ferris Wheel. The "wonder" at 264 feet high was about 26 stories!

As Sioux City and other communities were suffering from floods and failures, Chicago flourished. It created the greatest show on earth, the World's Columbian Exposition of 1893. Even as the country was sinking into the worst Depression it had ever seen.

Chicago erected not just a building that covered a square block. It built "The White City" of 200 buildings brightly lit at night with electricity. It previewed inventions and products and architecture and entertainment. And Little Egypt, the belly dancer who at the time seemed scandalous.

Among the lesser introductions were the first zipper, the first all-electric kitchen, and a new chewing gum called Juicy Fruit. Today, one might compare the zipper with the NASA space programs spin-offs like teflon, freeze dried food and velcro. In the 1893 Chicago Fair, the equivalent would be showing the future of electricity.

Inside the fairgrounds were some of the biggest museum buildings ever built.

The fair's "Midway" introduced the rest of the world to Americans. Or, as some said, "The world came to Chicago."

Just outside the fair were other exhibitions. One was a vast Wild West Show put on by Wild Bill Cody, featuring Annie Oakley, the world's most famous female sharpshooter.

Buffalo Bill promised 450 horses of all countries "In addition to Indians, cowboys, Mexicans, Cossacks, Arabs, and Tartars are detachments from the Sixth United States Cavalry, French chasseurs (calvary), German Pottsdammer Reds (infantry), and English lancers (more calvary).

These representatives of trained mounted soldiery are fully as hardy as the barbarous riders, and many of the feats they performed were quite as wonderful." And Buffalo Bill promised "genuine illustrations of life on the plains." Today you could spend hours visiting the hundreds of websites covering the Fair.

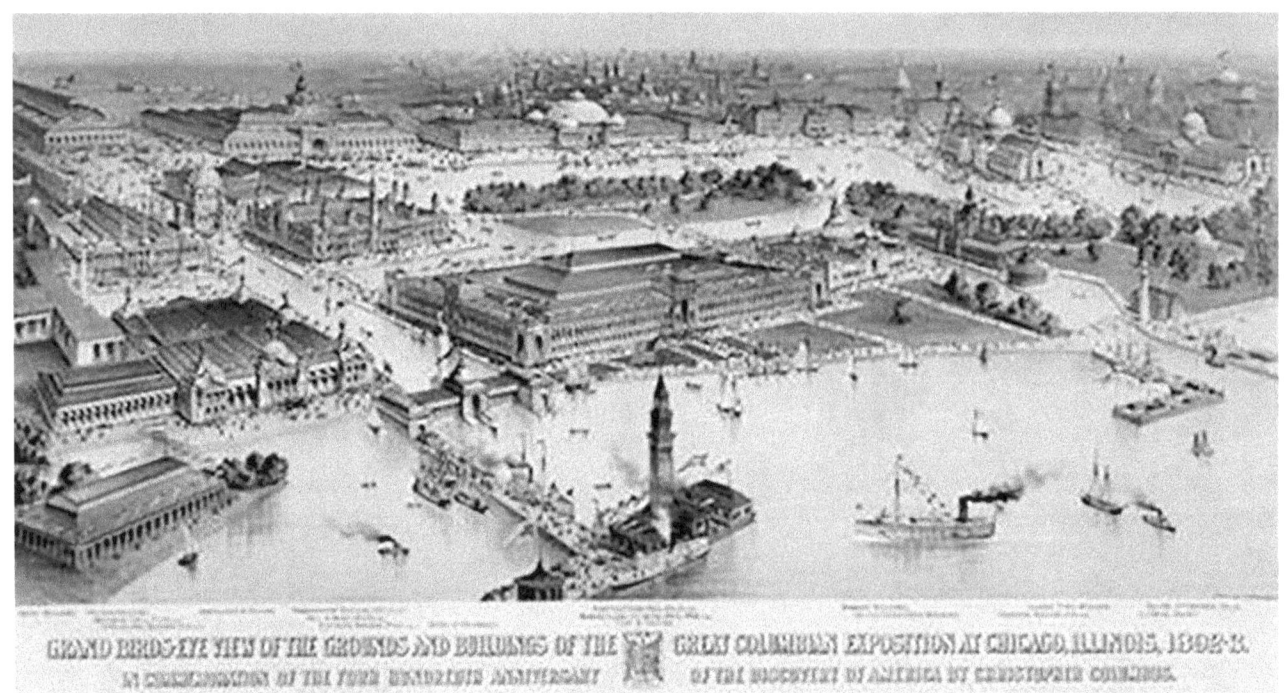

THE FAIR ... DAY AND NIGHT

Why many left Sioux City when the economy was bad.

Why they later returned to Sioux City.

After the first few from the Slutsk-Kapulia area arrived, the attraction of the existing Sioux City support group of friends and relatives from the Old Country was a huge pull.

The Helfets, Dobrofskys, and Levys, who had been reared in Liverpool, Warsaw, or Chicago, were well aware of the highs and lows of big city living. For quite a while, they, too, preferred the smaller setting of Sioux Falls, Sioux City, Council Bluffs, and Omaha.

Like the rest of the nation and of the world, Sioux City was subject to severe economic swings. They called economic Recessions "Panics" in those days.

Sometimes, the Sioux City relatives didn't just wait out the storm, hoping for better times to return. Sometimes, they left for good.

Others, like my paternal grandparents, Sarah Helfet Kroloff and Sam Kroloff were bounce-backers. Not long after what must have been a religious wedding in Sioux City, they left with Sarah's sister Esther and brother-in-law Jacob (Jake) Dobrofsky for what they expected to be greener pastures in Chicago. The official record of Sam and Sarah's marriage shows it took place in Chicago. Their photo, from I don't know where, sure looks like a wedding picture more than a year after she left Liverpool, England, for Iowa. I suspect they had a religious wedding in Sioux City and a civil wedding in Chicago.

Reading Uncle Jake's autobiography, I was surprised at how many relatives returned to Sioux City and stayed, at least through the First World War. (When that war ended, much of the Midwest's rural economy tanked for a while when the US government cut back on the purchase of food essentials like corn, wheat and potatoes once bought to feed the troops who returned from Europe. And then came the Great 1930's Depression.)

As noted, the relatives felt comfortable with Sioux City, in part because some of the same people who had provided the support system for them in Russia and Liverpool were living in Sioux City, and there was no way those would, or could, return to Russia.

More random background

- Improbably, this exercise in figuring out why Sam and Sarah did what they did began with a three part question. *Since my grandmother and grandfather met in Sioux City, why was my dad Archie born in Chicago, October 27, 1905? Why in 1907 was his brother Max born in New York? And why, by 1915 were they were back in Sioux City, where daughter Ina Leah Kroloff was born? The answer is on the next page.*

- Right is a picture of Max and big brother Archie. I can't imagine why, with such bitter memories of The Old Country, both would be decked out like miniature Russians. The family tried to remain "different" in Russia, but I recall Sam working hard to be a "real" American in Sioux City.

- My father was one of several Archie Kroloffs. An essay about Kapulia explains why there were so many Archies in the Kroloff and Herzoff families, along with other recurring names among the relatives' first-borns.

- On Feb 10, 1903, the three Helfet girls arrived at Ellis Island in New York and immediately went to Sioux City to join up with brother Harry (Isaac), who preceded them by two months. Sarah, Esther and Minnie, raised in Liverpool, were very proper Victorian strait-laced young ladies when they arrived. Just look at that picture of Sarah and Sam on the previous page.

- A cousin, Arnie Levin (whose mother was Sam's sister Helen), once stayed with Sam and Sarah for a while. If I recall correctly, it was while Arnie's mother and father were setting up their grocery/general store in Rosalie, Nebraska, just over 30 miles south of Sioux City. Their customers primarily were from the nearby Winnebago and Omaha Indian reservations. One day, over lunch, the often jovial Arnie turned deadly serious when talking about Sarah, who apparently was a very stern disciplinarian.

- Aunt Ina, the younger sister of Archie and Max, eventually married Irving Levich. Irving's father, Morris, was born in or near Kapulia and was an early emigre to Sioux City. He's the one who tried potato farming in South Dakota for two growing seasons. One good, the second disastrous.

- My late sweet sister Susan swore she heard the following right. One of the young Kroloff boys, Archie or Max, became ill, and a trip from Sioux City to Liverpool had to be delayed. My grandmother Sarah was determined to return to England and show off her young sons to the family. They eventually went and returned, apparently without incident. However,

Sister Susan's version of the story is that the original return booking was on the Titanic. It's more likely the Lusitania, which also sank, but either way, it's a good story.

Meanwhile, back in Sioux City.

As promised, I will occasionally refresh your memory. Esther Helfet married Jacob Dobrofsky. They were from different parts of Ukraine. Both families had settled in Liverpool, where Esther and Jake met. She left first, and Jake later followed her to Sioux City. Her ship from Liverpool had docked in New York. He docked in Philadelphia.

From Uncle Jake's long memoir, I learned that the two sisters, Sarah and Esther, and their husbands, (Sam and Uncle Jake), moved to Chicago before my father Archie was born because they thought they could get better jobs. That was not a successful move.

Jake and Esther returned to Sioux City. My grandparents Sam and Sarah and my toddler dad wound up in New York City where Sam had signed up for a traveling salesman job selling equipment to laundries. He was recommended by a family friend in Sioux City, Joseph Wolfson.

According to Jake, Sam was on the road a lot. His territory extended from New York to Ohio. That explains why Uncle Max was born in New York. Sam, Sarah, (and the two boys) were back in Sioux City before the 1910 census.

Uncle Jake Dobrofsky wrote that Sam had a new successful enterprise. He made (maybe at home) and then sold punch boards to stores as far away from Sioux City as Wyoming.

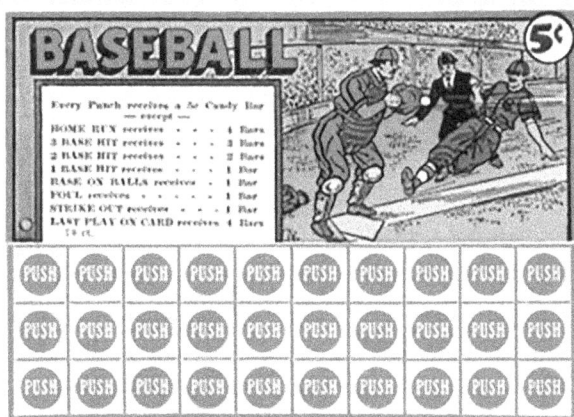

Punch boards were an early form of The Lottery. A store would buy a large, printed, thick piece of cardboard with many holes in it. Inside the holes were little pieces of paper that told the "puncher" how much he or she won for the small price of gambling. Or the paper would say there was no prize. The store owner might buy a card for $3 and know the total payout would be $10. By determining how much to charge per punch, the owner could know the profit.

Jake said Sam made a lot of money until there was too much competition. The business itself was not a fad. A small grocery store in my Chicago neighborhood had punch cards as late as the 1950s.

I heard a different story about Sam's leaving the gambling business. Strait-laced Sarah was sick and tired of her husband once again spending so much time on the road, among them were untamed places like Deadwood, South Dakota (home of Boot Hill, Calamity Jane, and Wild Bill Hickok).

A surprisingly large number of downtown Deadwood stores were owned by Jews from The Pale. I wouldn't be surprised if some were from around Kapulia, and that's what attracted Sam to the burg.

Sarah told Sam to stay home, or she would take the kids, go back to England, and stay. Sam opened a Sioux City grocery store.

EUPHORIA

There was something else going on in Sioux City and in other towns across the country during the late 1800s. The greenhorns quickly bought into it. The "it" was a national euphoria about America and its unlimited future. It was like they had boarded a train that could take them anywhere they wanted, and along the way, they could stop and check out the surroundings and maybe stay. If that didn't work out, they would move somewhere else (greener pastures). The newly minted Americans were convinced they had  left Europe's organized governmental oppression behind, and they quickly saw others around them beginning to live the American Dream. Notice that a public school is in the forefront of the painting at https://commons.wikimedia.org/wiki/File:After_Frances_Flora_Bond_Palmer,_Across_the_Continent_-_%22Westward_the_Course_of_Empire_Takes_its_Way%22,_1868,_NGA_66574.jpg

They believed in Manifest Destiny, which is the idea that America's growth and individual growth and welfare were unstoppable because it was "God's Will." Manifest means "obvious to the eye or mind." I can't get my head into the heads of people of color, but for the whites who came to America or thought about living in America, Manifest Destiny could have personified the aspirational aspect of the American Dream.

African Americans, Asians and Native Americans were segregated out of areas and jobs. The few black, brown, red and yellow skinned residents in Sioux City were in that category. Sure, there were restrictions on Jews, Catholics, or other tribes getting into clubs and some schools. But the aspirational aspect of "America" was strong, although it appears to be weaker today than in the 1800s, it lingers across the world.

The American Eagle is much brighter than the dark vulture that soared over The Pale of Russia

My mother and other Sioux City girls of the time feared people of dark color. There hadn't been any blacks where their families came from, so the fear must have been picked up from neighbors in Sioux City. (Although they loved their "negro/colored/schvartze maids.) Note: I use the word colored when referring to Americans and coloured when discussing non-white residents of South Africa in other essays. Neither are words I would use in conversation.

But, above all, Little Chicago was still on the edge of the frontier and was bubbling with optimism that was contagious. Therefore, the bottom line was that the residents of Sioux City who were having a hard time "knew" that they could "make it" somewhere else in America. If the new venture failed, they could return to the Sioux City safety net before foraging out again.

They had broken out of the dreary Pale's nightmare into a brighter dream.

SETTING THE SCENE FOR THE FAMILY'S EARLY DAYS IN SIOUX CITY

What was there before and just after our relatives arrived

It wasn't just the wings of a butterfly that brought a whirlwind of change to the land and people along the Missouri River bordering the Dakotas, Wisconsin, Nebraska and Iowa. Native American medicine men forecast bad times with the sighting of a new insect, the Honey Bee.

The Sioux and other tribes could tell that hordes of white men were approaching (maybe in three years) as the Honey Bees advanced into their territory.

In the 1700s, a few French and Spanish fur trappers and traders, "blue beards," started to move up and down the Missouri River coming from the south (New Orleans) and north (Canada). Unintentionally, the farmers who followed attracted the bees as they moved west.

By 1850, Kapulia, Warsaw, Ukraine, and other European locations where our ancestors were born had a recorded history going back hundreds of years. But Sioux City, Iowa, where so many of our relatives resided in the 19th and 20th centuries, simply didn't exist on paper or in legend. What became Sioux City was an occasional home for splinter groups of two or three Native American tribes. Painting from collection of George Catlin artwork. https://pueblosoriginarios.com/recursos/colecciones/catlin/mandan.html
Bee is from hundreds of Pinterest accounts.

It was located on an amorphous and contentious border between mostly Sioux tribes. In the area were Otoes, Omahas, Iowas, Winnebagos and others who were being forced to move west by the men with skin the color of light corn. This precipitated several wars among the tribes as alien Native Americans were pushed into their territory. Picture is of a Lakota Sioux tepee.

At mid-century, the only permanent structure in the Sioux City area was a wood cabin built by a French-Canadian fur trapper for his wives, two of whom seemed to be sisters. Nearby were a few tepees, occasionally filled with the family of Chief War Eagle of the Yankton Sioux. The chief was a friend of the trapper, and the chief was his father-in-law.

The area's single claim to fame among Caucasians was the 1804 death of US Army Sgt. Charles Floyd. He was the only fatality during the famous Lewis & Clark Expedition sent west by President Thomas Jefferson. The expeditions were to document what actually was in the newly purchased Louisiana Territory that more or less doubled the size of the United States. Rumors of a water route across the Territory to the Pacific Ocean were proven false.

Sgt. Floyd had a fatal stomach or bowel catastrophe near present-day Sioux City and was buried there. The remaining explorers headed west.

By 1870, before our ancestors arrived, Sioux City had about the same population as Kapulia … a bit over 3,000. By 1890, when the Krulevitsky/Kroloffs and the Kauffmans were settling in, Sioux City had over 30,000 residents, soon to be an expected 50,000. In addition to its boosterism, the city grew in fits and starts for two main reasons. (1) The arrival of railroads. (2) The greater economic forces across America and the world. Important fits were The Panics of 1873-79, the one in 1893 and then just after World War I. Today, we call economic fits "depressions."

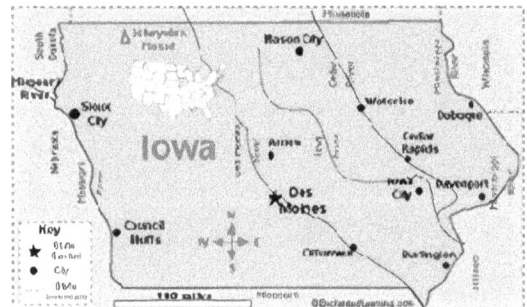

Map: https://www.guideoftheworld.net/iowa-cities-map

The 1873 Depression had many mothers. The first allegedly surfaced in Vienna, Austria, where a bunch of financial shenanigans caused banks to fail. Even then, tiny Sioux City and smaller cities across the Midwest were part of the national and international market economy. They suffered fallout just like the big cities thousands of miles away where stock market manipulators and speculators lived.

Joseph Kauffman arrived in 1887 with his parents. Sam Kroloff immigrated in 1890 but probably first was in the NY garment trade (family legend says he was a buttonhole maker), and maybe in Chicago, before Sioux City.

FOR ALL THE PROBLEMS OF DAILY LIFE

Sioux City continued to be awash with sometimes irrational exuberance ... even after floods and panics

A persistent positive attitude about the future probably is the underlying reason immigrants were attracted to the sometimes flooded, sometimes desert-dry, almost always wet (as in liquor) and wicked Sioux City ... and its wetter and wickeder city directly across the Missouri River, South Sioux City, Nebraska.

As of this writing, it remains unclear how and why the very early adapters of our family chose the Missouri Valley. The Midwest was not the East Europe they left and where they had no chance or desire to return. That unbridled optimism about the American future, their future, and Siouxland's future may have been the key factor. The openness of the land and most of the people may be what drew our ancestors to the Missouri River like a bee to pollen. Or maybe it was just that a respected aunt or uncle came first and convinced some others in the family to follow.

During its first decades, Sioux City was a classic, somewhat rough frontier town and a steamboat port. For at least one year, armor was placed on a paddle-wheel boat moving north to shield it from attacks by Native Americans who had been forced out of their homes. The Indian Wars in South Dakota upstream from Sioux City occurred in the mid 1860s when soldiers were stationed in Sioux City.

At one point, St. Louis lost its lead as the Missouri Valley's steamboat capital to the tiny Sioux City river port 770 miles upstream. By 1868, when the first railroad thundered into Sioux City, it was a well known jumping-off-spot for people seeking fortunes in the Wild West where (hopefully) money was to be made in mining, farming, grazing cattle and everything that was meant to be rosy. Starting in 1874, there was actually "gold in them 'thar' hills" a few hundred miles to the west near Deadwood.

Painting is of the steamboat Omaha at the Sioux City Landing, arriving from St. Louis in 1856. https://www.siouxcitymuseum.org/sergeant-floyd-river-museum-our-history?itemId=2v3wmmxiwwbkj4ehvzzu789hoqt18x

The Sioux City that Sam Kroloff and Joseph Kauffman knew in the 1880s and 1890s had always been a pretty transient community. Many stopped there a year or so to work and save some money before heading West to seek their gold or other fortunes in the fertile Great Plains or the barren but mineral rich, Dakota Bad Lands. Some US Army soldiers garrisoned there during the Indian Wars apparently liked it and stayed after being released from duty.

GLOBALIZATION IS NOT NEW. OUR FAMILY WAS PART OF THE EVOLUTION

Similarities, Sioux City, Iowa, Calvinia, South Africa

Sometimes, wars make for good business among local merchants. See the essays about Calvinia South Africa. He ... Great Uncle Leon Helfet... prospered by supplying British soldiers during the last Boer War in South Africa around 1900.

Curiously, Leon and later four of his siblings (Minna, Sarah, Esther, Isaac/Harry) left Liverpool within about five years of each other. Leon, still a teenager, went first and settled in a small South African town (called a dorp in the Afrikaans language). His four siblings were also in their late teens or early adulthood in 1903 when they began their off-and-on residence in the American "dorp" called Sioux City.

Our Sioux City relatives, much like Leon in South Africa, also tended to work in stores selling food, furniture, and fashions to residents hundreds of miles from the big cities, at the edge of what Europeans thought of as the wilderness. The people who lived in the wilderness thought it was home.

The US Civil War and Reconstruction and the earlier French and Indian Wars had impacts similar to The Anglo-Boer War. The festering indignities of Apartheid were similar to white-black-brown relationships in the Americas, although arguably slightly worse.

Antisemitism generated by the Klu Klux Klan in Sioux City during the early 1900s was not as bad as the activities of Fascist supporters of Germany around WWII who forced Leon and his family to leave Calvinia.

One of our relatives from Kapulia operated a grocery store in a suburb of Sioux City. Across the street was a large empty lot the KKK used to demonstrate. He kept the store open because it was good for business, and many of the KKK were his usual customers who were happy to come in to refresh themselves after the demonstration.

Nonetheless, memories of previously being uprooted from their homes in The Pale of Russia with sometimes hostile neighbors must have been fresh and painful.

The recipe for that tasty stew in Sioux City's ethnic melting pot included Scandinavians, Germans, Poles, Canadians, British and a smattering who had been born in the USA further east. In 1885, there were just enough blacks to form a small African Methodist Episcopalian Church (AME).

This paragraph is where I may lose you yet again

Arnie Levin's mother was my great aunt Helen, one of my grandfather Sam Kroloff's sisters. In the 1940s-50s Helen Kroloff Levin, a widow, lived with her sister Ida Kroloff Herzoff, also a widow. Coincidentally, their apartment on the first floor of 1214 Pierce Street in Sioux City was next door to my mother's father and mother, Joseph and Mary Kauffman. A few summers I would see Sam visit the Kauffmans, share some schnapps, have a good natured argument with Mary and then go next door to spend time with his sisters. The argument was in Yiddish and I had no idea what it was all about. That helps to explain why, especially as a youngster, it was difficult to understand family relationships. They all were related to me, but not each other.

For a long time, there were more white men than women in Sioux City, Iowa and probably in Calvinia, South Africa. It was not unusual, even in boom times, for white men to follow reports of free land, better jobs, or just a chance to move about a vast country. Something that was almost unheard of in Eastern Europe. Later, the men might bring over families from the old country to join them.

In the USA, the transcontinental railroads did not go through Sioux City. To get there, travelers had to go through cities like Omaha or St. Louis or St. Paul and change trains. Nonetheless, Sioux City was a portal to the South Dakota Bad Lands, the Montana gold rush, and a host of towns that became famous through Wild West pulp magazine stories of the time. (Pulp refers to the cheap wood pulp that was used to create the paper on which the magazines were printed. Magazines on higher quality paper were "glossies" or "slicks.")

Deadwood, South Dakota, was a Wild West town. It welcomed Wild Bill Hickok, Calamity Jane, and others of some fame and is remembered just as various cities revere Wyatt Earp and Doc Holiday. The picture (left) shows Deadwood, SD, 1876, a few years before Sam Kroloff arrived there as a traveling salesman selling to stores what today probably would be depicted as harmless gambling games. Photos of Deadwood: https://cdrhsites.unl.edu/diggingin/historicimages/di.rg.2573-3-1.html and Sioux City Rapid Transit https://www.quia.com/jg/2242363list.html

Like most small towns in Europe and the USA, Sioux City had horses and manure in the streets, and some of the smells, outhouses, garbage, sewage, and yuck that was left over from occasional floods, plus the stinks from slaughtering of animals in the stockyards area and sporadic garbage pick up. But, compared to Chicago, New York, London, et. al., it was clean.
1888-sioux-city-iowa-state-perspective-view-map

Typical of most port towns like Sioux City, there was still some scumminess. For example, the time bar owners put out a "contract" on a crusading preacher who wanted to ban booze. His assassination gave the city a reputation similar to that of Chicago (a few years later) during the Al Capone Gang era.

Down by the docks (appropriately called "The Bottoms") and across the Missouri in South Sioux City, Nebraska, it truly was the Wild West where alcohol and other vices reigned supreme.

Above is a very hi-res map of Sioux City in 1888. It can be blown up much larger. Notice the use of steam engines pulling trains on land and a Corn Palace.

Nearly a dozen railroads stopped at Sioux City, which housed the third largest stockyards in the country (after Chicago and Kansas City). Sometime after 1900, I was told, the Sioux City residents with noses that pointed skyward complained about the stench. As I heard it, the mayor commissioned a big sign near the stockyard's manure pile. It said, "THE SWEET SMELL OF SUCCESS."

(Not discussed in these essays are the thriving Kroloffs who moved from Sioux City to Arizona, primarily for health reasons… or the many family members in Council Bluffs, Iowa and across the river in Omaha, Nebraska. Although many were Krolevetsky's in Europe, they had other last names in the USA, like Pill, Richards, or Davidson.). Many moved to southern California.

PRE-WWI

The farmland for miles around was highly fertile. Until the railroads whistled into and through Sioux City, local farmers did not have a year-round way to ship products to the world (river ice!).

Sioux City was also the center of business, banking, bartering, bars, brawls and boasting. By mid-1891, it had an elevated railroad, only the third to be built in the US (after Boston and New York City) and before Chicago's "L" was running.

The importance of the railroads to our Midwestern ancestors can't be overestimated. They were how the family arrived, whether from the East Coast or down from Canada.

A few years after the "ribbons of steel" hit Sioux City, one local meatpacker was selling as much as $1.25 million in meat products headed to Liverpool and London, England. Might that Iowa meat have been a factor in the travel to Sioux City by four children of a kosher butcher who fled from Ukraine to Liverpool named Helfet?

In the 1890s, there were cable street cars like in San Francisco, plus electric powered street cars, a Grand Opera House, scores of active businesses, and a spreading web of modern utilities like phones, a sewage system, running water, and public schools (very important for the Americanization of immigrants). Photo is of Central High School, built in 1883, where our relatives studied. It offered a strong classical education. My dad pretty much shamed me into taking Latin, which turned out to be a good idea. Fortunately for me, he didn't take a lot of math in high school. I don't do math. Post card: https://rememberingletters.wordpress.com/2012/01/01/the-castle-on-the-hill/

In the 1880s growth years, the city fathers expected and planned for a city of 250,000 people. One local construction company bragged it had made 14 million bricks in a ten-month period.

There were a few wooden sidewalks and partially wood-plank streets, but the sewage was still in the streets or running downhill in trenches that sometimes choked up before dumping their loads into the river.

So, the wayfaring Europeans arrived and took on sometimes brutal jobs. For the rural immigrants from all across Europe, their introduction to Sioux City might have been their first long-term experience with a money economy, not a barter economy. Bank checks were new to them.

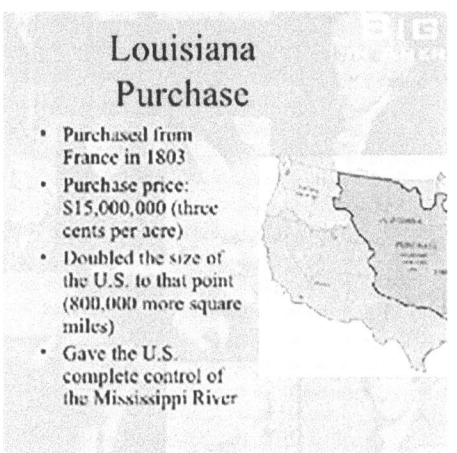

Money was a stem cell from which Sioux City grew.

In 1803, the US paid bargain-basement prices for much of the land between the Mississippi River and the Rocky Mountains, including the site where Sioux City would be built.

Into what we today might consider minor but pesky spats between the Native American tribes, in 1804 arrived the Lewis and Clark "Corps of Discovery" expedition. They tied up their boats and camped near today's Sioux City. There Sgt. Floyd died.

The Corps was an Army group that had been ordered to chart the great unknown of the Louisiana Purchase and report back to President Thomas Jefferson what the country had acquired. Jefferson especially wanted to know if there was a water route to the Pacific Ocean. There wasn't and still isn't. Maps and background: https://www.sutori.com/en/story/an-expanding-nation-timeline--2WahzdbkGPAGV3CBmqqtgZH2

Lewis and Clark had to negotiate with about a dozen tribes on their adventure to the Pacific and back. Some were friendly, some fierce. Cooperation with the Native Americans may have been the most important aspect of the successful trek.

Several fur trappers, mostly beavers, and traders in manufactured goods, like guns, had been in the Sioux City area, but it wasn't until about 1848, that anyone of European descent set up a permanent camp there. As might be expected, the first person was a fur trader who lived among the Indians. He had two Native American wives (supposedly sisters). Teepees of their relatives dotted his land, including one housing his father-in-law, a prominent tribal chief. By 1854, a town of about 400 people had been incorporated as Sioux City.

It was a rough and tumble town that grew larger as the trade with the Dakotas and Minnesota blossomed. That would be the states and the tribes by those names.

There was sporadic military action in the vicinity because of the years-long Indian Wars. If the Indians did not give up peaceably, US government policy was to drive them from their property to areas west of the Mississippi River and then west of the Missouri River. Eventually, there would be tribal reservations north, south and west of Sioux City.

What became Sioux City was an area frequented by Sioux tribes who met to plan raids to take out the trespassers. Later, US Army troops who had been stationed in Sioux City to protect the newcomers went on the attack.

During the American Civil War of the 1860s, the US Army was fighting the Sioux tribes, and for a while, Sioux City was an army headquarters. In one 1864 campaign, the troops marched north along the river, accompanied by two steamboats with supplies. Thus, Sioux City businesses had a ready customer in the US Army. And the city needed employees to serve the troops and more employees to serve the people serving the troops.

Years before the rails came to Sioux City, stage coaches were not a rare sight, nor were wagons full of crops or other "goods" and steamboats that had docked at the river's edge. A few steamboats were built there, too.

Like many a port town, it had its "genteel" element and people in the "Bottoms" near the riverfront who not only were low geographically but also were considered the lowest level of society. Rough people, evil people doing evil things to each other, it was said. When the railroads came to Sioux City in the late 1860s, and fewer steamboats arrived, the bottoms remained somewhat raucous. Picture shows Sioux City saloons about 1885 when our family was beginning to arrive.

Sometime after 1920, Helen Kroloff Levin and her family operated a general store about 30 miles south of Sioux City in Rosalie, Nebraska. It was on the Omaha tribe's reservation and very close to the Winnebago reservation. The Winnebago, whom tribal historian Lee Sultzman claims were tossed around like a "piece of unwanted luggage," was squished into the Omaha reservation, and the two had enough serious issues that the land ceded to them finally was divided into two reservations, one for each tribe. Another large group of the "unwanted luggage" (many from the Winnebago tribe) was contained in a Wisconsin reservation land hundreds of miles away. Inside the Levins' general store, its clientele must have had some interesting encounters.

In terms of the Kroloffs, Kauffmans, Herzoffs, Robinows and myriad other cousins, Sioux City, Iowa, in the late 1800s and early 1900s was a "destination." It is not clear who came first, but word obviously spread that the town was a reasonably good place to work and live.

Certainly, settling in a frontier town was more appealing than being in a back-tier community in feudal Russia. So they came and, for the most part, stayed for a relatively long time because they were optimistic about their future there. Then some left in bad times, some came back … and some found "greener" pastures in Chicago, Arizona and California.

It took over ten years for Sioux City to fully recover from the 1893 Panic, which helps explain why, in 1905, several Dobrofskys, Kroloffs, and Helfets had gone to Chicago as a group to seek jobs or start a business.

RIDING THE RAILS WEST

In the 1940s, when the equally young Chuck Kroloff and I visited relatives in Sioux City, occasionally, we were downwind from the stockyards. It was mostly filled with cattle and pigs waiting to be killed, sliced and diced and repackaged as protein and fat to feed the masses. The smell was about as intense as being back in our hometown of Chicago, which had much bigger "yards."

Chicago's stockyards had wrestled the title of "Hog Butcher for the World" from Cincinnati during the not so Civil War Between The States because of its expanding web of railroad tracks.

Sioux City's stockyards opened over a generation later in 1887. By 1973, it was the largest stockyard in the world, based on salable receipts, according to The Sioux City Journal newspaper. That was two years after the previously bigger stockyards in Chicago closed. A monotonous, almost unending chain of railroad cattle cars brought millions of sheep, steers, cows and pigs to the stockyards.

Once Sioux City obtained its rails in 1868 and a stockyard 20 years later, it could begin to work on its booster's dream to grow up and be the "Little Chicago." Photos show a group of pre-TV people, like sister Susan, my folks and I, at the Devon Ave., railroad crossing, a couple miles west of where we lived. We/they were waiting to see and wave at The Hiawatha headed for Sioux City. Also, the Chicago Union Station was a cathedral for railroading. https://chuckmanchicagonostalgia.wordpress.com/2010/12/07/photo-chicago-train-hiawatha-crowd-gathered-to-see-the-train-pass-outside-the-city-lines-ofc-parked-cars-c1940/ and Union Staton https://www.facebook.com/ZachTaylorDavis/posts/2457570244262391/
Train tracks were the sinews that held America together.

The railroad's most important days occurred in 1862. Abraham Lincoln and Congress were deep into the Civil War and trying to reunite the North with the "rebellious" Southerners. Unlike the dysfunctional Washington, DC of the early 21st Century, the not-quite-as-dysfunctional Washington of that year could do more than one thing at a time.

In about six productive weeks, Congress passed, and President Lincoln signed into law, bills that made it possible to construct the railroads that would irrevocably bind the states east of the Mississippi River with those to the west … all the way to the Pacific Ocean.

Without the railroads (and the roads and telegraph lines they attracted), the chances of some or all of the Western states sticking together and joining the United States of Western America were high. Maybe the country would have been called the Disunited States of America (DSA).

Historically, the railroads were big. Probably bigger was the means used to finance the building of the railroads and populating the lands between the Mighty Mississippi and "Big Muddy," which was a nickname for the Missouri River, America's longest river.

The railroads (after much wheeling and dealing and bribes and who knows what else) received the rights to much of the public land surrounding where the tracks would be laid. The sale of that land actually helped finance the laying of the rails all the way to the West Coast. Of course, the earlier owners, Native Americans, strongly disagreed and fought bitter battles that they eventually lost. The practice of selling land to finance transportation, like canals, was already well known.

State and local governments also sold some land to investors, farmers and whomever would buy it. Towns were created and promoted by the railroads around places where there was coal, wood, or water for the engines. The homes, businesses, and farms on those properties provided new people, produce and products to haul to new markets.

While the use of land grants was not new, the brilliant addition to the mix was that Congress also made such a huge amount of public land around the railroads available for sale. The proceeds of those land grant sales went to finance state colleges, which assured that women and men could get higher education at a reasonable price. Eventually, some of that money was made available for what became a few traditionally black colleges.

Arguably, land grant colleges/universities have been the brightest stars in the universe of America's higher education. They made higher education possible for the young and poor, unlike other nations.

Typically, "railroads established stations about every 20 miles in the Midwest and West so that farmers could bring their crops or cattle to the depot within a one-day wagon ride," according to railroad historian Rudy Daniels. The depots, in effect, were seeds planted by the railroads. As noted above, towns grew up around most of them. It was an interesting business strategy, the side-effect was an expanding economy that, like a train, sometimes went fast, sometimes slowed and stalled before it could build up a "head" of steam.

Of course, there was "wheeling and dealing" over where the railroad tracks would be placed. Some of the deals were made in the daylight, some were in the shade, and others in the smoke filled dark behind closed doors.

BACK TO THE WHITE CITY

The Corn Palace period ended because Sioux City didn't have the cold, hard cash to clean up from a flood and build another palace. Its glory was frozen in the past as yet another financial Panic enveloped a cooling economy. The elevated railway had fallen on hard times.

Meanwhile, the fabled Chicago "L" elevated trains, streetcars, railroads from far and wide and boats brought millions of people and many more millions of dollars to The White City, as the 1893 World's Columbian Exposition was called. Sioux City had been content to invite America to see its Palaces. Chicago invited the world. This was in the face of a worldwide economic panic.

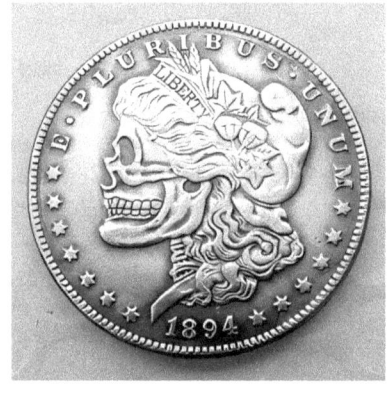

The industrial, agricultural, and increasingly electrical revolutions were transforming America. Arguably, the American way of life was not built on a rural farm base but on finance, factories and urban centers ... the so called "Incorporation of America."

Thus, there was a noticeable shift of social control from the people and government to big business. America became the prototypical consumer society. The incredible growth of corporations led to further cyclical financial instabilities and then boomed. It seemed that everybody, everywhere, was chasing the Almighty Dollar. But, not all dollars were equal. The skeleton fake dollar is still being sold all over the Internet.

Recessions like the devastating one of 1893, the violent Homestead and Pullman labor strikes and others that soon followed accentuated the widespread unemployment and homelessness that plagued the early years of the decade. The frontier was filling up, immigration, technological advances, and railroads had reshaped the country's face, and suddenly, Americans were at once confused, excited, and overwhelmed.

It has been argued that Chicago was America's most important city between 1880 and 1920. Or, at least, a well deserved Second City. But, in 1893, it was the focal point.

About 27 million people visited the fair or a quarter of the USA's population. In theory, Chicago's Exposition was a celebration of the 400th anniversary of Columbus' voyage to the New World and the rebuilding after the Great Chicago Fire. It was more about the future than the past. Where 46 men hammered for a few weeks to build one of Sioux City's Corn Palaces, over 40,000 workers built the lagoon and over 200 temporary buildings at the Chicago World's Fair. The 14 main buildings covered a total floor space of 63 million square feet.

It looks like the on-site railroad station (pictured above) could handle at least 20 trains at a time. Many arrived by public transportation and by boats that off-loaded at piers on the Lake Michigan side of the Fair. The picture is a ship of The World's Fair Steamboat Co.

The nearly one square mile Fair helped to craft the modern world. It was where manufacturers promoted products, where states and provinces competed for new residents and new investments, where urban spaces were organized into shimmering utopian cities, and where people from all social classes went to be alternately amused, instructed, and diverted from more pressing concerns.

The Columbian Exposition attempted to redefine America for itself and the world, and in doing so, introduced themes and artifacts still in American life: the connection between technology and progress, the predominance of corporations and the professional class in the power structure of the country; the triumph of the consumer culture, as well as the more pedestrian legacy of Juicy Fruit Gum, Pabst Blue Ribbon beer, ragtime music, and Quaker Oats.

The exhibition's influence on architecture is seen on the Mall in Washington, DC. Both were projected and headed by Daniel Hudson Burnham, who famously said, "Make no little plans. They have no magic to stir men's blood." It is my all-time favorite quote.

The White City was the prototype for what Burnham and his colleagues thought a city should be. It included carnival rides. Among them was the original Ferris Wheel, built by George Ferris. The structure towered 264 feet high and had 36 cars, each of which could accommodate 60 people, 2160 at a time.

The Midway entertainment area was the prototype for today's amusement parks and the birthplace of a uniquely American carnival industry. Today, it houses the U of Chicago, a huge museum, and neighbors like the Obamas.

Although denied a spot at the fair, Buffalo Bill Cody decided to come to Chicago anyway, setting up his popular Wild West show just outside the edge of the exposition. Historian Frederick Jackson Turner gave academic lectures reflecting on the end of the frontier that Buffalo Bill represented.

One reason Chicago could pull off such a dramatic and influential extravaganza is that financial heavyweights in New York invested huge amounts of money. The White City was a clear illustration of how business was already running in America. The Fair was a success, and investors made a profit.

 Inside the Iowa building, the exhibition hall's walls, pillars and ceiling were covered with colorful scenes and designs made of the seeds, grains, grasses, corn shucks and kernels of Iowa. There were 1,200 bushels of corn and three-and-a-half carloads of  other Iowa-grown products. At the center was a scale model of the state capitol. Illustrations are of Iowa building from inside and outside.

Interestingly, Iowa considered itself, just as Sioux City did with its Corn Palaces, a feeder first and a manufacturer second. Essentially, Iowa sold, sent, and fed its raw products into the manufacturing and processing colossus of Chicago (and, to a lesser extent, Omaha). In return, it bought "value added" products from the cities like clothes, tools and other goods not produced locally.

The Corn Palaces and the World's Columbian Exposition were examples of the self promotion or boosterism that Chicago and Sioux City used to become richer and encouraged immigrants to come, stay and, hopefully, prosper.

The last two decades of the 19th Century significantly helped shape what we are today. I guess, in an odd way the Fair must have infuenced me. It wasn't until researching for this book that I discoverd my parents were living across the street from the southern boundary of the Fair when I was born.

WHAT MARY SAW

Above is The Midway Plaisance of the 1893 World's Columbian Exposition that now is the home of the University of Chicago.

This mile-long spur off the main exposition site had, novelty acts, scientific and technological oddities, rides, food, and sideshows. From that point on, "Midway" was the generic term for the part of any American fair containing the rides and sideshows."

The following is courtesy of The History Channel from the post, https://www.history.com/authors/barbara-maranzani?page=12

Seven Things You May Not Know About the 1893 Chicago World's Fair. By Barbara Maranzani

On May 1, 1893, the gates opened at the World's Columbian Exposition, also known as the Chicago World's Fair. Over the next six months, more than 26 million visitors would flock to the 600-acre fairgrounds and 200-plus buildings full of art, food, entertainment and technological gadgets. The fair, ostensibly meant to celebrate the 400th anniversary of Christopher Columbus' first voyage to the New World, served as a showcase for a fully rebuilt and vibrant Chicago, just two decades removed from its devastating fire. On the 120th anniversary of its opening day, here are seven facts you may not know about 1893 Chicago World's Fair

1. Chicago had to beat out a number of other cities to get the fair.

In the late 1880s, Chicago, St. Louis, New York and Washington, D.C. all submitted bids to host the 1893 fair, but the race was soon narrowed to New York and Chicago. Big Apple financial titans including Cornelius Vanderbilt, William Waldorf Astor and J. P. Morgan pledged to raise $15 million to cover the city's expenses, with Chicago's mercantile and meatpacking millionaires Marshall Field, Philip Armour and Gustavus Swift following suit. But when Lyman Gage, president of one of the largest banks in the Midwest, arranged for millions more in financing, momentum swung Chicago's way and the U.S. Congress, which was in charge of the selection, awarded the city the exposition.

2. The fair produced a number of firsts.

Among the well-loved commercial products that made their debut at the Chicago World's Fair were Cream of Wheat, Juicy Fruit gum and Pabst Blue Ribbon beer. Technological products that would soon find their way into homes nationwide, such as the dishwasher and fluorescent light bulbs, had early prototype versions on display in Chicago as well. The U.S. government also got in on the act, issuing the country's first postcards and commemorative stamps and two new commemorative coins: a quarter and half dollar. The half dollar featured Christopher Columbus, in whose honor the fair had been staged, while the quarter depicted Queen Isabella of Spain, who had funded Columbus' voyages—making it the first U.S. coin to honor a woman.

3. A Ferris wheel saved the fair from financial ruin.

Despite the money raised by private investors and the U.S. government (through the sale of the commemorative coins and stamps), squabbling amongst the organizers and numerous construction delays resulted in a huge budget deficit. Another costly mistake was the refusal to allow showman William "Buffalo Bill" Cody and his troupe of sharpshooters, cowboys and Native American performers to appear at the fair. A disgruntled Cody brought his Wild West extravaganza to Chicago anyway, setting up shop right outside the fairgrounds and siphoning off visitors. The fair's precarious finances received a boost in June 1893 with the long-awaited debut of a new invention from Pittsburgh-based bridge builder and steel magnate George Washington Gale Ferris Jr. intended to rival the highlight of the 1889 fair in Paris (the Eiffel Tower), Ferris' 264-foot-tall wheel was an engineering marvel. It could fit 2,160 people at a time, and cost 50 cents to ride—twice the price of a ticket to the fair itself. The world's first Ferris wheel proved so popular it was moved to Chicago's North Side, where it remained in operation for 10 years before it was sold to the organizers of the 1904 World's Fair in St. Louis, Missouri.

4. It was the first exposition to have national pavilions.

Nearly 50 foreign countries and 43 states and territories were represented in Chicago. American pavilions touted the country's diverse history, food and culture with exhibits like Virginia's replica of George Washington's Mount Vernon estate, a century-old palm tree from

California, a massive stained glass display by Louis Comfort Tiffany and a full-service Creole restaurant from Louisiana. Philadelphia even sent the Liberty Bell, as well as two replicas: one made of rolled oats and one made of oranges. Not to be outdone, Norway sailed a full-sized replica of a Viking ship across the ocean for the fair, and German industrial giant Krupp spent the equivalent of more than $25 million in today's money to mount a massive artillery display including a number of weapons that would later be used in World War I.

5. Chicago was home to both a serial killer and a political assassin during the fair.

Unbeknownst to festival-goers, there was a mass murderer in their midst. For several years before and during the exposition, Dr. Henry Howard Holmes was busily luring victims (including a number of fairgoers) to a three-story, block-long building called the "Castle," where they were tortured, mutilated and killed. Although H. H. Holmes' heinous crimes weren't discovered until after the fair ended, it's believed that he was responsible for dozens of deaths in Chicago. It was another murder, however, that made headlines during the fair. On October 28, just two days before the exposition was set to close, Chicago's recently reelected mayor, Carter Harrison Sr., was shot and killed by a disgruntled—and deranged—office seeker, Patrick Eugene Prendergast, who believed he was owed a political appointment by the mayor. With the city in shock, the fair's organizers quickly decided to cancel the lavish closing ceremony in favor of a public memorial to the city's popular slain leader. See book and movie The Devil in the White City.

6. The Prendergast case was the first murder trial for famed lawyer Clarence Darrow.

Darrow, who defended Prendergast, would go on to build a career as one of the nation's preeminent criminal lawyers, representing murderers Leopold and Loeb and famously sparring with William Jennings Bryan while acting as defense attorney in the Scopes Monkey Trial. He wasn't so lucky in the Prendergast case, however, unsuccessfully arguing that his client should be declared mentally unfit to stand trial. After his insanity defense failed, Prendergast was hanged on July 14, 1894. It was the only murder case in Darrow's career to end in his client's execution. (Darrow figured prominently in the union vs. business trials that dramatically affected life and work in Hazleton, PA, where wife Susan's dad, John Gordick, grew up.

7. The Chicago World's Fair played a key role in the creation of the City Beautiful movement.

At the core of the fair was an area that quickly became known as the White City for its buildings with white stucco siding and its streets illuminated by electric lights. Buildings and monuments by Charles McKim, Daniel Burnham, Augusts Saint-Gaudens and Richard Morris Hunt and lush landscaping by Frederick Law Olmsted, the designer of New York's Central Park, left a lasting impression on municipal planners looking for a way to bring open spaces and grand public buildings into crowded cities. Chicago itself was one of the first cities to adopt aspects of the new City Beautiful movement. Dozens of other cities across the country followed its lead, most notably Washington, D.C., where by 1902 plans were in place for a redesign of the city center that would result in the creation of the National Mall and its surrounding monuments.

In theory, the fair commemorated Christopher Columbus. At that time, not much was written about the Jews being expelled from Spain in 1492, that Columbus and the royal couple funding his voyage had Jewish blood coursing through their own veins, as did those of key crew members. Or that one rationale for Columbus' voyage was to find places with wealth that could be plundered to help the Spanish mount a new Crusade to recapture Jerusalem from Muslims. - A comment by George Kroloff

Photo:
https://commons.wikimedia.org/wiki/File:Aerial_view_of_National_Mall_15847v.jpg

ANOTHER QUICK RECAP

As the 19th Century hurtled into the 20th, Russian "authorities" were on the lookout for about a dozen young draft dodgers with names that sounded like Krulevitsky. They had lived in or near Kapulia, in The Pale of Settlements.

For several of the peak emigration years, any young, relatively healthy Jewish kid could be inducted into the Russian Army for as much as a 25-year term. Based on what they heard, the teens and pre-teens didn't expect to live through the experience. Their parents thought they would never see them again. It was brutal. Draft quotas for each shtetl needed to be filled.

There were severe consequences for the families of those who escaped the dragnet, whether they were caught or not. Fines were stiff. Knowing their escape to America would be hard on their families must have weighed heavily on the Krulevitsky lads. Each boy who went missing usually had to be replaced by another young male. That could be a neighbor, brother, cousin, friend, whomever. In some places, raiding parties would kidnap youngsters from another village. The picture is of a shtetl home.

If the Tsar's police had searched near the shores of the Missouri River and its tributaries along the 200 miles from Sioux Falls, South Dakota, down through Sioux City, Iowa and further South to Omaha, Nebraska, they would have found the culprits, and many of their cousins or friends on the lam from Kapulia, Slutzk and Hlusk, Hresk, Hrozova, Snov, Liuban, Pohost, Romanove, Starobin, Timkovitz, Uretche, Verkhutin, and Vizne.

Sioux City, which housed quite a few of them, was a very different, chest-thumping, optimistic kind of community than Old World Kapulia. Its 1889 population was over 30,000, certainly much more than Kapulia's estimated 4,450.

Unlike the immigrants' hometowns, citizens in Sioux City were looking towards a bright future. For example, Sioux City was the birthplace of the Corn Palace, a temporary building built with a different design each year as part of the local Corn Festival. Of course, the walls were covered with corn cobs. The first was built and taken down in 1887. Picture is from https://www.siouxcitymuseum.org/history-website/1889-corn-palace The website contains volumes of information about the Corn Palaces and the community's history.

The concept must have been interesting, maybe bewildering, to the newly arrived greenhorns.

The Corn Palaces became larger and grander every year. The last Sioux City Corn Palace was built in 1891. It sprawled across the city's largest downtown avenue and was about a block wide on either side. That palace had three towers, one stretched about 20 stories high. It also had a large tunnel, which allowed traffic to pass beneath its center.

Downtown Sioux City also had a permanent seven-story office building, undoubtedly higher than anything the relatives in and around Kapulia ever saw while growing up.

The palaces became world famous. See essay on Boosterism Sioux City-and-Chicago.

Before the Krulevitsky cousins went missing, they lived in a mere sliver of the Russian Empire about 55 miles southwest of Minsk. Their homes had been in, or near, a town they all called Kapulia. (Today, Kopyl is south of the K in MINSK). Evading the draft was only one reason for them screwing up their courage and leaving. Pale map at: https://www.jewishvirtuallibrary.org/the-pale-of-settlement

The life they fled was about as rustic as it would have been about the year 900, a thousand years earlier.

While Kapulia was 5000 miles from Sioux City, Iowa, in the 19th Century, it was also 1000 years away. The community, for the most part, was just emerging from the Middle Ages.

The Krulevitskys and their relatives grew up in that part of western Russia known as The Pale of Settlements. (Pale means "border.") Though its size varied over several decades, The Pale was well over 400,000 square miles and, by the 1880s, encompassed much of what later was called Eastern Europe. The Kruelvitskys lived in Byelorussia, which now is the country of Belarus, just north of Ukraine. (Curiously, for a few weeks in the 1990s, the Belarus ambassador to the US was a client of mine. It was a very bizarre experience, to be explained if I ever get around to it.)

Nearly five million Jews were in The Pale, according to the 1897 Russian census. They made up about 12 percent of the total population. Although about two million of them emigrated, mostly to the USA, a population explosion created more new souls than those who left. (Population figures presented herein from various sources are elastic.) Pale map at: https://www.jewishvirtuallibrary.org/the-pale-of-settlement This website has a huge library of essays about the Jewish experience over the centuries.

Please read the captions on the map. About 1880, when some of our relatives were making plans to flee, Russia was moving well over a million Jews into The Pale and was shuffling hundreds of thousands from rural to urban areas and still others from urban to rural. Family legends tend to discard all the moving around before emigrating. Most written records were destroyed in wars and The Holocaust.

Jews were political prisoners of a sort because it was very difficult for most of them to move from one place to another on their own unless the government wanted them to move. The map above shows only some of the forced relocations into The Pale.

There was a bushel basket full of reasons for creating The Pale. High among them was the longstanding European effort to keep Jews away from the rest of the population, especially citizens who might compete with them ... thus limiting the kinds of work Jews could do.

Most of the Tsars wanted Russia to be even more European than the French, who started the Inquisition in the 12th century when the Catholic church was worried about heresy within its ranks. Europe, since well before the Spanish Inquisition, had persecuted Jews and sought conversion to Catholicism. When the Tsars got themselves whipped up, it was conversion to their form of Russian Orthodoxy from traditional Judaism. Artwork left, painted 1878: This picture is on the cover of a book written centuries ago about Judah Halevi https://www.barnesandnoble.com/w/the-book-of-kuzari-judah-hallevi/1103757898 The Kuzari takes place during a conversion of some Khazar nobility to Judaism, as conflict was increasing between the Muslims in the south of Spain and the Christians in the north, with the line moving back and forth.

As the Christians advanced, Jewish communities came under pressure to convert in order to survive. Judah Hallevi ended up in Christian Toledo in his later life, and The Book of

Kuzazri is a product of that period: a defense of the Jewish religion and people, with a unique philosophical underpinning based on Hallevi's studies and views.

Like their successors, Joseph Stalin and Vladimir Putin, the Tsars expanded into Europe and built a buffer zone to protect their homeland from invading armies.

The 1897 census showed 4,463 people in Kapulia, of which 2,671 were Jews. Nearby, some cousins lived in Starobin, which had 2,315 (1,494 were Jews) and Timkovitsh 2,393 (1,523 were Jews). All told, about 60 percent of the people in the Kapulia area were Jews. In small towns (shtetls), there were ethnic neighborhoods but not real ghettos. In cities, ghettos might be surrounded by walls.

My wild guess is that a quarter of the Jewish residents of The Pale were relatively new arrivals who had been expelled from communities from the territory controlled by the Tsar. Many were young. Like most poor areas of Europe, births were increasing, and deaths were decreasing.

The DNA of Kroloffs, Herzoffs, Leviches, Robinows, Pills, Davidsons, and hundreds of other USA cousins twists directly back to Kapulia and several other nearby towns. It is possible they were not more than one or two generations away from somewhere else. Where? Why were they in this small village? How did they get there?

THE SIMMONS, THE SOUTH, AND US HISTORY 1608 - 1945

First, there were the American colonies, followed by several wars, including the Civil War. Fifty years later, my dear wife Susan's grandparents were in a depressed little town called Blue Mountain, Mississippi. Even today, some people refer to the burg as BM. There never was a time when the town had as many as 1000 residents. That's where her birth father, Robert (Bob) Bernard Simmons, was born in 1914.

Bob died 32 years later in an accident the very same day he was released from active duty in the Navy. At that time, Susan was seven years old. The family lived about 60 miles west of Los Angeles in San Bernardino.

We know that Susan's mother, Edith Miriam Marks Simmons (later Gordick), had a strong Boston accent. Her husband Bob probably had at least a touch of a southern drawl since all of his closest family came from the Deep South, mostly near the northeast corner of the state of Mississippi, which borders Alabama and Tennessee. Listening to Bob and Edith's dueling accents probably would have been of interest to older children. But, neither Susan nor her brother Robert M. remembers their birth father's voice nor much about him.

Accents are superficial evidence of a place where the speaker was born or lived. They arise out of the culture of that place. The cultures of people and places where a person grows up tend to unconsciously shape the way people make decisions throughout their entire lives. Neither Susan, brother Bob, nor other members of our family talked about Robert L. Simmons, which is why he is such an interesting subject for "WHY DID OUR FAMILIES DO THAT?"

This essay also looks at the people and history that enveloped them and shaped the decisions they made that affect us today. History caused Robert L. Simmons to be born in Blue Mountain, Mississippi, to be in the US Navy, to be in the port of Boston where he met his future wife Edith Marks, and for their two children to be born in Southern California just before the Second World War.

Before his tragic death, their father was a presence, but not always around most of Susan and Brother Bob's young lives. Either he was away in the Navy or working as a policeman in San Bernardino during their waking hours. Or he would be asleep during the daytime if he worked nights.

The repercussions of the accident that killed Robert left Edith broken hearted and cut off from her family 3000 miles away. As was written in early English literature, "ere long," Edith married John Calvin Gordick, who adopted Susan and Robert M. In fact and practice, he was their father. The Simmons family completely faded from their family culture.

This essay is a look at a large slice of American history more or less through the eyes of the Simmons family. One of the very first British settlers on soil, which eventually became the United States of America, was a man named William Simmons, who arrived in Virginia well before the Pilgrims landed in Plymouth, Massachusetts. He probably was an indentured servant. After viewing numerous family trees, it looks like he was Susan's great, great, and a few more greats, grandfather.

This timeline is followed by the history and people behind the bullets.

- **300 million years ago,** a meteor, about the size of a football field, crashed into the newly formed Appalachian Mountains near the point where today, the Kentucky, Tennessee, and Virginia borders come together. That mountain gash is known as The Cumberland Gap.

- **1492** Spanish Inquisition.

- **1492** Columbus was the first European to curl toes in warm Caribbean island sand. Thinking he had found India, natives became known as "Indians."

- **1492** (clearly, it was a big year in Western history) The Columbian Exchange begins.

- **1607** Richard Simmons' was aboard one of the three ships that dropped anchor at Jamestown, Virginia. The passengers create North America's first British colony to survive a few years. Alas, Richard, promptly died.

- **1608** William Simmons, a laborer who must have been an indentured servant, arrives at Jamestown.

- **1600s and 1700s** Simmons and Mitchell families settled along the Atlantic Seaboard. Quite a few resided just west of today's Jamestown, Virginia.

- **1754** Brutal French and Indian War. Simmons soldiers first saw a Land of Milk and Honey west of Appalachian Mountains. Some were paid in "patents" or land grants in the "unsettled" area and eventually move west.

- **1776** Revolutionary War. More Mitchell-Simmons soldiers got land grants for service.

- **Around 1800** The Cumberland Gap's narrow Indian trail was widened to accommodate wagons. Family members moved west across the Appalachians. Several into Tennessee and Georgia, some near what became Tippah County, Mississippi.

- **1830s** Most Native Americans were forced out of Mississippi. Millions of acres were opened for settlement by whites and their slaves. More of Susan's ancestors moved in.

- **1860s,** Tippah County, was decimated by waves of Civil War battles. Nearby towns changed hands over 50 times. Great suffering. Tiny Blue Mountain (Susan's ancestral homesite) never really thrived.

- **1910** Lemuel B. Simmons married Susie/Suzie Mitchell in El Paso. (Why El Paso?) He was not the first Simmons to marry a Mitchell. The two continue west to Los Angeles and then to nearby towns where "Lem" worked as RR conductor.

- **1930s** Lem, Suzie, their sons William M and Robert B settled in San Bernardino, California, where Lem was a home builder.

- **1937-38** Robert B, in the US Navy, with his enlistment about completed, met Edith Marks while his ship was in Boston port. She moved to his home port, San Diego. They marry. The Simmons soon have two children, Susan L and Robert M. Once out of the Navy, Robert B, became a carpenter and then a policeman in his hometown, San Bernardino.

- **WWII 1945,** Robert B returned to active Navy duty.

- **1946** Robert B died in accident on way home after being released from Navy in Los Angeles.

- **1946** Edith marries John Calvin Gordick who adopts Susan L and Robert M. and was a strong presence in their lives.(**Note: Some relatives are identified by their middle initial to differentiate them from other family members with similar names.**)

UNMASKING A FAKE VOLDEMORT MAPPING A ROAD TO TIPPAH

Discovering a story about an American family that also is a family story about America.

We start where this essay ends. Southern California, 1946.

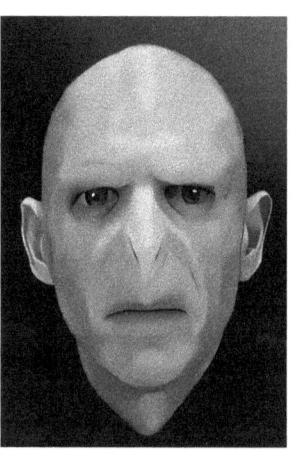

If you followed the Harry Potter books and movies, you should remember Lord Voldermort, the most evil character of all time. Voldemort was so powerful that people feared to speak his name. Thus, they referred to him as "He Who Cannot Be Named."

For the first 50 years of our marriage, I envisioned Susan's birth father as being someone like the elusive, dreaded, supremely ugly Voldemort. He just wasn't talked about. Susan's father and his family were non-existent.

I learned online that her birth father's full name was Robert Bernard Simmons. They called him, naturally, Bob.

And then facts and a few pictures began to appear. There was no evidence of him being evil; in fact, his military records depict him as a genuinely nice person. Pictures of him showed six-feet-two inches of happiness, a really good looking family guy. (Pictures are Robert B. and son Robert M, also Bob's dad Lemuel B and Susie Mitchell Simmons, from the Hill Family Tree.)

Bob Simmon's parents were from Tippah County, Mississippi. They were living in Southern California when Robert B was born. For an unexplained reason, Susan's grandmother was back in Blue Mountain, Tippah County, when Robert B was actually born. That was 1914, a half century after the northeastern Mississippi county was crushed by the Civil War. The year he was born and for a long time afterward, Blue Mountain did not have a single paved street or road.

Susan's grandmother was variously known as Suzie/Susie/Susan/Sue Mitchell Simmons. In 1920, she and Lemuel, a train conductor, lived in Riverside, California. Almost every adult male on their street also worked on the railroad, according to the census. William, the oldest son, was born in California. Robert B was born in Mississippi. Suzie obviously went back "home" for a while.

Fast forward to the early-1930s. Several people had written notes in support of teenage Robert B enlisting in the US Navy to learn a trade. They described him as a hardworking, decent individual. The trade he learned was how to be a "signalman," communicating by flags and searchlights between ships nearby. It was not much of an education for a future job, but the pay was steady.

In December of 1937, while Robert B's ship was docked in Boston, he met Edith Marks, a local girl, some of whose family had immigrated from Canada years earlier. They were Scotch and Irish. (An oft repeated family legend claims that some ancestors were Native Americans. A DNA check in 2017 did not find any Native Americans in the family. Nor has any evidence been found to verify a family myth, claiming President James Monroe was a relative. Apparently Edith's grandmother loved "spoofing" the younger ones.)

When they met, Edith was about to be 18 and Robert B about 22. In less than a year, she had moved to San Diego, the last port of call for his ship. They married.

He was at sea when my wife Susan was born in February 1939 in San Diego, probably at the navy base. Robert B was honorably discharged (That was before WWII when he again served in the Navy). Bob, Edith and baby Susan moved to San Bernardino, California, about 100 miles away. There, he first worked with his father, Lemuel B, and his older brother, William M, building houses. Susan's brother Robert M was born in 1940 in San Bernardino. (Photo; Bob, Edith, Susan)

Railroading was deeply rooted in the Simmons family, all the way back to Blue Mountain in Tippah County. It appears Lem worked for the Southern Pacific RR, and the family moved from LA to other cities along the line … including Riverside and San Bernardino.

William, Susan's uncle and Bob's brother, remains a mystery. He married a "Ruth" who, so far, has been impossible to trace online. William's main presence in history seems to be that he died in 1971 and was buried in a military cemetery because he had been in the Navy, like his brother.

Robert B, Susan's father, had attended school (through 12th grade) in San Bernardino.

Most of WWII, he was a San Bernardino policeman. Late in the war, he was re-inducted into the Navy. (Photo: Robert B in police uniform, Edith, Susan, Robert L.)

Not surprisingly, after Robert B was back in the Navy, Edith felt isolated in San Bernardino, with two youngsters and few friends, according to a diary in which she sporadically wrote. Her in-laws still lived there. Edith anxiously waited for Robert B's final return as a civilian on April 24, 1946.

Then tragedy.

By midday, as planned, Robert B was mustered out of the Navy in the Los Angeles area. He died in an accident on the way home to San Bernardino. It seems he tried to save some money … attempted to hop onto a freight train headed to San Bernadino … and missed. He died.

To Susan and her brother Bob, the events of April, May, June, and July 1946 remain a bit murky. Susan does remember the terrible Wednesday evening and the scene when policemen arrived to report her father's death.

Edith's later marriage to Army Air Corps Sergeant John Calvin Gordick lasted 30 years. (An early picture of them is at right.) He adopted Susan and her brother Robert M. Later, the family grew to include a brother, John, and sisters, Jody and Shelley Gordick.

The adventures of the core Robert Simmons/Gordick family (Susan, Robert M. and Edith) should be told in another essay. This essay is primarily about what happened during the 430 years before the sad incident in the Simmons' San Bernardino doorway. Susan's mother's family was from the area that became the United Kingdom. John Gordick, her adopted father, came from a central European family. See The Smart Elek?

Simmons ... picking up the trail

Susan and I have three adult children. Three adult grandkids. We are about three inches from being happily SuperGlued forever together at the hip. That's partially false news. We are donating our bodies to science and will be cadavers at a medical school.

From early in our relationship, it was clear that there was a mystery about Susan's past. She just didn't remember much about her birth father and his family. I was curious. Who were the Simmons? Who was her father? Why was he, whose family lived in Southern California, born in Blue Mountain, Tippah County, Mississippi? What did his voice sound like? Did he have a Southern accent?

This is my effort to fill in the blanks and conjure up a somewhat revisionist researched view of how the Simmons family influenced American history and, more importantly, how history influenced the family … including Susan, her siblings, their kids and our kids.

There were two American Simmons.

They were at Jamestown, VA. Richard, an original settler, arrived in 1607.

The Susan Constant, Godspeed and Discovery, had set sail from London on December 20, 1606, bound for the New World. The fleet reached the Virginia coast four months later, in late April of the next year. After two weeks of exploring the seacoast and inland waterways, the voyagers selected a site on May 13. It was at a point where marauding Spanish ships could not easily bombard the fort they would build. They were afraid of the Inquisition. (See painting, right.)

Richard died within four months of landing in Virginia. I found no evidence that he and Susan were related.

But William Simmons arrived in 1608, just a year later. He arrived on the first supply ship sent from London to the Jamestown settlement. The ship's record claims he was a laborer. That probably means he was an indentured servant.

After hours of examining family trees online, William, the Jamestown laborer, is the most likely candidate for planting the first American root from wife Susan Lee Simmons Gordick's family tree.

He probably worked out his indenture, which was a contract to be a slave for several years and then be freed.

One of the misplaced facts about the American colonies is that up to about 1800, most of the white British colonists arrived as indentured servants like William. Thousands were petty criminals whom the British wanted to clean out of their filthy prisons (called gaols).

Some were children picked up on the streets and delivered to ship captains who would sell them in America. (Thus, the term kidnapping.) Like many black slaves, indentured servants were not allowed to marry and could be bought and sold. Unlike black slaves, the white indentures knew that if they could keep themselves alive at a certain date in a few years, they would be freed.

Within a generation or two of William's arrival, there were several Simmons living in Virginia just west of Jamestown.

It wasn't until about 175 years after the first Southern Simmons arrived that they were able to move west over the Appalachian Mountains to Tennessee and Kentucky and then down to Mississippi. Geography and global geopolitics, hostile Native Americans and crafty bandits kept them close to the Atlantic Coast.

THE TREK TO TIPPAH BEGAN WITH, AND WAS PUSHED ALONG BY, THE COLUMBIAN EXCHANGE

Tippah County (yellow), in fact, the whole Mississippi Territory, was as alien to the early British settlers as Lesotho in Africa is to most white Americans today.

A short horseback ride from Blue Mountain, where Susan's birth father was born, is the tiny town named Mitchell. Simmons' and Mitchell's families still lived in the area late into the 20th century. Probably still do.

Susan's ancestors from Mississippi and Massachusetts were involved in the French and Indian Wars and the Revolutionary War. As soldiers, they first saw some of the lush, fertile land west of the Appalachian mountains. Later, they would fight with and against each other in the Civil War, when some died of disease in prisons and hospitals. They may even have fought each other in Tippah County around Blue Mountain.

Germs, groceries, gold, gems, globalization

First germs. Unwittingly, Christopher Columbus started the Columbian Exchange in 1492. He brought germs to the Americas. Well, he did not return to Spain with gems, although he did bring a few germs Europeans didn't know of. But it was the beginning of an "exchange" that changed much of civilization.

The Columbian exchange, in a very few years, brought to Europe, Asia, and Africa the American potatoes and corn so important to feed a rapidly growing world population. The Exchange eventually brought new kinds of cotton to protect humans' skins, as well as rum and tobacco to eat away the innards of billions of new users.

Germs were, arguably, the most important element in the history of the New World and the Simmons' trek to Tippah.

The islands Columbus visited in the Caribbean were outposts of an ancient, sophisticated and amazingly healthy network of civilizations. Using new techniques, historians have concluded that in 1492, the three Americas, North, Central, and South, as well as the Caribbean islands, could have been home to as many people as Asia. The indigenous Americans were isolated from Europe, Asia and Africa. They also were isolated from germs and diseases that other cultures had become immune to.

One of the biggest threats to the newly exposed Native American population was rats. The rodents escaped from European ships along with the vermin that lived on the rodents skins. They infected the nearby indigenous people, who, in turn, infected others of their tribes and distant tribes with whom they traded or fought.

Maybe the most deadly of all killers were pigs that Spanish and Portuguese explorers and conquerors brought with them for food. Many broke free and became feral. Ugly, oozing, gurgling pig pox jumped species to humans. The pox and other imported European diseases spread up and down the Atlantic and Pacific coasts and relentlessly worked their way inland. The gnats, rats, lice and other creepy-crawlies spread the pox, decimating entire villages along the Indigenous American's trade trails.

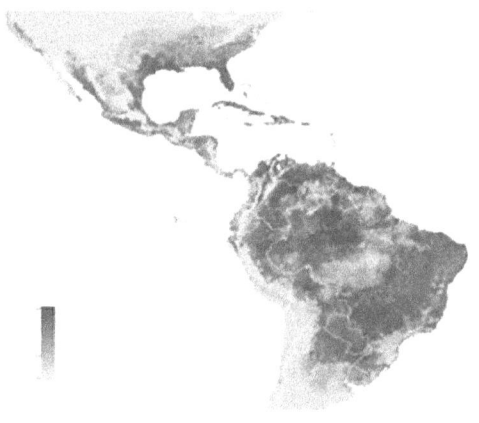

Germs help explain why a very small number of Europeans were able to conquer the American continents. Teeny-tiny microbes were much more lethal than swords or muskets. Scientists now estimate upwards of 80 million inhabitants of the Americas died of the pox and a few other European diseases. The pandemics took several generations to run their course, and the surviving Native Americans around Plymouth and Jamestown were still trying to figure out what hit them when the oddly clothed, bearded, inexperienced and often very hungry pale faced English settlers arrived.

Other diseases, especially Malaria and Yellow Fever spread by mosquitos, were huge killers of the white indentured servants who soon were working tobacco fields and later the rice paddies and cotton fields. (Mosquito zone map from old NYTimes)

The importation of African slaves who could survive in the mosquito zone (between Baltimore in North America and Buenos Aires in South America) had two causes. First, they were immune to some tropical diseases. Second, slaves were considered to be a cost-efficient way to obtain needed labor to produce and meet the expanding demand for North American agricultural products and the hoards of silver from South America.

The northern and southern extremes of the American Continents were relatively free of disease-bearing flying insects. In the Mosquito Zone, the bugs were major reasons for decisions affecting civil rights (or lack of them), business and battles. The pandemics that cut down so many of the indigenous Americans still bug world politics. And they dominated the Simmons' country.

(In the Revolutionary War, Malaria weakened the British soldiers south of Baltimore to the point that, at the end of the war, the King's generals reportedly couldn't find enough healthy men to fight. George Washington's success in the Revolutionary War was due, in large part, because he forced his troops to be inoculated against "the pox." Even as tobacco plants were sucking up the nutrients in the Seaboard soil, the fields continued to be fertile breeding grounds for the bugs that delivered the deadly germs to the local populations. Germs, not bullets, were the main killers of soldiers in the American Civil War and WWI, too.)

When the first Simmons settler (Richard) died a few months after arriving in Jamestown, it is likely that one or more diseases led to his demise. He was an investor, not an explorer, and like his compatriots, he had no clue how to survive in the alien environment of Virginia. There were just too many human, inhuman, and unhuman predators who didn't want their domain disturbed by outsiders with hairy faces.

Groceries. An academic explanation of the Columbian Exchange tends to read like this ... It was "The widespread transfer of plants, animals, culture, human populations, technology, and ideas between the Americas and the Old World in the 15th and 16th centuries."

The Columbian Exchange drove European colonization and trade after Christopher Columbus' 1492 voyage. Invasive species of flora and fauna and communicable diseases were a byproduct of the Exchange. But, without the corn and potatoes from the Americas, there likely would not have been the population explosion that occurred a couple hundred years later. Or the Potato Feast and then the Famine in Ireland.

Gold and gems. Gold is what the European kings wanted. There wasn't near enough to satisfy them in the Americas. For the Spanish, however, there was Silver. Lots of it, and Chinese warlords and traders were willing to pay or barter for it. Silver made Spain rich, most of it was dug out of deep mines near the west coast of South America by indigenous slaves.

Globalization. Trade in manufactured and agricultural products, humans (slaves), and gunpowder exploded after 1492. A snapshot of how globalization worked could have been taken when the Spanish hired Japanese samurai warriors to protect the caravans of mules and llamas, hundreds of thousands of them carrying silver to Pacific Ocean ports. Bandits were stealing the silver before it could reach the ships waiting to take the riches to China.

ON THE ROAD TO BLUE MOUNTAIN

The colonists, including Simmons, along the Atlantic really were stuck.

For Southern Simmons families and their neighbors, tobacco was initially the main cash crop. Addiction to the weed was growing in the Americas and, more importantly, Europe. It literally lit up the economy in the 1600s.

American lumber shipped across the Atlantic burned up in fireplaces and built up Europe. Back in America, European farming methods were used to grow tobacco and other crops. That form of agriculture was gobbling up the land's nutrients, making the soil unfit for farming. A few years later, cotton and rice became cash crops. As demand for the crops grew, there was a push to find new and fertile land. The vast area west of the Appalachians was a magnet pulling people like the Simmons.

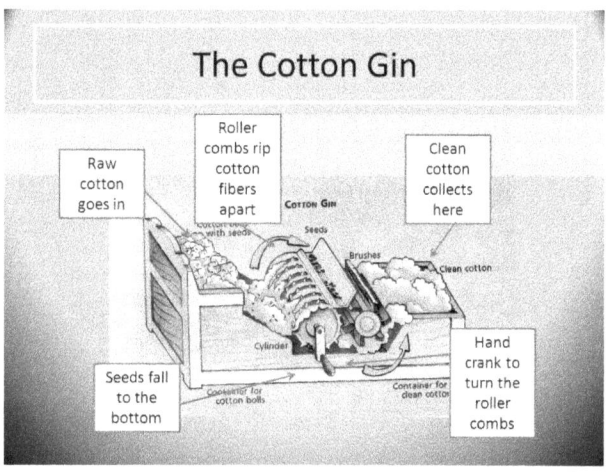

Then, in the 1790s, Eli Whitney invented the Cotton Gin (gin, as in engine). The machine greatly speeded the production of cotton by cleaning out the dirt, seeds, and other imperfections that were caught in the sticky cotton bolls (bunches of cotton growing on the plants, like big seeds). The market for American cotton sky-rocketed in the Northern states and Europe. As did the demand for slaves to work the fields and process the cotton.

England's economy was heavily invested in US cotton. The South grew it. The North processed it and shipped much of the cotton East to Europe. Cotton mills, which turned the cotton fibers into cloth, sprouted up along the Atlantic Coast, with many in North Carolina and New England. (Lowell, Mass. textile mills, undated etching.) Coincidentally, it was in Lowell that John and Edith Gordick settled after he retired from the military. By then, however, Susan was in nursing school in Chicago.

The approximately 1,750 largest plantation and slave holders were to the South, what the Robber Baron industrialists and investors were to the North. In Mississippi, "Cotton was King." The plantation super-slavers controlled just about everything, including governments. Just as the Robber Barons did in the North.

Much more about that in the essay about John Calvin Gordick's Pennsylvania family.

While I found records of one or two Mitchell families who probably were Susan's relatives owning as many as 20 slaves, one goal of poor Southerners was to own at least one slave. Thus, they could have someone under their control to look down upon … a slave was a status symbol.

But that gets us ahead of the story.

The Simmons were caught in a bind. As mentioned, several had fought in the French and Indian Wars on the western side of the Appalachians. In the Ohio River Valley, they had seen a new Promised Land.

As a reward for their service in the earlier wars and later in the Revolutionary War and the War of 1812 with the British, there are records of Simmons, along with thousands of others, receiving a piece of paper (a "patent" or land grant) entitling them to property in the west. They wanted to claim their land, but they couldn't get there. If you read about the use of land grants in building canals and railroads and the American education system in previous essays, you will see an interesting pattern. Governments and businesses used vast acreage of land Native Americans thought belonged to them to fuel America's Destiny.

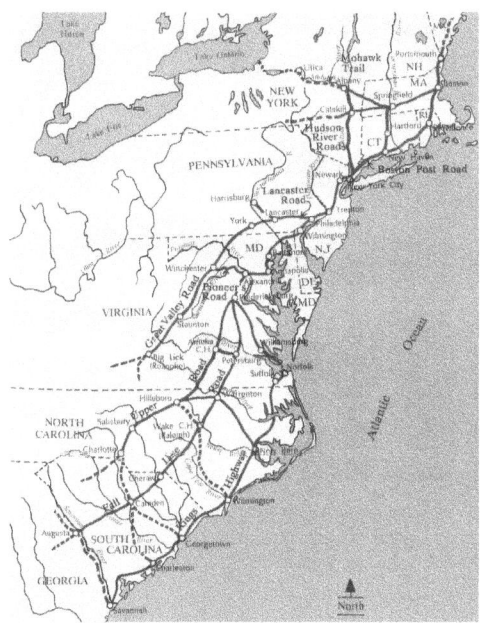

The big bumps in the roads. The Appalachian mountains are nowhere near as high as the far-off Rockies to the "real west." Although, most colonists probably hadn't heard much, if anything, about the giant Great Plains, the deserts, or the soaring peaks of the Rocky Mountains.

The Appalachians were uncrossable except by foot or horseback using Indian or animal pathways too narrow for a wagon. A favored means of travel was rivers, but rivers refuse to flow up over mountains or hills. The gravity of the situation was obvious.

Therefore, almost all migration in the Eastern American colonies was north/south, as the map of major trails and rivers shows. Map and more information from https://www.nettally.com/jameson1/williamjameson/,,RevwarForts-talk2a.pdf

The Appalachian mountain barrier wasn't breached until the late 1700s when a group that included the legendary frontiersman Daniel Boone, also a land speculator, was responsible for widening the narrow Cumberland Gap trail so that it could accommodate wagons.

Among the relatively few people who walked the Wilderness Trail, which led into the Cumberland Gap, were President Abraham Lincoln's parents. They settled in Kentucky, where Honest Abe was born in a one-room log cabin on Sinking Spring Farm near Hodgenville.

US EXPANSION GEOPOLITICAL BARRIERS.

There were the French to the north and west and the Spanish to the south.

In 1608, even as the British were establishing their first colony at Jamestown, the French were digging in at Quebec, Canada. They commanded the St. Lawrence River and started domination of the fur trade.

The centuries-long European battles between the French, English and Spanish washed over the North American shores. By the early 1700s, France and its allies, among several large Native American tribes, effectively blocked the British colonists, including the Simmons and Mitchells, from settling in the Ohio Valley.

A ring of French forts, settlements, churches and trading posts started in Quebec, ran down the St. Lawrence River, along the Great Lakes, and then further down the Mississippi to the Gulf of Mexico. There, they mixed it up with the Spanish, who off-and-on controlled New Orleans, the Gulf Coast and Florida.

Then, in 1754, something with huge unintended consequences happened. It was one of The French and Indian Wars.

Europeans looked at the North American wars as a part of a worldwide and bloody series of battles raging from Europe to Pacific islands like the Philippines to India, as well as the Americas. It is known as The Seven Years War. European kings just couldn't stop trying to flex their muscles (armies).

Susan's ancestors from New England to the Carolinas were in the thick of the skirmishes, mostly in colonial militias. They also became caught up in the movement that led to the American Revolution. (Painting is based on the French & Indian Wars.) It was not unusual for these citizen soldiers to be paid, not in money, but in grants for some land west of the Appalachians.

In 1753, a 21-year-old Virginian named George Washington led the Virginia Militia into battle. Washington had been appointed by a colonial governor with a great name … "Dinwiddie. "

Young George did not initially have a stellar performance. His troops suffered severe casualties, and Washington was forced to surrender. But he and others, including some Simmons, saw first-hand the brutality of the British military.

They saw the mean-spirited treatment by British officers of their own troops, the brutality of the British against the "lowly" colonials fighting alongside them, and cruelty against their Indian enemies, who they matched a-scalp-for-a-scalp and worse.

Another essay in this series is about the Helfet relatives half a world away in South Africa. It reports on similar brutality by the British in the Boer War 150 years later. In 1900, they still wore the red coats that made them relatively easy targets for guerrillas like the Native Americans and South African Boers (descendants of the Dutch).

Not long after George Washington suffered the 1753 humiliation, he and others returned to battle and beat up the French.

Globally, including in North America, the Brits won The Seven Years War.

The North American territory lost by the French almost doubled the amount of land over which the British claimed control, and they were opened to white colonists. But, soon, the British found they were governing an enormous chunk of North America, which, along with paying off war debts, was an immense financial burden for England. See this website for a teacher's view on how to explain what happened. http://mrstolentinohistory.weebly.com/google-classroom.html

So, the Brits instituted a series of taxes and tried to force the relatively few colonists who had settled in the Ohio Valley to return to the Atlantic Seaboard. That was bad news for the several land speculators who eventually signed the Declaration of Independence. The so-called "Fathers of Our Country" couldn't make money by selling land they claimed they owned to any new settlers if the "King" would only let settlers buy land that England controlled.

Thus, The Declaration of Independence, which challenged the age-old feudal system in Europe, includes phrases that spell out the grievances the signers felt. For instance, the government can't just grab people's land willy-nilly. Yep, Washington's family, Thomas Jefferson and Ben Franklin, were land speculators.

Separately, the British didn't think that the colonial militias they had forced into service during the French and Indian War pulled their own weight. Cash-strapped London thought the colonies should contribute to easing the debt and pay for the continued "protection" provided by the British. They were taxes, pure and simple. It was sort of like the protection racket by mobsters who had been part of the Al Capone Gang in Chicago when I was growing up there. "I will protect you, but you have to pay for it." Of course, that was on top of whatever was being paid for Chicago police, colonial militia, etc.

America's War for Independence officially started at Lexington, Massachusetts, in 1775 and ended in 1783 … about a generation after the French and Indian War. The Boston Tea Party (1773) was just one of many protests generated by the taxes. Bales and boxes of highly taxed tea were grabbed from a British ship and dumped into Boston Harbor. (See old print above.)

The war began in Massachusetts and ended in 1781 when British General Cornwallis surrendered to General George Washington in Yorktown, Virginia. It is interesting that Washington's introduction to warfare was his defeat as a young man during the French and Indian wars. There are many illustrations of the Yorktown ceremony. A few have captions that are very hard to decipher, identifying the men on horseback who led troops to defeat the British. Two thoughts come to mind.

First, Yorktown is very close to Jamestown, where Susan's ancestor (assumedly an indentured servant named Simmons, arrived at the first sustaining British settlement in what became the USA and also close to where her brother Bob and father John served in the US Air Force). Second, how many of the officers who supported General Washington were French military? Susan's mother's family came from what now is Great Britain. Some settled in French Canada and eventually oozed south into New England. My grandkid's father's family (son-in-law Glenn) came to the New World on the Mayflower. The anti-semitism that burst out of the French Dreyfus Affair at the end of the 1800s helped force some of my ancestors to act on long festering hope and fears of escaping the Pale of Russia's tyranny (politely described as emigrating) to the As. America (north and south) and Africa.

This, in a convoluted way, brings me back to the paradox of Cornwallis, the British general, surrendering to Washington at Yorktown. For my immediate family, our history is intertwined with American and European history in large part. This, along with scientific advances, is a key background for WHY DID OUR FAMILIES DO THAT? The almost undecipherable captions on drawings of Cornwallis's surrender indicate an exceptionally large number of French military officers on horses overseeing the ceremony. They were Washington's allies.

As noted before, in the 1790s, The Wilderness Trail, which led to the Cumberland Gap, was widened enough to let wagons pass through. Then some Simmons and Mitchells (Susan's birth parents) moved west and, after a few years, settled in Kentucky and Tennessee near the Northern border of Mississippi in what became Tippah County.

Because it was hilly, the area around Tippah featured small family farms, small towns and relatively few plantations because plantations generally required large acreage of flat land. Below is a fantasy painting of Daniel Boone leading a group through the Cumberland Gap… (notice the armed scout in the woods on the left of the artwork.) cumberlandgapregion.com. Copies of painting available from artist at "Info@davidwrightart.com"

THE GAP AND ANOTHER RECAP

The good news for the Simmons and other families trapped on the East side of the Appalachians was that over 300 million years ago, an errant meteor about the size of a football field crashed into the still-growing Appalachian Mountains and created a valley that became known as the Cumberland Gap. It is in the general vicinity of the point where the states of Virginia, Tennessee and Kentucky come together.

The bad news is that it took 300 million years for people and technology to progress enough to widen the deer and Indian trail through the Gap so that wagons could be hauled into the Ohio River Valley.

Sorry for the repetition. The Gap is long forgotten, but quite important not just to the Simmons but all American history. It pushed westward the goalposts at the end zone of the frontier. That movement didn't stop until, at the great Chicago World's Fair of 1893, a somewhat obscure Wisconsin academic named Frederick Jackson Turner declared that there were no more domestic frontiers. He said it was the end of the frontier, the West had been won. (See essays discussing the Fair, America's and the Russian Tsars' ideas about Manifest Destiny above.)

The French lost the French and Indian Wars. In the long run, the British lost much of North America. In another context also discussed in other essays, King George lost the American Revolutionary War and some of his colonies. Tsar Nicholas lost to the Bolsheviks in the Russian Revolutionary War, where he lost not only his country but also his wife and his life. Some of my ancestors at that time exited Russia and went to America. Some remained and died.

History is complicated. It affected our families and why we are what they were. About a generation after The French and Indian Wars, with French help, George Washington, his troops, and widespread malaria helped defeat the British and end the Revolutionary War in Yorktown, VA, just 20 miles from Jamestown and home of the first American Simmons. Washington, forcing his troops to be vaccinated, helped win the war.

Then, within a historical blink (1803), the young American Republic paid the cash-strapped French a pittance for the Louisiana Purchase, which doubled the size of the fledgling USA in almost every measure (square miles, economy, food production, resources, world prestige, etc.).

In the next century (the 1900s), at a great loss of life, America rescues the French and British from the Germans (WWI and WWII). Just to round out the ironies, the Germans also contributed to the colonials' victory.

A circle of history.

Susan appears to be in the bloodline of the Simmons (sometimes only one m) mentioned above, who arrived at Jamestown aboard the first supply ship from England and settled nearby. Online family trees seem to directly connect her to a John Simmons in Surry County, Virginia, the county where Jamestown is located.

History has a way of looping back upon itself. Jamestown today is about a half-hour drive from Yorktown, VA, the site of the battle where the British surrendered to Gen. Washington. That occurred less than 200 years after Jamestown started as the first permanent British settlement in what became the United States of America. There was Simmons in Jamestown when it all began in 1607, and Simmons participated in the American War for Independence, which ended in nearby Yorktown in 1781.

Susan's brother, Air Force Master Sgt. Robert Mitchell Simmons Gordick and his family lived in that area for a long time. Bob was at Langley Air Force Base, oddly enough, before World War 2. Bob's father, also a Master Sgt. John Gordick also was stationed at Langley. The same John Calvin Gordick married the widow Edith Marks Simmons and adopted Susan and Bob.

A HISTORY FOR DUMMIES MOMENT

Just like the History for Dummies books, another recap goes a long way.

The early French, English and the Dutch (who founded New York) didn't just get up, leave Europe, and go west. Often, they were financed by investors who expected the settlers to work, plant, trade, trap … and then ship back items that would be sold at a profit in Europe and elsewhere. The Germans seemed to have more interest in Africa than America.

The Spanish were different than the Brits and, to some extent, the French. Their explorations and exploitations were aimed at converting the heathens to Catholicism as well as providing royalty with wealth. One explanation of Columbus' sales pitch to King Ferdinand and Queen Isabella of Spain was that he might find enough gold to fund a new Crusade, probably to be led by King Ferdinand, to capture Jerusalem from the Muslims.

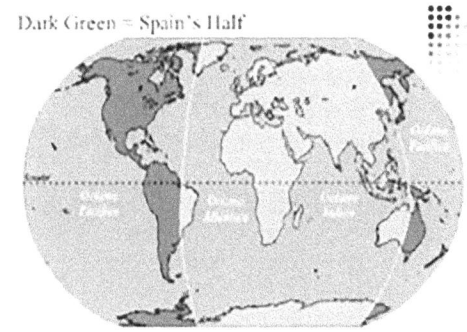

Curiously, without a real understanding of world geography, and in an attempt to settle arguments among powerful Catholic families in Spain and Portugal, the Pope of the time chose a north-south line circling the globe and said everything on one side would be Spanish and the other side Portuguese.

In the New World, Spain got almost all the land and mineral riches. Portugal has some steamy jungles in Brazil and frozen Greenland. As you probably know, countries like Britain, France, and what later became Germany and Holland said, "pshaw!"

How the Spanish conquests affected Southern California, where Lem and Suzie Simmons settled, will be skipped in this essay.

It is probably safe to assume that most of the Simmons who landed North of Philadelphia fought for the Union in the Civil War, and those who landed in the South fought for the Confederacy. (Except for those in Maryland, who were all over the place politically … and still are.)

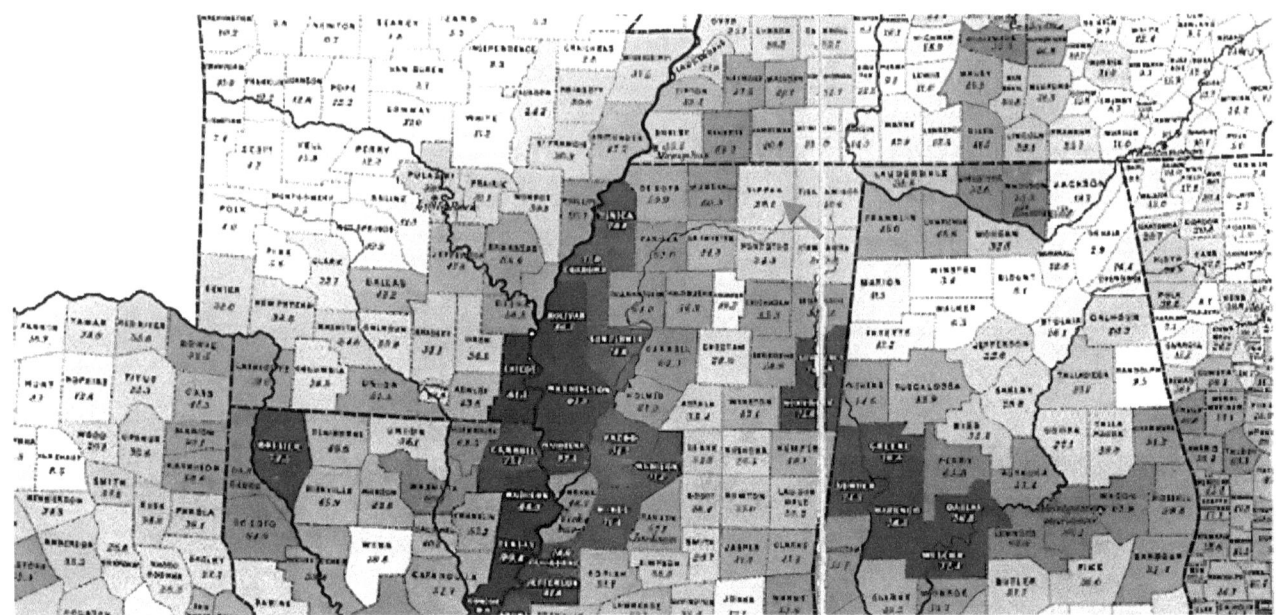

1860 MAP PRESIDENT LINCOLN USED SHOWING SLAVERY BY COUNTY

The arrow points to Tippah (28.1%). But, why Tippah?

Good question, I'm not totally sure of the answer, but there are strong clues.

In the late 1700s and early 1800s, Tennessee and Mississippi were attractive. America was still predominantly an agricultural society. When things "got" bad, people "up and went." When possible, they moved westward, seeking new lands to till or to provide services for the farmers.

As repeated above, the tobacco farmland in Virginia was worn out by poor agricultural techniques. The world market for American tobacco was also softening. Everyone, including farm families, had to eat, and rich earth that produced abundant crops was available in Kentucky, Tennessee, Georgia, Alabama, and Mississippi. There was a phenomenon called The Great Migration to the Mississippi Territory, 1798-1819.

Cotton was in demand, big time. Mississippi, which had the appropriate land and climate, claimed it was the center of the Cotton Kingdom. Of course, there were similar reasons for people to settle elsewhere. But this essay is not about them.

Maybe the magnet that attracted people to the Tippah area and nearby Tennessee was as simple as the answer to why my own grandparents and dozens of their relatives and neighbors moved to the Missouri River area North and South of Sioux City, Iowa. A relative or friend arrived and wrote back home that it was a good place to set roots. The postal systems of the 1700s and 1800s were slow, but they often worked. Usually, people lived near someone who could read.

In 1798, Congress created the Mississippi Territory, the combined population of white Europeans and black African slaves in that territory was fewer than 7,000. All but a handful were living in the south near the Gulf of Mexico.

The Territory was "Ch-land," the home of Chickasaw, Cherokee and Choctaw tribes until the 1830s when treaties forced the tribes to walk about 600 miles west along "The Trail of Tears" to what now is Oklahoma. If you get history from watching old "Western" movies on TV, you would think the Cherokee always lived in "The Wild West."

Anyhow, a bunch of Mitchells (Susan's grandmother's family) and Simmons settled around what became Tippah County. A small town near Blue Mountain is named Mitchell, the maiden name of Susan's grandmother. (I know it was mentioned above, but this is to reemphasize the family's roots in the Deep South.)

Not everyone was a farmer. One of Susan's great-grandfathers ran a boarding house. Nearby were shopkeepers, doctors, clergy, and maybe a few Indian chiefs in retirement. Literature about the area indicates no lack of lawyers.

A few in Tippah were supporters of The North. It appears that most whites just wanted to be left alone.

The Tippah area was to be devastated by armies from the North and South and bands of thugs who roamed across the land, preying on already-plundered families. Many of the local men were off to war. Some males fought nearby and occasionally came home. Some fought far to the North and East.

Armies had to be fed, and they often looted any food they could find nearby. In one report, military marauders around Tippah even took the popcorn strings from a Christmas tree. An example of troops "foraging" or "living off the land" is depicted in the illustration of General Sherman's troops in Georgia. (Above) Picture and much more civil war information at https://reparationscomm.org/tag/civil-war/

Towns close to Blue Mountain, like Ripley and Holly Springs, home of the famous NAACP founder, Ida B. Wells (Right) Picture and background at https://www.womenshistory.org/resources/video/womens-history-minute-ida-b-wells, were ravaged and several, reportedly, changed hands between North or South, or raiders, over 50 times.

Among those who served was William A. Simmons, Susan's great grandfather, who was a corporal in the 26th Regiment, Mississippi Infantry. William and his wife had moved to Tippah before the Civil War.

William A's family originally moved to Tennessee from Bedford, Virginia. Some of his wife's family can be traced from New Jersey to West Virginia, to Pennsylvania, and to Tennessee, according to sometimes accurate online family trees.

An example of the unreliability of sources is that, depending on the record, Susie Mitchell Simmons was born in nearby Alabama, not Mississippi. In any event, the Mitchell and Simmons paths to Tippah do not appear to be unusual.

Another part of Susan's grandmother's family, the Robinsons of Tennessee, had 10 slaves, according to the 1820 Census. As mentioned, at least one member of the Mitchell family had more than 20 slaves.

Near Tippah County's Blue Mountain were the tracks of the Mobile, Ohio and the Mississippi Central railroads. As roving bands, and then full armies, marched back and forth across the area, trains, tracks and ties were continually destroyed and only partially repaired.

The picture shows a train with reinforcements for Confederate General Joseph E. Johnston, commander of forces in the west, running off the track in the forests of Mississippi. (The Illustrated London News) This picture and description of the travails of common citizens during Civil War at https://www.mshistorynow.mdah.ms.gov/issue/jackson-the-capital-city-and-the-civil-war

For Tippah, about one year after the start of the Civil War, the Battle of Shiloh was more than a wake up call. It was a call to arms, along with a dose of panic because the war, to that point, had not really hit home. Shiloh was less than two days ride by horse from Blue Mountain.

The blood left at Shiloh, on the Tennessee River in Tennessee, was staggering … 23,741 casualties (13,047 Union and 10,694 Confederate) and 3,800 captured or missing.

The Confederates stopped to lick their wounds in Corinth, about 30 miles from Blue Mountain. Corinth was the scene of several battles and skirmishes (small battles) between Union and Confederate troops.

A large number of "able bodied" Tippah young men were conscripted (forced to join the army) or volunteered. At least one Tippah soldier's death was recorded as far away as the Battle of Bull Run (also known as the Battle of First Manassas). It was the first major battle of the American Civil War (1861), about 25 miles from Washington, DC.

In his book, "History of Tippah County, Mississippi: The First Century," Andrew Brown estimates about 2,000 men left Tippah County to fight the War. That was out of a white population of nearly 16,000. Several died of disease and poor medical treatment in northern prisons. (Disease killed more Civil War soldiers than battles. Same was true of WWI.)

As in the rest of the South, uncounted thousands of blacks fled their "masters" and headed for clusters of Northern troops. Some became Union soldiers. Others lived in what today would be called "refugee" camps the Union had set up. There are reports that after the war, a number of suddenly "former" slaves returned to their plantations, where some may have expected to find family.

Here are a few excerpts from Brown's account. *"There were skirmishes across the county … Tippah County was in fear after Sihloh … and as the war went on, and northern Mississippi became a no-man's land overrun by both armies but held by neither, more and more stragglers drifted into the area and lived off the country by any means they could."*

The citizens of north Mississippi were thus stripped of much of their food and forage not only by the two armies but also by outlaw bands that followed the armies. At least some of the blame… must be laid at the feet of northern General Halleck, whose letter to Grant makes it plain that the idea of all-out war against the entire population was conceived not by Sheridan in Georgia in 1864, but by Halleck… in1863"… and tested in west Tennessee and north Mississippi, where Tippah rests.

After the Union and Rebel armies moved east. In the last half of the Civil War, Tippah continued to stumble through the "fog of war." Newspapers were few. There was no regular mail service. The general collapse of all forms of transportation made it impossible for the citizens to have more than a vague idea of what was happening only a few miles away. Often, word-of-mouth was wrong … an early version of fake news. It was a bitter, nerve-racking experience.

Occasionally, the matriarchy left in Tippah was visited by male loved ones. They were on furlough or had deserted, or they were among the relatively few encamped nearby. Losing the use of the last horse and eating whatever hidden food was left led to personal disasters in rural areas. Even if there was someplace to walk to, it probably was in dire straights. (Picture shows abandoned BM depot.) Photo at https://railfanguides.us/stations/ms/#bluemountain

After the Civil War, in 1866, a Tippah County census reported 19,361 people, of whom 14,671 were white and 4,710 "colored." In the six years since the federal 1860 Census, the county lost 1,535 white and 1,621 colored residents.

Even though a railroad went through Blue Mountain in the 1880s and brought news and notions from afar, it took generations to recuperate from the battles and from the hatred and frustration that lingered after the war. As of this writing (2019), it must be assumed that wounds continue to drain.

Slavery was outlawed before the end of the war. Nonetheless, many poor blacks and whites remained under the control of the large plantation owners as they became sharecroppers … a form of economic slavery without the whips. Few, if any, sharecroppers ever made enough money to buy their way out of debt to the large landowners on whose land they farmed.

During "Reconstruction" (1865 to 1877), the victorious North took over and upended the old Southern Way by trying to give the black slaves relatively equal rights. The Simmons and Mitchells were there, but their reactions, as far as I can determine, went unreported.

I have been unable to find anything online of the Simmons and Mitchells who settled around Tippah ever doing or saying anything unusually positive or negative about anything. I would love to find some letters from that period.

Not long after the war ended, the mostly Baptist KKK rose up to discipline blacks, Jews, Catholics, union members, white Union and Reconstruction sympathizers, and anyone they just didn't care for. Like French beheadings in the 1800s, Southern lynchings drew big crowds.

Once, Susan and I were in Costa Rica and drove through a banana plantation with very dark green, almost black, plastic bags covering the banana bunches hanging from trees.

My brain was flooded with the haunting song "Strange Fruit" about lynching, most notably sung by Billie Holliday. Check it on YouTube.

Here are the lyrics:

Southern trees bear strange fruit.
Blood on the leaves and blood at the root.
Black bodies swinging in the southern breeze
Strange fruit hanging from the poplar trees

Pastoral scene of the gallant south
The bulging eyes and the twisted mouth
Scent of magnolias, sweet and fresh
Then the sudden smell of burning flesh

Here is fruit for the crows to pluck
For the rain to gather, for the wind to suck
For the sun to rot, for the trees to drop
Here is a strange and bitter crop.

Mississippi has had more recorded lynchings than any other state.

AND THAT IS A SHORT HISTORY OF THE AMERICAN SOUTH SEEN THROUGH THE EYES OF A FEW OF THE SIMMONS FAMILY.

BACK TO THE BEGINNING

Life in the sparsely settled Tippah County, Mississippi, must have been hard for Lemuel Simmons and Suzie Mitchell, otherwise, why would they leave? Lem and Suzie stopped in Texas, where they were married, moved to Los Angeles, and later moved to towns east of LA. They finally settled in San Bernardino before 1930. And that's where this essay about the South began … in Southern California, where Edith Marks and her husband Robert Bernard Simmons were living after my dear wife Susan Lee Simmons Gordick Kroloff was born.

Bob Simmons and Edith.

A FINAL REVIEW

Columbus, Simmons, Pilgrims, then Greed, Glory, Gory, Gold, Germs and Gems

In the earliest 1600s, Spanish royalty had their eyes on Holland. During that time, a group of "Reformers," Pilgrims and Puritans who had escaped persecution in England fled to Holland. Rapidly, many became disenchanted with Dutch urban life. They also were afraid that the Spanish would become the rulers of Holland and bring the Inquisition to them. If that happened, they figured they would be tortured unless they converted to Catholicism. Some made their way back to England. About the same time, another group of Englishmen, also afraid of the Spanish, had set up camp in Jamestown at a site they thought would be safe from the guns on any passing Spanish ships. About a decade later, some of the Puritans/Pilgrims sailed to North America and dug in around Plymouth Rock. (The details are too complicated and irrelevant for this essay. However, it is important to note that the English folks who financed people going to the New World usually expected them to pay back with crops, furs and the like.)

The first two American Simmons were in Jamestown, Virginia. One promptly died. The second survived.

The Columbian Exchange is named for Christopher Columbus. His mission, historians report, was to find a sea route to India, discover gold, and bring glory and riches to Spain's Catholic Spanish king and queen. Those riches, in turn, would finance a new Crusade and capture Jerusalem from the heathens who practiced Islam. The Columbian Exchange is his legacy. It generated the global transfer of plants, animals, culture, human populations, technology, invasive species, diseases, and ideas that are the basis of our lives today.

Not knowing any better, Columbus and his crew decided that the Carib Indians they met were Indians from India. That's how Native North Americans became known as Indians.

The Mayflower was overloaded because she took aboard passengers and stocks of her leaking sister ship that had set out with her on the voyage to America. That caused a delay in their plans and meant the winds that would take the Mayflower to the warmer South had died down for the season.

The Pilgrims in Massachusetts and their earlier English counterparts in Virginia had serious problems surviving in an environment for which they were not prepared. The nearby Native Americans, who recently had been devastated by deadly pandemics brought to America by the Spanish and Portuguese and various traders, were not sure about the new white people who wanted to stay rather than trade and leave like earlier Europeans who had visited them.

So, the Indians wavered between accepting the white colonists, repelling them, and trying to figure out how to use them for their own purposes.

Greed, glory, gory, gamers, groceries and germs. Most school kids know the greed and gory part of history. Rulers, insecure and/or delusional, wanted "more" … more land, more people to rule, more power, more wealth and more glory. History leaves the impression that the word "enough" was not in their vocabulary.

There always were winners and losers … and gamblers who wanted to "game the system" to "get a piece of the action."

One of the gamers was an Italian whose English name was Christopher Columbus. The Greeks and others, including Columbus, had known for 1500 years that the world was round. Columbus "knew" that if he could get someone to fund him, he could sail west to India and return with valuable spices and maybe cloth, maybe gold, plus glory and wealth for himself.

After years of shopping his ideas around, Columbus eventually convinced the king and queen of Spain to finance a fleet of three small ships, which he would lead. The Nina, Pinta and Santa Maria.

In 1492, Columbus set foot on a small island in a new world.

His one small step for man was a giant leap for mankind.

Leap is a tricky word.

It can mean up or down, as off a cliff.

End notes about Cousin Eugene's capture by Canadians soldiers in World War Two and his mother, Auntie Mushie, along with a South African coincidence.

EUGENE:

My maternal grandmother, Sarah Helfet Kroloff, arrived in Sioux City with two sisters and was met by their brother Harry. One sister, Minnie (Minna), eventually married Joe Cohen and lived in Chicago. Uncle Joe and Aunt Minnie had three kids, Eugene, Rhea and Leona. On rare occasions, my dad, mom, sister Susan, and I would take a street car to the elevated, change trains halfway there, and finally exit at a station near their residence. It took a long time to get back and forth. They lived in a house. At that time, every other Chicagoan I knew lived in an apartment.

Joe was a big man. He was a furniture mover getting on in years and having trouble lifting. I was told the company "moved" him from the back of the truck to the front, and he became a driver, and that's how he was listed in the census. He had the thickest eye glasses I had ever seen, and I wondered how I could be warned if he was driving in our neighborhood so I could send out an alarm.

Eugene, a very nice young man, was the child I remember best. He was a WWII veteran who became caught up in the month-long infamous "Battle of the Bulge," which began in December 1944. It was Germany's last major attack on the Western Front.

Alas, in the middle of the battle, Eugene was captured by the Canadians. Yes, the Canadians. I think he was a prisoner for over a week.

It seems the surprised Allies had a lot of trouble coordinating a response to the German onslaught of over 400,000 troops. Early on, the Germans had captured a bunch of Americans, donned their uniforms and went out hunting Allied units.

For some unknown reason, the Canadians surrounding Eugene thought he might be a German who spoke English with a perfect Chicago accent. Like others who were afraid of being captured, he had ditched any form of identification. Eventually, Eugene was returned to his home unit.

IT WAS MUSHY BUT WE FINALLY IDENTIFIED MUSHIE

The day Susan and I married in Chicago was almost a generation after WWII. We hosted a small reception in our tiny basement apartment. Susan, the beauty queen of the event, wore a nifty white dress and a long white veil. One of my well meaning older cousins came up to her and said, "Oh, you must be the bride. You look just like Auntie Mushie!"

It has taken well over 50 years to come to the conclusion Mushie was Minnie, one of the sisters who accompanied my grandmother from Liverpool to Sioux City, Iowa in 1903 and then lived in Chicago. She was Eugene's mom.

The picture, thought to be humorous in 1962, was taken on the wedding day. One reason our marriage survived, so far for over 60 years, is that we went into the escapade with our eyes wide open. The book Susan is holding is titled "The Boss."

Well, it took a lot of people putting up with a lot of tumult and tedium to make this book possible. Of course, most of them are dead, so the usual thank you at the end of a book is impractical. However, Susan, our kids Abigail, Adam, and Amy plus a slew of cousins, along with some expensive genealogy sites, and the nice people at Amazon/Kindle/Franklin, have been very patient with this old man. I couldn't have done it without them.

gmkroloff1@icloud.com

The most important person mentioned above is Susan Lee Simmons Gordick Kroloff, wife, mother of our three kids (Abigail, Adam, Amy) and the inspiration for everything good.

I was born in the Depression, attended three Big Ten universities, finally graduated with a degree in journalism, served in the US Army and held senior positions in Administrative and Congressional branches of the US government, private and not-for-profit sectors in Chicago and Washington, DC.

Some of my work is in the collections of The Smithsonian Institution and the Newseum.

ABOUT THE AUTHOR

In high school, George Kroloff spent a lot of the time running each year for some office or another and occasionally winning. He worked in a laundromat, delivered groceries by bicycle, and, with his dearest right-wing friend, snuck into the Chicago Republican Convention that nominated Dwight David Eisenhower.

We went to support him, but the crowd outside the convention hall was so large that the Chicago Police and Fire Departments started limiting attendance. So, as hundreds of prospective candidate celebrants were told to walk backward to make room around the entry doors, we pretended to walk backward but really were heading forward and eventually snuck into the hall. We were too late for the IKE demonstration, so we ditched our IKE signs and joined the MacArthur partisans screaming up and down the aisles. They seemed a bit different. We read in the newspaper the next day that several had been hired off of Skid Row, and at least one delegate's pocket was picked.

My introduction to Chicago's down-and-dirty politics was later while working for a small PR firm that told me to cheat on my expense report or get stuck with a miserable salary. That also was my introduction to Chicago business while elements of the Capone Mob still rode grey-to-black horses in parades.

But I did learn a couple of lessons, for instance. Male newspaper photographers like to take pictures of sexy-looking girls, and their editors tend to put them in the paper. My boss signed up a car washing gadget company as a client. I was tasked to get them "ink" … published in papers. My first hint of serving the news media is to help a client evolve from that. The circus was coming to town. I called the press agent and asked if I could borrow an elephant and a skimpily clad circus beauty on top and declare the nation's first "Go Wash Your Elephant Day" with this unremembered company's product. It was my first news service hit! Pictures of the pretty girl, the suffering elephant, and somebody pointing a spritzing hose with a soapy nozzle made it into papers all over the USA.

At the time, I was just trying to make enough money to live on, have some left over for my mom and dad, and figure out why half the world seemed nuts.

I quit the PR firm after they assigned me to a client who was the sacrificial lamb Republicans put up to counter the man who ran Chicago, Richard J. Daley, the last of the big city bosses.

Later, patching together some low-paying clients, I became the "booker" for Chicago's top interviewer of show business giants, scheduling them for his afternoon show on WAIT Radio.

A couple of times, Phyllis Diller asked me to go shopping with her in a trendy Chicago area. Fans came up to us and saw a shining star out about town. I was about the age of her oldest son, who was a worry to her at that time. Unlike the other fans on the street, I saw a Midwest mother in a strange city with no real friends trying to keep her sanity.

I wasn't much of a help, but apparently, she thought I grounded her.

Then, there was the mob-run auto dealer, a sponsor of the show. One day, I went to the dealer with my boss and stupidly mentioned my interest in a used car. Big mistake, the knuckle daggers among the salesmen seemed like twins of the knuckle dagger union dues-collectors when I worked at a warehouse to make money to continue college after my dad had serious heart problems and like the knuckle draggers at the illegal night club next to the illegal gambling establishment across the road from a Cook County prison. Boy, oh Boy, did the auto "salesmen" have a deal for me. Rather than having my knees crushed, I accepted the transaction. Reluctantly.

Separately, and I think unrelated, I promoted some has-been performers at a night club that also turned out to be mob run. One early morning, I was stopped by a cop for speeding in Jackson Park, the site of the great Chicago World's Fair late in the 19th Century and across the street from where my parents lived when I was born deep in the Depression of the 1930s.

First thought ... Is it good the cop doesn't know I have a couple hundred dollars in small bills in my pocket, or is it bad?

Second thought ... Since the police and the mob are hand in glove, is it good the mob knows I have all that money in my pocket or bad?

Third thought ... The cop needed some money for a birthday present.

I slipped $10 dollars in his hand with my driver's license. He returned the license and warned me not to have such a heavy foot on the accelerator.

Good experience for Washington a few years later.

I also had a client who managed big-time stars while in Chicago ... Belafonte, Bernstein, Judy Garland, etc. Their shows were always sold out, but the contracts must have a clause that required a press agent, and I was really cheap.

Then there was the Chicago Association of Industry and Commerce (The Chamber Of Commerce). My first real job. Visits to Washington to lobby, promotion of the Western Hemisphere's biggest trade fair, introducing Bossa Nova to North America, and meeting smart people from everywhere. Also, my first encounter with the White House.

A South American nation was exhibiting its export goods and sent the president to puff up the promotion. Unfortunately, he was a drunk. Something I had not been briefed on. I saw him floundering in the get-together period and yelled out, "Is there anyone from the State Department here." It was the Kennedy Administration and who should show up, but Angier Biddle Duke who smoothly eased The Ecuadorian President out of the room

About the same time, I had written the speech for the Chamber president at the ceremony where O'Hare Field was turned over to civilian aviation after years as an Air Force Base. I was in the elevator with Vice President Lyndon Johnson and had the most pleasant Secret Service pat-down ever.

The Chicago Trade Fair was important. I was the only single male working for the Chamber of a certain age. So, I was assigned to be a liaison with the beauty queens from each country. One said, "George, I have a girl for you." She did. Soon, Susan and I married. Susan, who had been a Navy then Air Force brat, was somewhat disturbed about moving to a new base each year, which meant a new school, new friends, etc.

Once married, she made me promise never to move again. So, of course, I accepted a job that reported to the Department of Agriculture, Agency For International Development, State Department and White House Food for Peace offices in Washington. I was in great shape, walking between offices and waiting for signatures on papers that already were out of date.

I received an offer from the White House to monitor the Food For Peace efforts. That meant a trip around the world for a naive Midwesterner. Big deal. Of course, I accepted. The head of the office is a chap later known as Senator George McGovern. Hey, I grew up in Chicago alleys and Iowa corn fields. A trip around the world was pretty special.

Loe and behold, the next day, an old friend who was a top official in the US Postal Service continued to pressure me to join his staff. Come see the Postmaster General, he said. I did, he convinced me to join the staff and promised to call George McGovern. "I out rank him," he said.

Learned a lot there, especially under John Gronowski and Larry O'Brien. Later, while working closely with George McGovern as a senior staffer on the US Senate Foreign Relations Committee, I never mentioned that I was the guy Gronowski stole.

At the post office, I had many assignments, but the one that made the Smithsonian was the national campaign to convince 80 million Americans, most of whom were furious because they were becoming numbers, not people … to use ZIP Codes. I received a huge amount of help from local post office information officers, but nonetheless, I think I won a $50 award for changing American habits and saving millions of taxpayer dollars.

From Post Office, I went to my Post Office, as I created a school, community, and public relations office before the Pentagon Papers Scandal, Watergate, and a lot of other stuff. Yes, I worked with Kay Graham, Ben Bradlee, Woodward and Bernstein, and a lot of other fabulous Washington Post individuals. But it was the school publishing effort to ween kids from TV to learn about the world from newspapers that made the Newseum. Don't want to denigrate the names above, they really are great Americans. I took me about three years to convince the newsroom reporters and editors that I wasn't some show business flack that would embarrass them.

Then, the Senate. Got a call while lying on the family room rug watching some sitcom asking me if the Chairman of the US Senate Foreign Relations Committee were to call me to suggest an interview to be his assistant on the committee, would I be receptive. I accepted the call. Was hired. And the first couple of years were weird. I had a couple of political assignments that I couldn't figure out how to accomplish without the Chairman having fingerprints on them. Then, a Washington Post reporter told me that around the time I left the paper, the newsroom was beginning an investigation into my boss. Was he a crook? According to the reporter, the paper dropped the investigation. I was wondering why my leaving The Post was so subdued.

Anyhow, my chairman, my boss, Senator John Sparkman, gave me little guidance. So, on my own, I created a morning foreign news report for senators, a system of showing red, yellow, and green lights so a person testifying would know how long to talk and when I could punch my Senator in the ribs to wake him up and move on to the next person to testify. Don't snicker. This was a big deal.

Not that anyone cares now, but my well-researched THE NEW WORLD INFORMATION ORDER report for the Committee and hearings I put together to expand upon it convinced many governments, including the USA, to reevaluate how they assigned frequencies for microwaves, modern missile targeting devices, and much more. I was pleased when the CIA asked for a briefing because, following the report they set up a special office to evaluate my suggestions in the future. One of the things I hated about visiting the CIA was that every time I had to pee, someone would follow me into the mens room to make sure I didn't plant a bomb or take pictures. It was a bit too cozy.

Some of the hearings I put together created quite a stir. Senators McGovern and Percy were big fans. Percy offered me a job if I wanted to switch parties, and I never told McGovern I was the chap that The Postmaster General pulled rank on and stole me from his White House staff. I occasionally had second thoughts about that gig because my office would have been the same one as General Douglas MacArthur occupied between the First and Second World Wars. It had an impressive fireplace in the Executive Office of the President on the White House campus along Pennsylvania Avenue.

Later, as a consultant, I tackled how to improve donations of blood to keep people alive, why people had to understand that nuclear waste from hospitals has to go somewhere, and dozens of other tasks that had to do with science, numerous non-profits, war, disabilities, and even American taxes on Brazilian booze.

Aside from running a business, dealing with clients, and solving their problems, there were many hours of public service work. Among them was being on the board and then president of the board of the Pan American Development Foundation. Chair of the organization was the Secretary General of the OAS, The Organization of American States. It is the UN of our hemisphere. Together, we met a slew of heads of state. That was kind of old school after being on the staff of the US Senate Foreign Relations Committee.

But, when I look back on a career of big-picture tasks ... changing the way Americans communicated (ZIP Code), Watergate while at the Washington Post, reorienting all kinds of thinking about communications (news, propaganda, telephones, satellites, etc.), and showing that they are interconnected, the silliness of the half-dressed Ringling Brothers circus showgirl on top a a huge elephant, or even figuring out how to create the credibility of the newly formed Commission on Presidential Debates after my former client, The League of Women Voters flamed out ... I think there is one thing I am most proud of ... even after ZIP CODE, The Washington Post, and Presidential Debates.

According to Wikipedia, The Chernobyl disaster began on 26 April 1986 with the explosion of the No. 4 reactor of the Chernobyl Nuclear Power Plant near the city of Pripyat in northern Ukraine, near the Belarus border in the Soviet Union.[1] It is one of only two nuclear energy accidents rated at the maximum severity on the International Nuclear Event Scale, the other being the 2011 Fukushima nuclear accident. The response involved more than 500,000 personnel and cost an estimated 18 billion rubles (about $68 billion USD in 2019).[2] It remains the worst nuclear disaster in history.

Within a few minutes, news of the disaster circled Earth's northern hemisphere, and American fearmongers were convincing us we all would die as the radioactive cloud drifted over the US. Having dealt with nuclear matters while working in the US Senate and later as a consultant to companies and non-profits dealing with the mineral so dangerous to humans, I was shaken.

Suddenly, my brain was yelling at me to call my former client, the College of Nuclear Physicians (Radiologists), to get a report on how individuals should react.

I called.

They agreed to be ready to report to all humanity the next day what they could discover about the nuclear cloud headed towards North America. They found that the further the cloud was from Chernobyl the less would be its effect. By the time it passed the California coast there would be virtually no damage. Americans and Europeans and most Russians and Asians were safe.

I scheduled a news conference at the National Press Club, and naturally, the room was packed, and a lot of psychiatrist officers weren't. And a lot of people slept well that night because the experts, the scientists, the doctors, were right. Even on TV they had a great bedside manner.

Information is the key to conception, survival, death, and all that is human. If I live long enough, I will work on my nascent theory that nearly 14 billion years ago, when an event we know as The Big Bag occurred, the only thing it produced, the only thing that our universe is composed of, is a form of information that is like LEGO Bricks. It rearranges itself into different forms.

The exact same kinds of things creating the atoms that construct a grain of sand, also build your brain cells, and the water on the moons of Saturn and Jupiter.

Son-of-a-gun. I knew my father, Archie Kroloff, was smart but didn't, until recently, understand he was brilliant. He said everything is the same thing but different. He really didn't know what he meant, nor do I. But it seems plausible. And clearly, information is precious.

I hope the information about our families in this book is useful and entertaining for you. **I also hope you appreciated … not depreciated … my intermixing the stories or essays in an odd and incomplete manner so you could pick up on a topic you found interesting and not have to wade through matters of less interest. … and that darned repetition of some matters to remind you of something you may have read days ago,**

George Kroloff, December, 2024

Maybe it will encourage you to search your families' histories with the hope of understanding why they did what they did that causes you to do the things that you do.